_____SELF-ESTEEM

SELF-ESTEEM

THE KEY TO YOUR CHILD'S WELL-BEING

HARRIS CLEMES & REYNOLD BEAN

G. P. PUTNAM'S SONS
NEW YORK

LIBRARY OF CONGRESS CATALOGING IN PUBLICATION DATA

Clemes, Harris.
  Self-esteem.

  1. Children—Management. 2. Self-respect.
3. Child psychology. 4. Parent and child.
I. Bean, Reynold.   joint author.   II. Title.
HQ769.C62 1980   649′.1   80-23661

ISBN 0-399-12529-9

PRINTED IN THE UNITED STATES OF AMERICA

TO OUR PARENTS

Now that we understand what it takes

ACKNOWLEDGMENTS

Many of the ideas in this book have come from our students, who shared their experiences as teachers, parents, and adults concerned with children.

A special and deep thanks goes to Hamilton Brannan, who, as a close friend, challenged our thinking, refined our ideas, and gave encouragement when needed.

Both of us have a warm place in our hearts for Selena Clarke. She guided the production of the manuscript through its many revisions with patience and a deep interest.

We wish to thank Rohanna Muth, Rachel Kaiser, and Psyche Pascual for their typing of the manuscript and Lucia Lemes for duplicating the manuscript.

Finally, we acknowledge the very special support we received from our wives, Halimah Bean and Maya Clemes. They were patient with our late hours and urged us to produce as fine a book as possible. We think we did.

CONTENTS

FOREWORD   **11**

SECTION 1—INTRODUCTION

CHAPTER 1 Self-esteem—What It Is and Why It's Important   **17**
What is Self-esteem? The Characteristics of High and Low Self-esteem.
Self-esteem and Self-concept. Self-esteem as a Motive for Behavior. Self-
esteem and School Performance. Self-esteem and Interpersonal Relations.
Self-esteem and Creativity. How Parents' Self-esteem Affects Children.
CHAPTER 2 The Four Conditions of Self-esteem   **34**
Self-esteem and Children's Needs. The Four Conditions That Insure Self-
esteem. When a Child Has a Sense of Connectiveness. When a Child Has a
Sense of Uniqueness. When a Child Has a Sense of Power. When a Child
Has a Sense of Models. How the Four Conditions Interact. Identifying the
Critical Condition. The Three Domains.

SECTION II—THE WHOLE CHILD: FEELING CONNECTED

CHAPTER 3 Do Children Feel They Belong?   **79**
How Children with Connectiveness Problems Behave. How Children's
Sense of Connectiveness Is Threatened.

CHAPTER 4 At Home: Being in the Family   **91**
Building Your Child's Sense of Connectiveness. Building Your Family's
Sense of Connectiveness. Handling Change That Threatens a Sense of
Connectiveness.

CHAPTER 5 **Improving the Way Children Communicate   117**
The Communication Tapestry. Building Strength into the Communication Tapestry. Adding Richness to the Communication Tapestry. Building Flexibility into Your Communication Tapestry. The Three D's That Hinder Communication and Destroy Connectiveness. Building Communication Skills.

SECTION III—**THE WHOLE CHILD: BEING SPECIAL**

CHAPTER 6 **Individuality: Plus or Minus?   131**
How Children with Uniqueness Problems Behave. How Children's Sense of Uniqueness Is Threatened.

CHAPTER 7 **At Home: Do You Know Who I Am?   145**
How to Relate to Your Child to Build a Sense of Uniqueness. Building Your Family's Sense of Uniqueness. Handling Threats to Children's Sense of Uniqueness. Confirming Children's Sense of Uniqueness: A Special Way of Communicating.

CHAPTER 8 **Stimulating Children's Talents and Creativity   174**
Creativity: How Do You Recognize It? Creativity and the Sense of Uniqueness. Creative Children—A Problem or Blessing? Fostering Creativity.

SECTION IV—**THE WHOLE CHILD: DOING THE JOB**

CHAPTER 9 **Feeling and/or Exercising Power   185**
How Children with Power Problems Behave. How Children's Sense of Power is Threatened.

CHAPTER 10 **At Home: I Can Do It!   197**
Building Your Child's Sense of Power. Building a Sense of Power in Your Family.

CHAPTER 11 **Teaching Children to Be Responsible and Competent   216**
Hazards That Hinder Teaching Responsibility. Remembering. Building Responsibility Through Limits and Rules. Building Responsibility Through Feedback.

SECTION V—**THE WHOLE CHILD: KNOWING WHAT'S HAPPENING**

CHAPTER 12 **Good Models/Poor Models   235**
How Children with Models Problems Behave. How Children's Sense of Models is Threatened.

CHAPTER 13 **At Home: Having Good Sense**   **246**
How to Relate to Your Child to Build a Sense of Models. Building Your Family's Sense of Models.

CHAPTER 14 **Values and Goals:**
                Getting From Here to There Safely   **256**
What Are Values? Helping Children to Know What They Want and How to Get It.

SECTION VI **THE WHOLE PARENT: YOUR SELF-ESTEEM**

CHAPTER 15 **Nurturing Your Own Self-esteem**   **265**
Treating Yourself Well Will Raise Your Children's Self-esteem. Assessing Your Self-esteem. How People Destroy Their Self-esteem. How Poor Marital Relations Can Lower Your Self-esteem. Enhancing Your Self-esteem Through Everyday Actions. Mind Pictures That Enhance Your Self-esteem.

This book is about the way children develop into healthy, happy adults, and how you can help them do so. It will show how you can improve your own self-esteem, at the same time you encourage high self-esteem in your children.

Self-esteem is the feeling of satisfaction with oneself that arises when a person's (adult or child) needs are satisfied. Our needs are met in two ways: (1) By using our own *inner capabilities* and resources to influence events, or, (2) By our *environment* providing the necessary conditions so that we can accomplish our purposes.

Self-esteem, therefore, has to do with both the way we handle our world and the way the world influences us. People with high self-esteem have developed many skills and attitudes that help them accomplish their purposes effectively. They either have, inside themselves, what they need, or they know how to get it.

At every stage of life our self-esteem determines how we act, how we learn, how we relate, how we feel, and how we work. Self-esteem can be observed in an infant as well as an adult.

In this book you will discover how to observe and understand self-esteem in your children and in yourself, by understanding the four conditions that are necessary in order to have it. It is essential we have each of these conditions to a high degree in order to have high self-esteem. These four conditions are:

1. *A sense of connectiveness*—which has to do with how we relate to people and things.
2. *A sense of uniqueness*—which has to do with how we feel about our differentness (our unique attributes) and how we express those feelings.
3. *A sense of power*—which has to do with how effectively we influence the circumstances of our lives.
4. *A sense of models*—which has to do with how we clarify and manifest our goals and purposes.

In this book you will learn how to enhance these four conditions in your children at every stage of their lives.

We describe many important things you need to know about children. In doing so, we have tapped the latest scientific findings, and have integrated them with our many years of professional experience as family therapists.

But that's not all. In writing any book, especially one about children, it is interesting to examine the authors' motives. In this regard, we wish to use this introduction to reveal something about ourselves that may not come through clearly in the text. This is the fact that a very large part of our lives has been devoted to being parents.

Between us we have had a hand in raising ten children. At the time of this writing, their ages range from four to twenty-seven; five are boys or young men, and five are girls or young women. We know that we have devoted more time, energy, thought, and action to this gang than to almost anything else.

We're still learning!

In doing the planning, research, and writing that have gone into this work, not a day passed in which we did not take some time to reflect on our own children, and on ourselves as parents. Many times we have said, "I wish I'd known *that* when they were that age," or "I've got to remember that for the future." Never once in the preparation of this book did we depart from this most central activity of our lives—being parents.

Early in our careers as parents, long before our professional credentials became important, we sensed that the most important feelings our children had were how they felt about themselves. It would be apparent in the expression of infinite delight on one of our toddlers' faces when he or she experienced some new-found skill. The total expression of good feelings they demonstrated when being held was a sign of satisfaction with themselves. Later on we noticed how strongly their liking for themselves influenced their schoolwork, relations with playmates, and their interaction with teachers.

In spite of having made working with children and families our profession, we don't believe we're much different from most parents in what we want to see in our children. We want them to get along with people; we want them to know they're special and have other people think so; we want them to use the skills they have and learn new ones; and we want them to have values and beliefs that make them respect themselves and be worthy of the respect of others. We know they won't be happy all the time, but we'd like them to know how to be happy and to deal effectively with stress. We want them to believe that they're important, and to conduct themselves accordingly. We want them to be responsible, and to handle their own lives well.

As parents we've had our fair share of successes and failures along the way. Most of our failures have resulted from our own unrealistic expectations, or not being in tune with a child's needs. We have felt successful when, to our surprise and delight, they have gone beyond our estimates of their capabilities.

We worry, just as you do, that things might not turn out well for them. We spend time talking and thinking about what to do for, about, or with them. And we sometimes seek advice or opinions from friends who are parents—to lend some perspective to our own personal experience.

What we, as parents, educators, and concerned adults, need

to do to help children have high self-esteem is mainly determined by the needs children have. We have devoted the main part of this book to discussing what these needs are and how to determine which are most crucial.

Just as it's important to know what to do to head off problems, it's important to know whether or not you have a problem. Many chapters will indicate what you will see when children are having difficulty meeting their needs and will give you clear direction as to what to do about them.

As parents, as well as writers, we have tried to make this material as direct, uncomplicated, and practical as possible. We provide you with a framework for understanding self-esteem. The basic principles that serve to define high or low self-esteem are universal and apply to people of all ages. An understanding of these principles will help you see yourself more clearly, in addition to helping you understand your children.

There are chapters on the many things you can do to raise your children's self-esteem. We have focused on things you can do in your everyday contacts with your child, whether it be in an individual, group or family setting. You will find chapters devoted to communication, creativity, responsibility, and values.

In a rapidly changing world, parents are challenged to determine what their children need *now* in order to cope with a future that is unpredictable. Because of this, we see increasing interest in developing personal characteristics that are necessary for effective living despite changing circumstances. Self-esteem is the one trait that, more than any other, influences the way in which a person deals with the world. When self-esteem is high, it allows a person to cope creatively with an uncertain future. It is a gift that parents can provide for their children, and in so doing, contribute to their future success and well-being.

SECTION I

INTRODUCTION

Self-Esteem: What It Is and Why It's Important

WHAT IS SELF-ESTEEM?

"My son is really a bright young fellow, and when left to himself is quite capable of solving really tough problems. But why does he do so poorly in school? Does he have a self-esteem problem?"

"I don't think my daughter has a self-esteem problem. Quite the contrary. She can become an obnoxious show-off, and always wants to be the center of attention. Her problem is that other kids don't like her. Is this a self-esteem issue?"

"My nine-year-old acts as if he's not very bright. School's a disaster, usually. And he's been in special classes for several years. He just can't seem to keep things straight. I know it makes him feel terrible about himself, but how can I improve his self-esteem if I don't make him smarter?"

"I have a student who is a terror. If there's trouble, you just know he's in the middle of it. I've talked to him, punished him, even bribed him to act better, but nothing works for very long. How does his problem relate to self-esteem?"

So many parents and teachers are confronted with curious, paradoxical, inconsistent, and seemingly irrational behavior in children, that questions about what kids do and why abound.

The concept of self-esteem explains much about children's behavior and is based on a rather simple premise. *Most behavior is motivated by a person's desire to feel good* about what he has, what he is, what he's done, or what he knows. When we feel good about ourselves, we have self-esteem. This is true for adults as well as children.

We will go to great lengths to feel good—even tolerate short-term pain in order to feel good later. For example, you push your physical limits to the point of pain in a game of tennis so that you feel good about winning, or at least trying to win. We often put up with a spouse's bad mood because we know that tomorrow things will be better. We will tolerate real anxiety when trying something new because having done it makes us feel great. A child will accept a spanking because he had to play that last game and, thus, arrived home late.

Can you remember times when you felt really good about yourself? Chances are that they were characterized by one or more of the following feelings:

- You felt important to someone who was important to you.
- You felt "special," even if you couldn't put your finger on what made you feel that way.
- You felt on top of things, doing what was needed, confident that you could handle whatever came your way.
- You felt purposeful—you were working toward goals that were important to you, that expressed your own beliefs and values.

The internal processes that result in "feeling good" are the same for children and adults, even though the specific experiences differ. A child who finally understands addition feels a satisfaction similar to that of an adult who discovers the correct way to balance a checkbook. If you are aware of what makes you feel good, you will be able to help children feel that way too.

Self-esteem is feeling good about yourself, and those feelings promote behavior that tends to reinforce them. A child who feels good about having solved a problem in class is likely to want to solve another one in order to feel good again. A young man who feels warm, secure, and happy with a certain young woman will want to see her again.

Because it's a feeling, self-esteem always expresses itself in the way people act. You can observe your children's self-esteem by seeing *what* they do and *how* they do it.

THE CHARACTERISTICS OF HIGH AND LOW SELF-ESTEEM

Self-esteem waxes and wanes. When children have high or low self-esteem they will say and do things that exemplify the characteristics listed below. All children will show these characteristics at one time or another. Yet rather than focus on any one characteristic, we need to observe the "pattern" of their behavior.

A child with high self-esteem will:

- be proud of his accomplishments — "Look at this; I really like this picture I painted."
- act independently — "I made my own breakfast."
- assume responsibility — "I'll water the plants for you."
- tolerate frustration — "Oooh, this model is hard to put together, but I know I can do it."
- approach new challenges with enthusiasm — "Wow, teacher said that we're going to start learning long division tomorrow."
- feel capable of influencing others — "Let me show you how to play this new game I learned."
- exhibit a broad range of emotions and feelings — "I feel so good when Daddy's home, and sad when he's gone."

A child with low self-esteem will:

- avoid situations that provoke anxiety

  "I'm not going to school today; there's a hard test in math."

- demean his own talents

  "Nothing I draw looks good."

- feel that others don't value him

  "They never want to play with me."

- blame others for his own failings

  "You didn't tell me where the broom was, so I couldn't clean up the mess."

- be easily influenced by others

  "I know I shouldn't have done it, but they dared me to."

- become defensive and easily frustrated

  "It's not my fault the kite won't fly—I'm just going to smash the stupid thing."

- feel powerless

  "I can't find the scissors. Where's the tape? I don't have the right book—I'll never finish this project."

- exhibit a narrow range of emotions and feelings

  "I don't care. It doesn't make any difference to me what you do."

BEN: A STORY THAT COULD BE TRUE

One day, a long time ago, a mighty prince was leading his victorious army through a poor rural province of a land he had just conquered. So mighty was his power, so stern was his visage, so threatening were the reports of his ruthlessness, that all the land around seemed deserted, as everyone ran from his path.

As the prince rounded a curve in the road, his mighty hordes trailing behind him, he came upon a young boy, standing alone, watching him from beside a berry bush. There were dark purple smudges on the lad's face and hands, witness to his recent feast on the berries. The prince was so startled to find anyone around, let alone a solitary child, that he reined in, forcing his officers and aides to come to a jangling halt. The sergeants shouted at their troops and wagons to stop, everyone to wait upon the prince.

Since the boy did not bolt off, nor even appear to be apprehensive, the prince's curiosity was piqued. He rode up close to the lad, and said, "What are you doing here, boy?"

"Picking berries," was the boy's simple and obvious answer.

"Why haven't you run away like all the others?" queried the prince.

"The berries are sweeter here than any place else in the valley," the boy said, with neither fear nor brashness in his voice. "Would you like some? I can pick them for you."

The prince, who was treated with more deference than this by everyone, was getting a bit miffed by the absence of fear in the lad's tone and manner.

"I am the mighty Prince Krondak, son of the Thunder King, and this is my great stallion, Sacamondae! All people and things under the heavens quail before our power and strength," he roared at the boy, putting on his most threatening face.

"My name is Ben, and this is my friend, Scratcher." And with the mention of his name, a most undistinguished little mongrel crawled from under the bush, stood, looked at the prince, and wagged his stubby tail in an audacious manner.

Even the prince was forced to smile at this show of composure on the part of Ben and Scratcher. He dismounted from Sacamondae, throwing his reins to a nearby general, and walked over to Ben, who held out a small basket of berries for Krondak to help himself to.

Squatting down to be nearer his adversary, Krondak engaged Ben in conversation, as his officers and aides looked on with growing impatience.

"Aren't you terrified by the size of my sword, Starflame?" the prince asked, as he pulled his renowned blade from its scabbard.

"Oh," said Ben, with admiration in his voice, "it's very nice.

One day I hope to have a wonderful blade like that. Right now, though, this knife does me just fine." And to demonstrate, he pulled a small knife from a sash tied around his waist. Picking up a piece of wood, he cut a long strip from it (not without some effort), and threw it over the bush for Scratcher to fetch.

"Can't you see my army of a thousand warriors, who are the most fearsome in the world? Don't they frighten you?" Krondak swept his arm around the horizon.

"I have never seen so many people in my whole life," said Ben with great interest. "In my village there are only a few families, but we all get along nicely. All my uncles and cousins live close by." And then turning to Krondak, he asked, "Do you get along with all those people, are they your friends?"

Krondak, quickly speculating on how his men would cease to follow him if they lost their fear of his might, didn't respond to Ben's question.

"My name is known the world around," Krondak pursued his point. "Everyone has heard of me and fears my power."

"That's just like me," Ben responded with affection. "Everyone around here knows me too. I won the boys' race at the last Harvest Day festival. Oh, it was a bit embarrassing to have everyone notice me that way. We're a lot alike," Ben said without a sign of insolence. "I bet we could be friends. I'd like to ride your horse."

With that, Krondak raised Ben up in his hands, and placed him in Sacamondae's great saddle. Leading the enormous stallion by his bridle, Krondak signaled his army to move forward.

"Follow this lad," he called. "He is also a prince, fearless and noble. I have not been able to conquer him."

SELF-ESTEEM AND SELF-CONCEPT

The terms *self-esteem* and *self-concept* are often used interchangeably. But there is an important distinction between the two. Self-esteem differs from self-concept in that the former is a feeling, while the latter is a theory, a set of ideas a child has about himself. Self-concept can be reported; a child can say what he believes about himself, even though his beliefs don't correspond to his behavior. A child has beliefs about himself regarding what he does well or poorly, the preferences he has about things, what he likes or dislikes, the roles he plays in relationship to others, and the standards he holds. He may believe he's friendly, but have no friends. He may have a preference for sports, but refuse to join teams at school.

How does self-concept affect your children's behavior? Their feelings of personal satisfaction are enhanced when they:

- *Express their self-concept in action.* For example, a child who believes she's a good athlete scores the game-winning goal; another who believes he's handy helps dad do some complex chore; and one who believes she's a math whiz solves a tough problem.
- *Live up to the personal standards associated with their self-concept.* For example, a child scores high marks in an academic area she believes she's good in; a child who believes he's neat and tidy cleans his room to "perfection"; another who believes he has a special "thing" for matchbox cars accumulates all the local toy store has.
- *Have their self-concept validated by what others say or do to them.* For example, a child who believes he draws well receives praise for a new picture; a child who believes she's a good student receives an academic prize; and a young "helper" gets praise for cleaning the car well.

SELF-ESTEEM AS A MOTIVE FOR BEHAVIOR

Self-esteem influences the way self-concept is expressed in children's behavior. The relationship between self-esteem and self-concept is complex and dynamic. Children may *believe* that they ought to do something, but *feel* powerless to accomplish it. They may have a strong preference for something, but feel apprehensive about stating that preference. Self-concept inclines children toward behavior that is consistent with their personal beliefs; self-esteem influences how those beliefs are carried into action, and whether they are at all. When self-concept and self-esteem are mutually supportive, children act decisively and spontaneously. When self-esteem is low, confusion and stress surround the way that children manifest their self-concepts.

Three major motives affect what children do and how they do it:

Children act in ways that increase their feelings of self-worth and personal satisfaction. They seek praise and approval; they try to do things they do well; they try to avoid failure; they try to please others if they can.

Children behave in ways that "prove" to themselves and others their feelings about themselves are true. They act well if they feel they're "good," and misbehave if they feel that others expect them to be naughty; they will be ready at all times to play games if they feel they're good at them; they will be reluctant to give time and attention to a math quiz if they feel they're incompetent at math, irrespective of their actual ability.

Children act in ways that help them to maintain a consistent self-image, even though circumstances may change. Even though children's self-images may change over time, they are unconsciously reluctant to alter them. While they may be offered new self-concepts by adults, their deeper feelings, those that represent their self-esteem, may not change. For example, a child may say it's luck or a "mistake" if she does something well that she has regularly failed at. "I can't"; "That's the way I am"; "I always mess it up" are protests to teachers and parents that justify failure. A child may read at home, but not do so at school, where he labels himself a poor reader.

Each of the above motives is important in understanding

children's behavior, but sometimes they operate simultaneous-ly and conflict with each other. When this happens children seem to behave inconsistently, and parents become confused about what they're doing and why. The following chart shows examples of ordinary situations in which conflict occurs.

I.Increase Self-worth and Satisfaction	II.Prove That Self-image Is True	III.Maintain Consistent Self-image
1.Tells mom he'll clean the garage (pleases others).	1.Works in a slow, inefficient way and doesn't finish because he believes (having been told) that he doesn't complete long, complex tasks.	1.Is told that he always makes promises but doesn't follow through.
2.Wants to be part of a group at school and moves into a group activity (seeks acceptance).	2.Thinks that other kids don't like him, so he tries so hard in a group that he puts off the others.	2.Experiences subtle rejection from others that proves once again that he's not likable.
3.Tells teacher she can't do some academic task (avoids failure); teacher says she can if she tries and shows her evidence from previous work.	3.Needs to prove that she's right and teacher is wrong, and wastes time thinking about it.	3.Hands in incomplete work, and teacher again indicates disappointment and displeasure in her.
4.Promises parents that she will not fight with younger sibling (seeks approval).	4.Needs to prove that she is bigger and more responsible, so she tries to make sibling do something and gets into argument.	4.Experiences parents' displeasure and is told that she's just not responsible enough to baby-sit.

Children can have a negative self-concept. They believe they are bad, dumb, sick, unlovable, incompetent, and so on—relative to specific issues or areas of their lives. When such negative beliefs are entrenched, children express them in the same way they would if they were positive attributes—seeking confirmation of them and maintaining their consistency. Many adults who lack assertiveness can trace this quality to criticism or punishment they received as children for being aggressive and assertive. Though there may be evidence in their lives to the contrary, they continue to see themselves as fearful, unaggressive, and placating—maintaining a consistently negative self-image.

Children with negative attitudes about themselves tend not to believe evidence to the contrary. They reject praise or approval for things they hold negative beliefs about, and are very resistant to changing. A child who believes he is not liked or trusted may reject attempts by adults to convince him that they like him and want to help. A child who feels that she doesn't measure up to her classmates in some aspect of schoolwork will likely reject evidence of success, dismissing it as luck or a "mistake."

When children have low self-esteem, it is reflected in characteristic patterns of behavior that become habits that are as intractable as any other.

SELF-ESTEEM AND SCHOOL PERFORMANCE

Self-esteem may determine your child's success in school. Children with superior intelligence and low self-esteem can do poorly in school, while children with average intelligence and high self-esteem can be unusually successful.

Children with low-self esteem tend to get little satisfaction from school, losing motivation and interest easily. Since they tend to be distracted by the issues that affect their feelings about themselves—their relationships with others, and their problems, fears, and anxieties—less interest is directed toward school tasks.

Low self-esteem perpetuates itself by hindering good school performance, and poor performance reinforces low self-esteem. It becomes increasingly difficult for a child to jump off this merry-go-round as time passes. As children fall further behind, greater emphasis is placed on remedial activities, and they become immersed in a continuing pattern of failure and self-denigration, while the origin of the problem, low self-esteem, is overlooked.

Typically, children with low self-esteem feel anxious. When anxiety is excessive, it interferes with learning. These children are usually anxious about approaching new tasks. They have trouble listening, concentrating, and thinking logically about a task, and their work suffers. Conversely, as self-esteem rises, anxiety diminishes, and motivation to accept challenges increases. These children then become more willing to tackle learning opportunities because their curiosity is less qualified by personal fears.

Danny's case shows how low self-esteem hurt a child of considerable intelligence.

DANIEL: A BRIGHT CHILD
WITH LOW SELF-ESTEEM

Danny comes from what is called "good stock." Both parents are teachers at the secondary level, well educated and highly creative. Danny had been quite precocious as an infant and toddler, and his parents had very high expectations for him; actually, they were very critical of any performance in academic work that was less than excellent. As an only child, Danny found school to be a great place for meeting his own social needs, and loved to interact with the other kids, often to the detriment of his schoolwork.

By the time he was in third grade, his parents' attempts to get him to live up to his intellectual gifts resulted in arguments, pressure on him, and criticism of the school. Caught between his desire to please his parents and his own need to socialize with others, Danny was usually in a state of anxiety and apprehension at school. At home he appeared to be fine, because he was not hampered by the pressure of socializing.

Danny was becoming convinced that there was something "wrong" with him. He couldn't seem to make his parents happy with him for very long. Knowing he needed to do perfect work, he usually didn't make an effort to justify being less than perfect ("I don't care!") He would only work if the teacher stood over him. Danny's relations with other children became ambivalent. He wanted to be liked, but knew that there was something wrong about wanting to relate to them so much. He would often become irrationally angry when anyone would approach him. He had become a child with both learning and behavior problems. When asked what he thought about himself, he would reply that he was stupid and naughty.

Children seek to fulfill their emotional needs wherever they are. Being accepted and respected by others, expressing oneself, being in charge, communicating successfully, and making big decisions are emotional needs that are often more important than schoolwork. Children will persist in meeting these needs despite parents' and teachers' expectations.

Children whose emotional needs are being met feel good about themselves and have lots of energy available to attack school tasks successfully. Their high self-esteem enables them to succeed, and every success strengthens self-esteem.

SELF-ESTEEM AND INTERPERSONAL RELATIONS

Children with high self-esteem generally have good relationships with others. Such relationships are self-perpetuating— we all *like* to spend time with someone who is pleasant. Children with low self-esteem are either overly aggressive or excessively retiring in interpersonal relationships, and offer little satisfaction to others.

Relationships are terribly important to everyone, especially to children with low self-esteem though their actions may belie this need. Children with low self-esteem seek support and approval from others which they can't give to themselves. Unfortunately, such children tend to distort communications and misconstrue people's attitudes, ultimately feeling that others believe about them what they believe about themselves. Befriending a child with low self-esteem is often frustrating and discouraging for playmates and teachers.

When children feel that they're not liked, relationships become problems sooner or later. Gloria's case shows how a child goes about undermining relationships that could be satisfying.

GLORIA: A CHILD WITH FEW FRIENDS

No one could understand why Gloria had such difficulties making and keeping friends. She was a cute, bright eight-year-old, had no defects that would make her unacceptable, and yet many people, adults as well as children, found it hard to like her or to be with her for very long.

The course of her relationships with others seemed to follow a pattern. Initially she would come home and be quite enthusiastic about a new friend she'd made. Such friends seemed, by her description, to have many virtues and no faults. For a while (anywhere from a few days to, at most, several weeks), she would be quite happy with her new friend, but submissive and very much the follower in the relationship.

The second phase of the relationships became more difficult. Gloria would become bossy and aggressive. Gradually the new friend would be seen less often, until, finally, Gloria would be talking about her friend only in disparaging terms. After the relationship ended Gloria would enter a friendless period, become depressed, and only come out of it when the pattern repeated itself.

Gloria, like all children, had a great need for relationships in which she could feel good. Her working mother and very busy father made real efforts to spend time with her, but, because of pressures on them, still could not meet the needs of a growing child. Her older sister and younger brother had their own friends and were involved in their own interests. Circumstances seemed to keep Gloria from having very satisfying relationships with her family.

Gloria had discovered that she could make a friend if she allowed that child to be the leader. Being submissive insured that her friend would want to continue to see her. But a strange thing would begin to happen. Gloria would begin to feel better when she had a friend, and her self-esteem would rise. As it did, she unconsciously became dissatisfied in the role of the follower. She would start to become more aggressive, and seek to have other needs met by the relationship. ("Let me decide what we're going to do this time"; "I don't want to play at your house again.") The tenor of the friendship would change, often to the chagrin of the other child. As Gloria's bids for leadership were rejected, she would push harder, leading to the inevitable end of the friendship, leaving her lonely, and convinced that she was unlikable when she tried to be herself in a relationship.

The key to understanding why children have poor relationships is knowing that they overburden friendships with needs that are not being met in other aspects of their lives. Unable to satisfy their own needs, children become dependent on certain relationships to make them feel good. They are bound to fail.

SELF-ESTEEM AND CREATIVITY

Parents and teachers like to see children being creative. Children who keep busy with imaginative play, who express themselves in unique ways, and who show artistic or intellectual talent are a delight to most adults. The tendency to act creatively is related to a child's self-esteem.

How does self-esteem influence creativity?

Creative acts always involve some degree of risk which demands a high level of self-confidence. To act creatively a child must trust others to accept him even if his imaginative solution to a task is unsuccessful.

True creativity arises from within your child. You cannot expect it "on demand." Creativity involves the integration of intellect, visual imagery, playfulness, and mental and physical dexterity. If a child's low self-esteem renders her excessively anxious or fearful, such integration is unlikely. Excessive anxiety interferes with the expression of all of these capabilities.

Being creative involves a high degree of clarity about our own mental images. These "mental pictures" are the imaginative reorganization of commonplace resources and events. Creative children take delight in acting out many of those images. If a child is overly dependent on praise and approval from other people in order to feel worthwhile he will want to conform to others' wishes rather than use his own imagination. Anxiety about how others will judge an act, can undermine a child's ability to experience such delight.

Children do not usually express creativity as some awe-inspiring talent, genius or precocious competence. Artistic and intellectually gifted "geniuses" are rare. Creative children express this quality in small ways; in their day-to-day activities, at play and work: decorating their room, playing spontaneous fantasy games, using creative imagination (a book becomes a wall of a fort, and sweeping the porch becomes a "war" against dirt). The level of their self-esteem determines the amount of creative behavior they express.

HOW PARENTS' SELF-ESTEEM
AFFECTS CHILDREN

Parents with low self-esteem often act in ways that promote self-esteem problems for their children. Such parents tend to "live" through their children. They want their children to achieve goals they haven't, and are disappointed when their children don't. Those children are caught between trying to live up to their parents' expectations and wanting to be themselves.

Parents with low self-esteem are often tense and anxious, especially about how they function as parents. Anxiety distorts communication. The result is they do not hear their children accurately and give ambiguous or contradictory messages. When parents are relaxed about how they're doing as parents, their children's self-esteem is helped because the parents can be better communicators and observers, and be more patient and tolerant.

Low self-esteem parents are often threatened by high self-esteem in their children, particularly when children seek independence and autonomy. These parents feel that their children are rejecting them, and may become aloof, excessively critical, or hurt by their children's independent behavior. When children experience their parents acting in these ways they become confused, frustrated, and angry.

Parents with low self-esteem tend to see many issues as problems or potential problems. When they try to head off problems that don't yet exist, they often create expectations that their children have a hard time meeting, and impose restrictions that undermine their children's self-confidence. Instead of helping their children to find ways to meet challenges, they encourage them to avoid risks.

Low self-esteem parents have difficulty expressing praise realistically. They tend to praise not at all, very little, or, conversely, excessively. But the praise they offer is general rather than specific. Children like and need praise, but if it is too general, it doesn't give them specific information about what they have done well, and leads to ambiguity and confusion.

Parents with low self-esteem tend to give their children mixed messages about success. They encourage their children toward success, but imply that it will be temporary or hard to reach. ("Keep trying, but don't expect to win!") If parents are really threatened by their children's success, they may go so far as to undermine it by withholding resources, criticizing, or breaking promises.

Parents with low self-esteem cannot avoid some of the above dilemmas but they must face themselves squarely before they can effectively enhance their children's self-esteem.

We all know that parents are models for their children, who are always seeking clues about how to act. Children often copy parents' feelings and attitudes, as well as language, mannerisms and actions. Children are sensitive to the subtle, nonverbal ways parents express feelings and attitudes. A shrug that is associated with a tense expression may tell a child that a parent is disappointed, even though nothing is said. Inconsistencies between what a parent says and the tone of voice in which it's said can communicate a whole message that is not spoken. It is almost impossible to hide a feeling, and children are acute observers of the subtle expressions that tell them about their parents' attitudes.

The Four Conditions
of Self-Esteem

SELF-ESTEEM AND CHILDREN'S NEEDS

Have you ever grown a vegetable garden or flowers? Sometimes it's not easy. The soil may be poor, drainage may be a
problem, or there may be too many insects; you need to
improve the conditions for healthy growth—add a little mulch
here, a bit of fertilizer there, water deeply but not too often,
trim and prune at the right time, and so on.

Insuring proper conditions for growth is as necessary for
children as it is for plants. If you try to grow sun-loving plants
in the shade, they won't prosper, nor do you expect to harvest
cucumbers from a tomato plant. Understanding what children's needs are is the first step to insuring proper conditions
for growth. As with plants, if the proper conditions are present, children will be able to manifest the splendid and unique
potential each of them is born with. Conversely, if the proper
conditions are not present, specific abnormalities develop
because many needs are unfulfilled.

When children get what they need to grow, the development
of good character, wholesome personality, positive human
relations, adequate goals, and necessary skills is automatic.

Departures from proper emotional and social development can always be traced to something that was missing in the child's experience. That missing ingredient will always be one or more of the four conditions required for self-esteem.

If self-esteem is the result of a child's needs being fulfilled, then it is our job as parents and teachers to understand what those needs are, at each stage of a child's life, so that we can insure they are met.

As we pointed out in the previous chapter, self-esteem is a feeling . . . a good feeling. When the needs of children are satisfied, they feel good. Promoting and maintaining the most important kinds of good feelings in children is achieved from an understanding of the four basic conditions required for self-esteem.

THE FOUR CONDITIONS THAT INSURE SELF-ESTEEM

The things children feel good about can be grouped into four major areas. Not all good feelings feel the same, nor do they result from the same kind of experiences. But good feelings do have a common feature—a generalized *sense of satisfaction*, which is evidence that something needed has been achieved.

Self-esteem occurs when children experience the positive feelings of satisfaction that result from having a sense of

CONNECTIVENESS—That is, a child feels good relating to people, places, and things that are important to her and these relationships are approved and respected by others.

UNIQUENESS—That is, a child acknowledges and respects the personal characteristics that make him special and different, and receives approval and respect from others for those characteristics.

POWER—That is, a child uses the skills, resources, and opportunities that she has in order to influence the circumstances of her own life in important ways.

MODELS—That is, a child knows that on his own, he is able to make sense out of things, make use of consistent and workable sets of values and personal standards, and have ideals and goals that produce a feeling of purpose and direction.

When these four conditions are met your child will have high self-esteem. Each condition is discriminable from the others, as we will show throughout the book. When all of these conditions are met simultaneously, a child is least aware of it—he just feels good, and people around him feel good too. But when any of the conditions are not being fulfilled, the child reacts in certain characteristic ways. In the following pages we will explore the essential components of each condition and how they interact to produce high or low self-esteem.

THE WHOLE CHILD

THE FOUR CONDITIONS OF SELF-ESTEEM

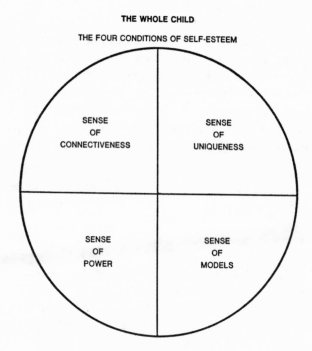

WHEN A CHILD HAS
A SENSE OF CONNECTIVENESS

We all have met children who are so easy to relate with that doing so makes us feel good. They seem to have an unusual talent for human relations. These children, like Sean in the following case study, have a high sense of connectiveness.

SEAN: A CHILD WHO FEELS CONNECTED

Sean is a delight! People are attracted to him, both children and adults, and can't quite tell why. Being seven years old, he is going through some changes, but he usually is happy and affectionate. His second-grade teacher would like to wring his neck sometimes, but invariably succumbs to his charm. From time to time he seems more inclined to socialize than work. He's no genius in school, but when he's brought to task for not having done something, he responds with good humor, often an unaffected apology, and usually gets the job done, albeit with some help.

He's easily the most popular child in class, invariably gentle and considerate with his peers, and evenhanded in his relations with others. He'll be as considerate of Sarah, a handicapped child, as he will be of Tony, the best athlete in second grade. He has warm relations with most of the children, but seems not to be dependent on any of them. He can be by himself, especially when caring for the class's pet hamster, which he does as often as teacher allows.

Sean can stand up for himself, though. He's never been in a fight, but his disarming charm usually persuades his adversaries to work out a compromise with him. His teacher has often seen him playing with someone with whom he had an argument just minutes before. Many of his conflicts seem to result from his taking the side of a child who is being attacked by others.

Sean's parents characterize him as a "scamp," always into

something. Sean's parents are very loving with him and his two younger siblings. They touch and hold each other a lot. Even at age seven, Sean holds hands with his parents, while shopping or going places. His teachers have had Sean's dad in class, and noticed that he rarely talks to his son without touching him at the same time.

Sean comes from a fairly large family, with many cousins, aunts, and uncles. The family does lots of things together, and Sean frequently talks about his uncle the airline pilot, and a cousin who's on the high-school football team.

One of the things that makes people like Sean is that he's a good communicator. He speaks clearly, says what he's thinking and feeling, and looks at you when he speaks. He says what he needs, and usually gets it because he takes others into consideration. He's a fair athlete, but a good team member. He gets as confused and frustrated as any child his age, but he'll probably do just fine, because he knows how to "connect" with people.

Sean wasn't born being friendly, but his innate potential to form close and intimate relationships blossomed in the warm, nurturing atmosphere of his home. Because he has a high sense of connectiveness, people like him.

A child's sense of connectiveness signifies that certain needs are fulfilled, primarily in relationships with people, and secondarily with places and things. When these needs are satisfied, a child feels good.

The following needs must be met in order for a child to have a high sense of connectiveness.

Children need to feel that they're part of something. This means they want and need to be *functional and important* members of a family, class, gang, team, work group, neighborhood, and so forth. Overall, they are aware that they have a place in the scheme of things.

Children need to feel related to people in positive ways. This usually is characterized by effective communication, being able to share feelings, and to experience warmth and caring from people who are important to them.

Children need to symbolize their membership with groups that are special to them. This means that children need to label their connectiveness in real and symbolic ways, for example, "I'm a Smith"; "a member of classroom 4-A"; "an American." Dressing like Dad, wearing the school emblem and team uniforms, having the same sneakers as friends, are ways that a sense of group identity becomes concrete and specific.

Children benefit from feeling connected to the past or a heritage. Acknowledging one's "roots" extends feelings of connection back in time and space, and deepens a sense of belonging and being a part of something. Patriotism, respecting one's ancestors, and feeling part of the ongoing stream of life are all related in this feeling. Most children are enchanted by stories of their parents' early days and of their own infancy and childhood.

Children need to feel that something important belongs to them. "Mine, mine," the young child cries. As he grows, the objects to which he feels attached (my ball, my stereo, my car), change, but remain important. Extraordinary interest in collecting and saving *things* is an expression of this need. The ways children go about satisfying this need should not be confused with excessive materialism, but is the way children symbolize feelings of "ownership," which ultimately result in mature feelings of commitment, responsibility, and caring.

Children need to feel that they belong to someone or something. This is not precisely the same as the feeling of being part of or identifying with something or some group, but has more to do with knowing that who or what one belongs to will care for, protect, and make one safe. Secure children sense that they belong to someone who will not disregard them or their needs.

Children need to know that the people or things to which they're connected are held in high esteem by oth-

ers. If a child senses that his family, school, friends, favorite things, race, religion, to name just a few, are disparaged or ridiculed, his own feelings of self-worth are undermined. "My daddy can *too* do that"; "My class is *so* the best." Children must insist that their connections are worthy of respect. Parents who disparage school or a child's teacher, and teachers who downgrade a child's friends are undermining the child's sense of connectiveness.

Children need to feel they're important to others. They want to know that they're noticed, that their opinions are heard, considered, and influence decisions, that their needs are weighed in decisions, and that they're wanted and respected. You cannot assume that your child feels important. It must be made concrete through specific action in which the child is involved.

Children need to feel connected to their own bodies. Having a sense of connectiveness also includes a physical/sensory aspect. Feeling at ease with and connected to one's own body results in being able to trust it to do what one wants, and to not do what one doesn't want. "I didn't mean to spill the milk!" Children with a poor sense of connectiveness often appear to be awkward and poorly coordinated. A child may tip his chair back from his desk, and fall over, because he cannot sense, in his own body, when he's reached the critical point-of-balance. Children learn to connect with their own bodies by being touched a lot and by taking some physical risks, such as climbing trees or jungle gyms, thus learning to enjoy physical activities and what their bodies can do.

The people, places, or things that your child feels connected to are enormously varied, and change over time. Children often feel strongly about associations that mean nothing to their parents and teachers. (Does Darth Vader turn you on?) The child who never takes his baseball cap off, except to shower, may not be demonstrating poor manners, so much as gaining some satisfaction from wearing that important emblem of connection. When teachers take some important

SENSE OF CONNECTIVENESS

CHILDREN NEED TO FEEL . . .

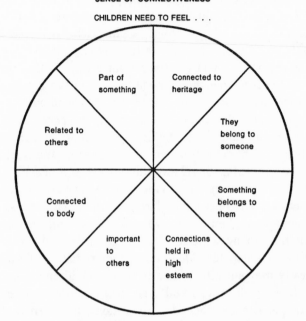

connectiveness symbol away from a child, they may prompt him to find another that produces similar satisfaction.

Similarly children need to feel connected to the important people in their lives, such as parents, relatives, siblings, friends, and teachers. A sense of connectiveness to these people is directly related to the degree of comfort, warmth, security, understanding, humor and goodwill that characterizes these relationships. Anger, frustration, and poor communications undermine a child's sense of connectiveness.

Your child feels connected to various categories of people, though the specific, personal relationship may not be close or intimate. For example, many children feel that all their classmates are important, though only a few are close friends. Children may actually know little about their teacher's personal life, but she may be defended, praised, pleased, and so on. Her attention is valued because she's the teacher, and simply by her role she's very important.

Furthermore, different relationships become important at different times. A child may play with someone she doesn't like, if no one else is available. A child who is forced into unfamiliar circumstances will seek relationships with others who share common characteristics that are important to the child at the time. An eight-year-old boy, for instance, will seek out almost any other boy, rather than befriend girls, even though he might share intellectual, social, and personal interests with them. Sometimes the people or things that children form bonds with seem strange or odd to parents and teachers. Often the motive for the relationship is the result of something that is important at the time to the child. A very bright student may become part of a gang of rough, unscholastic children, when equally studious peers are available, because he or she may be fantasizing some special "tough" role, and can act it out with the gang. It is likely to be a temporary affiliation.

Loyalty may substitute for affection in children's relationships. Loyalty to groups and even institutions may override and compensate for a child's frustrations, as when a child shows intense loyalty to a team on which he or she is the poorest player, thus fulfilling the need for a sense of connectiveness. All boys (or girls), all black people, all football players, all Catholics—each of these may be important sources of personal identification to a child.

Loyalty to race or religion may supersede (and interfere with) forming other bonds that may be rewarding. A minority child may band with others of his ethnic or racial group despite sharing interests with others outside the group. It seems that as children get older, such abstract loyalties become more and more important. Since feelings of safety are associated with the sense of connectiveness, associations that promote such feelings are given more and more importance.

Feeling connected goes beyond human relationships. The degree to which your child feels attached to places or things is also important. If children, for whatever reason, experience stress and anxiety in human relationships, they often compensate by forming intense bonds with places or things, and, these bonds often can take precedence over human connections. Because the sense of connectiveness is an ongoing need, any object may fulfill it when human relations don't. A hat, toy, article of clothing, blanket, teddy bear, old pot, or piece of wood may serve to increase a child's comfort, reduce anxiety, and allow him to feel a sense of belonging. When children have an intense, seemingly irrational, attachment to some object, it signifies that article to be important to their sense of connectiveness. Such attachments change over time—a toy that was special last week may be nearly forgotten today as more and more things satisfy your child's feelings.

A child's wish, dream, or fantasy may create the circumstances for attaching feelings to various places and things. Space has become an important place for many children due to science—fictional and real—TV, falling Skylabs, space capsules, and so forth. There are no objective limits to what children may feel connected to. A sense of connectiveness may result from strange things indeed. A friend of one of the authors was quite sickly and isolated as a child, and took up a passionate interest in insects, many of which became "friends" of his. He later became an entomologist, and ultimately transferred his important feelings of connectiveness to people, as a creative teacher and medical missionary.

Favorite places may arise and disappear. Your child's sense of connectiveness is activated by places where she or he feels safe and comfortable, and which serve to promote feelings of familiarity and belonging. Children are territorial creatures in that places may belong to them: "This is my house, you can't come in!" (Having something belong to us promotes a sense of ownership that, in turn, stimulates feelings of control.)

It is a constant challenge for parents and teachers to encourage children to place more value on human connections rather than place/thing connections—and the intention is frequently frustrated because at that moment a child's sense of connectiveness may be dominated by an object or a place. A room, his bed, a favorite corner, a special seat in class, the loft, parent's bed, underneath the kitchen table, a special desk, a closet, the seat next to teacher's desk, and many others, serve to activate and reinforce a child's sense of connectiveness.

A teacher had a "magic desk" in her kindergarten classroom. When a child misbehaved, he or she could sit at this special desk, which had been decorated and set apart from the others. The teacher told the children that if they sat in it for a while, they would calm down, feel good, and do better work. She had convinced them that it was really magical, and sitting in it invariably had a positive effect on the children—it satisfied their sense of connection to a special place.

Your child's sense of connectiveness is enhanced or diminished by circumstances and events he has no control over. Moving, changing schools, illness, death, divorce, babies, and the myriad of possible events in children's lives threaten a child's sense of connectiveness.

Parents and teachers must understand and respect the variety of ways in which children satisfy their need for a sense of connectiveness. A broad array of person/place/thing connections that produce satisfaction will go a long way to insure high self-esteem. When the range of satisfying connections is narrow, children will place excessive dependence on the few attachments that produce good feelings, running the risk of "wearing out" the ones they have. In Section II we will describe concrete and practical things that parents and teachers can do to raise children's sense of connectiveness.

WHEN A CHILD HAS A SENSE OF UNIQUENESS

Some children are "different." We can tell by the way they act that something unusual is going on inside them. This is not always a problem. Russ, the subject of our next case study, is different. He has a high sense of uniqueness.

RUSS: A DIFFERENT KIND OF CHILD

When Mrs. Bennett, the fourth-grade teacher, wants to "contemplate the mysteries of life," she lets herself think about

Russ, one of the most enigmatic children she has ever met. She really can't decide whether he is a problem or a blessing to her and to the children in her class. He frequently inhabits the gray area of "not quite being in trouble," although some of the things he does are not quite "normal."

Russ just never seems to react to things the way most children his age do. An example of this is the time that a speaker from the local fire department came to class. After the talk there were lots of questions about fire safety, firemen's duties, and so forth. Russ raised his hand three times and asked the same question each time. He wanted to know why the fire trucks were red. Each time the speaker gave an answer (easy to see, tradition, symbolic), Russ had a logical way of refuting the explanation. Finally, the fire official gave up, and said he really couldn't justify the color, that's just the way it was. Russ got a self-satisfied look on his face, and didn't ask any other questions. Mrs. Bennett wanted to wring his neck, but couldn't pin him with any specific infraction of the rules or decorum. And that's the way it would go, day in and day out.

Russ tends to do things his own way, and often when he wants to. There was the time he didn't do his math homework and was told to stay in during recess to finish it. During silent reading, just before recess, he asked to go to the bathroom and received permission to do so. He was out somewhat longer than usual, but not excessively, and when he returned he laid the worksheet on Mrs. Bennett's desk. He had done it in the bathroom! Suspecting that he had copied it from someone else, Mrs. Bennett took him aside and asked him straight out whether he had done so. Russ looked her straight in the eyes and said, "You know I never copy my work," and turned and went back to his seat. He was right—he had what amounted to a fetish about doing his own work. Of course, when Mrs. Bennett looked over the work, it was all correct. What's a teacher to do with a kid like that?

Russ shines in several areas in school. He's an exceptional artist, although his subjects are often a bit precocious. Nudes in fourth grade? But he never seems to do his off-the-wall things with the intention of gaining attention. Mostly he seems not to care what others think. His stories are fourth-grade masterpieces, well constructed and interesting. He loves to read, hates math (but can do it), and relates well to the other children—when he wants to. He's not a loner, but has no obvious pattern to his relationships.

Russ's parents don't give the appearance of being very unusual people. His father is a graphic artist, and his mother, who has a degree in philosophy, stays home with three young children. Their home is quite nice, and is filled with evidence of odd and special interests of every family member. They don't feel that anything is wrong with Russ. Quite the contrary. They seem to know what he's doing, and actually encourage Mrs. Bennett to give Russ lots of room for individuality. They rarely limit his explorations, provide plenty of resources for him, and rarely criticize him. They do insist that he treat other people fairly. They acknowledge his opinions, when he can justify them, and are willing to discuss things even when they disagree with him.

Russ is the kind of child who puts his unique imprint on everything he does, including the little bird that's his personal symbol—it's always next to his name on his papers. His unique view produces stimulating questions that often challenge his teachers. Despite his unusual behavior, he rarely does things that actually make trouble for others; his actions only create a bit of discomfort for them, because it's hard to tell where he's coming from. He doesn't react, he just does his "thing." He's a person who "hears a different drummer," and steps to that music.

Most children are not as unusual as Russ. He has a very high sense of uniqueness. But he does represent, in a dramatic way, the universal need of children to feel special and to express their feelings in a variety of ways. Russ is fortunate that his parents value his specialness and do many things to enhance it. Children with high self-esteem receive lots of support and approval for being "different."

The following needs must be met in order for children to have a high sense of uniqueness.

Children need to feel that there's something special about them, even though in many ways they're similar to others. Thus feeling special grows as a child's special qualities are pointed out and respected by others. Self-respect is a result of feeling special in positive ways.

Children need to feel that others think they're special. They learn this through things others say or do to them. Recognizing that a child is special and not telling him or her has little effect on the child's sense of uniqueness. Parents and teachers can treat children *as if* they're special, because they are—no two humans are exactly the same, even though they share many characteristics. Children cannot confirm what's special about themselves, unless others *whom they respect* tell them how they're special.

Children need to feel that they know and can do things that no one else can do. "See me; see what I'm doing. Watch me climb the tree!" Even though every child may do so, the child who takes such delight in and seeks acknowledgment of a special skill is enhancing his sense of uniqueness. *How* children do things, their style or approach, is what distinguishes a mundane act as unique.

Children need to be able to express themselves in their own way. Children cannot feel special unless those feelings are manifested in what they do. If children are held to rigid standards of performance, being told how to do things as well as what to do, and cannot safely explore alternative ways to behave, the outcome is a personality that is inflexible and conforming.

Children need to use their imaginations and freely expand their creative potentials. All children are naturally motivated to be creative, curious, and exploratory. When such behavior is acknowledged and rewarded, it becomes transformed into habits of creative thinking and acting. If the unique, fantastic, and unusual expressions of children's imagination and creativity are disparaged, their sense of uniqueness is restricted, and self-esteem suffers.

Children need to respect themselves. They need to value their performance and to learn to trust their perceptions.

Children learn to trust and respect themselves by being respected (taken seriously) by adults who are important to them. Parents and teachers who don't take children seriously undermine a child's self-respect—and very likely that of the adult that he'll become. Children who have little respect for themselves, can have little respect for others.

Children need to enjoy being different. Children need not interfere with the rights of others in order to do so. Children with a firm sense of uniqueness can respect other's rights to express themselves. Children with a low sense of uniqueness need to be the center of attention, usually at a cost to others. Young children will take delight in themselves if they find parents and teachers taking delight in them. If you and your child's teachers can't enjoy your children's uniqueness, they can't either.

SENSE OF UNIQUENESS

CHILDREN NEED TO . . .

Enjoy being different

Know there's something special about themselves

Respect themselves

Know and do things that no one else can do

Use imagination and expand creativity

Know others think them special

Express themselves in their own way

Although the need for a sense of uniqueness remains constant, that which your children feel is special about themselves changes with age and the conditions of their lives. A toddler's pride in his physical mobility changes into pride in his ability to climb fences as a preschooler. As new discoveries occur, the catalog of potentially special attributes grows longer and longer. But at each stage of development the qualities that children may take pride in must be met by approval and respect from others in order to build a firm and positive sense of uniqueness.

We all seek acceptance and approval for what we feel is special about ourselves. Children are often less restrained than adults to this end. "Look at me! See what I can do!" is an expression of a child's need to have his specialness acknowledged. Parents and teachers often dispose of children's behavior by saying, "Oh, he's just seeking attention." Just so. Children who seek attention really do need it! But not just any kind of attention. They are seeking to have their own sense of uniqueness enhanced by having *what they feel is special about themselves* recognized. If they don't receive such acknowledgment they behave in extreme ways in order to be noticed. A sign that a child's sense of uniqueness is low is when he seems to persevere in seeking attention for something that he is characteristically punished for.

Frequently children and adults don't identify the same attributes as special. Parents and teachers tend to value qualities that suggest emerging future virtues; children focus on what seems to make them feel good now. A very bright child may take his intellect for granted while seeking recognition for social and athletic prowess, while adults center their approval around his academic accomplishments. The disparity between the things a child is seeking recognition for and the things that adults are seeking to give recognition to creates conflict, and usually results in lowered self-esteem for the child. Perhaps the natural conflict between generations is a function of this dilemma.

A child's need for a sense of uniqueness is so strong that he will often seek acknowledgment for negative characteristics, if what he considers his virtues haven't been sufficiently recognized. When a child attaches negative labels to his uniqueness, he is as tenacious in expressing those characteristics as if he received praise for them. For example, a child may believe that he is the worst behaved student in his class. His special role of class clown, reinforced by his peers, may prompt him to take every opportunity to prove his special position in the class. He will say or do things to create trouble, even when he knows that he will be punished for it. When this type of behavior is met with excessive criticism and disapproval, the child develops a negative self-image.

To help your children feel special, give them many opportunities to express themselves: verbally, artistically, physically, at play, and in performing their duties. You can give them positive feedback by acknowledging that adults take pleasure in seeing such expressions of self. Specifically they need your help to *identify what it is about them that's special*. Children need to learn the vocabulary that helps them understand their positive characteristics. This requires parents and teachers to identify and label for a child those specific characteristics they find praiseworthy. For example, a child demonstrates compassion toward someone, but she may not know the word that describes what she did.

Your child's sense of uniqueness is experienced in many areas of his life. The qualities and characteristics he labels special may result from profuse approval received for expressing a specific attribute or competence with considerable skill.

Those things that make children feel unique are varied. They include:

- what they can do with their bodies (sports, dance, etc.)
- the special skills they have (building things, organizing, etc.)

- the special talents they have (artistic, singing, academics, etc.)
- their appearance (tall, fat, pretty, ugly, etc.)
- their background (race, heritage, place of origin, etc.)
- their hobbies or interests (collecting, camping, trains, etc.)
- what they know (animals, history, current events)
- what they do (take karate lessons, yell loudly, run fast, etc.)
- how they think (fantasies, imagination, humor, etc.)
- what they believe (religious beliefs, radical ideas, skepticism, etc.)

Because of the disparity between adults' and children's values about what makes someone special, enhancing your child's sense of uniqueness is not an easy thing for many parents and teachers. There are a number of stresses associated with being "different" or "special" in our society. We respect individuality, but not if it's too extreme; we value creativity, unless it challenges deeply held values; we respect imagination, until it departs too far from our own experiences; we accept originality, if we're not threatened by it being "weird." Children, of course, cannot make the subtle judgments that adults do about these matters. In seeking to enhance their sense of uniqueness, they may sometimes step beyond acceptable boundaries. Even though the need for a sense of uniqueness is a natural motive in children, we don't necessarily make it easy for them to fulfill that need.

Few parents want their children to be so different that they risk the disapproval of their peers or other adults. Parents who want their children to be good tend to mold behavior, rather than accept expressions of individuality.

Parents' and teachers' own fears about being different affect the way they respond to children's uniqueness. But it's important to remember that helping a child feel special does not automatically lead to his becoming an oddball.

WHEN A CHILD HAS A SENSE OF POWER

We all like responsible children. When they act appropriately, control themselves, and work successfully, we take pride in them and in ourselves as parents and teachers. We don't usually expect children to be as responsible as Lucia, the ten-year-old in our next case study, but, as you will see, there are good reasons why she is a child with a firm sense of power.

LUCIA: A CHILD IN CHARGE OF HERSELF

Her parents characterize her as ten years old, going on thirty-five. They, her teacher, and everyone who knows her are continually impressed by the depth of self-possession that this little girl expresses. She's bright, hard-working, responsible, pretty, stubborn, and independent.

She wasn't always that way. Lucia's infancy and early childhood were characterized by a great deal of illness and various maladies. She was hospitalized several times before she was five and spent long periods at home, bedridden.

Her parents handled her childhood illnesses in the practical, matter-of-fact way they go about most things. They always insisted that she do what she could to help herself. They gave her everything she needed, but required her to make her own decisions. When she was on a special diet, they told her all the things she could eat, and let her plan her own meals. Now, at ten, apart from some limitations on physical exertion, she is a healthy child.

At school Lucia is an excellent student. This seems to be more a result of hard work than of superior gifts. She tests in the bright-average range, but has the ability to focus on a task so that she is strong competition for children who have greater intellectual gifts but less stick-to-itiveness. She thinks about things before doing them, approaching most tasks with a clear plan that saves her time and energy.

She loves challenges. Her teachers only need imply that a task may be hard, and Lucia is ready to try. Often she's the only one to come up with the correct solution to a problem, because she will work at it longer than her classmates.

At home she exhibits the same characteristics. She has regular chores to do, as everyone in her family does, and her parents are diligent in seeing that they're done.

In addition to regular chores, her parents have a list of special duties for which the children are paid. If a job is done to the high standards the parents set, the children earn money and can do whatever they wish with it. Lucia regularly earns one to two dollars a week and is saving to buy a portable radio.

Her parents' attitude, as expressed to her teacher, is "We set the conditions and leave it up to the children how to live within them." Sometimes she complains about the rules at home, but she and her parents talk openly about any problems or disagreements they have with each other. Lucia makes lots of decisions at home. Lively family discussions also become planning times for trips, vacations, work days, and so forth. Everyone gets to speak, and anyone who has a good idea can influence events.

Because Lucia has the habit of thinking about what she's doing, she can be stubborn. She often rejects invitations to do things that interfere with her plans. When several of her friends pressured her to go to the movies one Saturday, she declined because it would interfere with a commitment she made to help her mother with shopping. She has an unusual capability to honor her obligations. It makes her seem older. By the way, she invited those same friends to come to her house after the movies, having figured out that she would be home by then. They did and, characteristically, Lucia got to be with her friends as well as fulfill her responsibility.

Lucia is often called upon by her peers to be in charge of things; she's usually elected to class office, and invariably gets the job done. Lucia knows how to make decisions and take responsibility. She's been taught to be in charge of herself.

* * *

One of the reasons other children like Lucia is that they see in her many qualities they would like to see in themselves. Lucia is unusual only in the sense that she puts her best effort into what she does and receives support and encouragement to do so. Your children are equally capable of doing so if their sense of power is adequate.

Children who have a sense of power feel that they can influence what happens in their lives. They know that their skills will be sufficient for the tasks for which they're responsible, that they have access to resources they need, and will have opportunities to use what they know.

The following needs must be met in order for children to have a high sense of power.

Children need to feel that they can do the things they set out to do. This sense of power is felt by the infant who can reach and hold her rattle; the preschooler who can safely ride his trike at breakneck speed down a hill; the school-aged child who can finish her math on time; the preteen who can take the right buses to a distant destination. This feeling is reinforced each time children successfully accomplish the tasks they undertake. It's important that parents and teachers help children succeed.

Children need to feel that they have the resources necessary to carry out their own purposes and those tasks set for them by parents and teachers. Children are not spoiled by having a large array of material resources available (toys, equipment, money, "stuff" of all sorts). Having such resources allows them to create and fulfill a greater variety of purposes (from play to work). When parents and teachers set tasks for children and don't provide the proper resources for completing them, the potential for failure increases. Children's ability to provide their own material resources is limited, although it increases with age.

Children need to feel that they are allowed to make or influence decisions about things that are important to them. In doing this they develop self-confidence. Requiring children to make decisions that are beyond their capabilities may undermine their sense of power because of the higher probability of failing. What's important to children changes as they grow, and are often issues they can handle if parents and teachers are willing to risk giving them decision-making power.

Children need to feel comfortable when fulfilling responsibilities. Obvious as it may sound, for children to become responsible, they need to be given responsibilities. Children can accept responsibility comfortably when parents and teachers insure that necessary resources are available; needed skills are taught effectively; and approval and rewards for success are built into the process.

Children need to feel that they know how to make decisions and solve problems. Allowing children to make decisions and teaching them effective ways to solve problems enhances their feelings of independence and personal control, and reinforces their sense of power.

Children need to feel that they can be in control of themselves when dealing with pressure and stress. The world of childhood is filled with potential stress—time limits, ambiguous situations, new experiences, deferred gratification, sharing limited resources (a toy), and trying to make sense of what's happening and what people mean. Children do not become stoic robots when they learn to control their feelings and express them appropriately. Parents and teachers can help children learn self-control by placing limits on excessive emotional outbursts, teaching children alternative methods for expressing themselves, and by being role models of self-discipline. If parents and teachers are too protective, it's hard for children to learn how to deal with stress.

Children need to use the skills they've learned. When children can do things, they need lots of opportunities to do them. Children become confident of their emerging capabilities as they use and refine them. Young children often do something over and over again until they are sure they know how, and then move on to something else. Children's sense of power is enhanced when they can do things that bring automatic success, providing a basis for exploring new skills.

Children need to feel that they can cope with failure. Failing is a normal part of childhood and children who fear it place limits on their experiences. Parents and teachers promote apprehension in children by overreacting to their failings. You can help them deal creatively with failure in several ways: (1) by teaching them to analyze failures so they need not repeat them; (2) by showing them how to set reasonable standards for themselves; and (3) by helping them understand that failure is an *event*, not a personal characteristic. If children fear failing, their chances of being successful diminish because they are more tentative and cautious.

We stress that having a sense of power does not necessarily mean having power in an absolute sense. Often recognizing and accepting limitations increases a sense of power. When children know the limits and conditions within which they live, at home and at school, their sense of freedom increases because they can make more realistic decisions.

The following points are critical factors in helping your children develop their sense of power:

- Reasonable and clear rules provide guidelines for children so that they know what kinds of decisions they can make, and can predict their parents' responses. Appropriate limits increase children's security.
- Learning to take responsibility, which includes decision making and problem solving, is the *most* important ingredient in school success. Responsible children produce rewards and praise for themselves.
- Doing chores and jobs at home and at school requires children to use the skills they have and to learn new ones, to develop organizing abilities, and to share in important activities. All of these add to a developing sense of power.

One of the most important skills children need is the ability to influence people. Stubbornness, attention-seeking behavior, aggressiveness, being demanding, saying no, and other forms of control are natural expressions of the toddler and preschooler's need to learn effective strategies for controlling and influencing other people. Your child's sense of power grows as she finds and uses appropriate and effective ways to get the things she needs from others, especially the important adults in her life. You and your child's teachers need to be receptive and flexible in order for her to learn that she can have influence.

The importance of enabling children to make decisions and choices cannot be overemphasized. It is the key to having a sense of power. Anyone, child or adult, who cannot make decisions about things that are important to them, or cannot carry out their decisions successfully is *powerless*—the antithesis of self-esteem.

Competence and power are closely associated, but a competent person may still have a low sense of power if he doesn't feel competent. Objective measures of competence do not guarantee that a child will feel good. On the other hand, it is difficult to maintain a sense of power without expressing competence in something. Teachers who set high standards, provide resources and alternative paths to meeting these standards, and convey support and approval despite children's failures can insure that children's competence grows.

An examination of those children we think of as spoiled is instructive. Though these children appear to control many situations, they have a low sense of power. If you watch a spoiled child closely, you will observe that his actions are quite predictable and patterned. He responds similarly to many events, and has little flexibility, while being manipulative. Spoiled children do not know how to handle pressure well, and since others solve their problems for them, have not learned to solve their own. If spoiled children begin to experience the consequences of what they do, and are not being protected by overly nurturant parents, their sense of power will begin to grow, and as their confidence in their own capacities develops their need to be controlling diminishes.

Handicapped children, those with learning disabilities, and

children with psychological problems that interfere with learning are especially susceptible to a low sense of power. Often a low sense of power, rather than the disability itself, is responsible for some of their learning problems. Section IV will identify many ways in which parents and teachers can enhance children's sense of power.

WHEN A CHILD HAS A SENSE OF MODELS

Some children just seem to know who they are and what they want. When children know what their goals are and work toward them, it lends a sense of purpose and direction to their lives. These children often seem to take care of themselves. Robbie, the subject of our next case study, is such a child. Most of us would be proud to have him as our own.

ROBBIE: A CHILD WHO KNOWS WHO HE IS

Robert Lainie Jorgenson IV has a favorite activity. He likes to lie in the hay loft looking down across the pasture toward the river, imagining how the land looked in the time of his grandfather and great-grandfather. He is the fourth generation of his family to live on this land, and he sometimes wonders how his grandchildren would see it.

Robbie remembers his grandfather with affection. Now eleven, he recalled how Grandpa Robert taught him about the plants and animals that lived in and around their river farm when he was only three or four years old. His grandfather would hold Robbie on his lap and sit as still as a statue, as he waited for birds and small animals to accept their presence and resume their ordinary activities that they could watch. Grandpa used to call all these creatures "the relatives," and told Robbie again and again that they had an important place on the farm. When Robbie was studying biology in school this past year, he learned how ecology proved Grandpa right. Robbie can't understand how his friends can use forest creatures for target practice with their .22's. He spends time watching them, feeding them in winter, and has learned where most of their nests and warrens are.

At eleven, Robbie is as good a farmhand as many men twice his age. He learned to drive a tractor when he was seven and knows and understands most of the processes used by his dad on the farm. He never questions that the farm is going to be his life. He also knows that he will be going to school in the future to learn new methods of farming in order to keep pace with changing practices. His dad and mom have talked with him on many occasions about it. He sometimes feels that his dad is overly concerned about whether he wants to be a farmer. Robbie knows that he loves the farm too much to ever leave it for long.

Robbie leads a full life for a boy his age. Work is a very important part of it, and there are always new things to learn. But school, Future Farmers of America, church, and sports also absorb his time. His mom always says, "There's always time enough for the important things. Let's just sit down and figure out what's most important."

Robbie knows that his folks are special, especially when he listens to some of his friends complain about their parents. He vividly remembers the time in third grade he got into trouble for being one of a group of boys who broke into the school's refrigerator and stole some ice cream. He'd been suspended, and his parents were told about what he'd done. Neither his mom nor dad said anything to him on the way home from school, but stopped the car where the road came close to the river. His dad got out and indicated to him to do so. His mom drove on home. Without a word, his dad walked through the orchard to a stand of trees just beyond it. Robbie remembers how scared he was, not knowing what was going to happen. His father stopped by a tree that was a favorite of Grandpa's and sat down on a root. He waited thoughtfully for a while, then told Robbie that his grandfather had taken *him* to this spot many times and told him about "the relatives." What Robbie needed to remember was "the relatives" also included all the *people* that Robbie had to deal with too. Then Robbie's dad became very quiet. He finally told Robbie to stand up and look out toward the river and the fields beyond. As Robbie did so, he was almost overcome by a strong feeling that was a mixture (as near as he could tell later) of guilt, anger at himself, and love for what he was looking at.

Behind him, his dad spoke and said, "There's only a few things you need to remember in this life, Robbie. And I'm going to tell you what they are. If you can remember them, you'll be worthy of the work and love that your ancestors have put into this place. They are these: One, understand why you're doing what you do. Two, do what you have to do the best way you know how. And three, think about the consequences of what you do before you do it." And then he rose and walked back home, leaving Robbie alone.

Robbie remembers staying in the grove by himself for hours after his dad left. During the next few days of his suspension Robbie worked hard for twelve hours each day, but nothing was said about the incident again.

Robbie hasn't forgotten what his dad said to him that day and he hasn't gotten into trouble again. Actually his life has become more organized and purposeful since then. He is beginning to integrate the strong human models and set of values that he experienced and is making them part of himself.

The strong role models and consistent set of principles that Robbie experienced determined the way he feels about life and his place in it. When your children make such models part of themselves, they are unconscious bases for choices. "I just feel that it's wrong to do that!" is a way of saying that a principle of ethics or morals has become part of the way we feel, and that our sense of models is becoming stronger.

People, ideas and beliefs, and your child's experiences all have an impact on his sense of models, and enable him to make sense out of life. Issues of personal values, goals, and ideals reflect children's sense of models, as does the ability to clarify personal standards and live up to them.

Three kinds of models that influence your child are:

- Human models—people who are worthy of emulation
- Philosophical models—ideas that guide a child's behavior attitudes
- Operational models—the knowledge that a child gains from everyday experience (how to do things such as talking, walking, opening jars, putting on shoes, etc.)

The following needs must be met in order for children to have a high sense of models.

Children need to experience people who are worthy models for their own behavior. Most of what children learn is the result of unconsciously mimicking parents, teachers, siblings, relatives and friends. People are *worthy* models when the attitudes and behaviors that a child copies from them, and uses, result in successful experiences for that child. Daddy's rough, aggressive demeanor may be quite acceptable for him at his job, but it may not be appropriate when junior acts that way in kindergarten. A parent or teacher who can effectively demonstrate what she wants children to learn is a better model than if she only tells them.

Children need to feel confident that they can distinguish right from wrong; good from bad. Moral and ethical standards are learned by observation and by listening to what people who are important to children say. Children then try to apply these standards to their own behavior to see how they work. If these experiences result in success, they will tend to adopt them. Your children will adopt family standards that are consistently practiced and positively reinforced.

Children need to feel that their own values and beliefs can successfully guide their behavior. A child's need to be aware of his own values is especially crucial at times of ethical dilemmas, such as choosing between loyalty and honesty in school situations. You can help your children clarify their own values by pointing out ways to express them effectively. As children experience success and receive praise for applying these values, they will become more confident in their own beliefs.

Children need to have a broad range of experiences, so that new experiences aren't intimidating. All experiences that children have build a framework, or "catalog," of memories that guides their behavior in future situations. When children have a broad range of positive experiences that are appropriate to their age and competence, they will have more confidence in facing new ones. Children who are forced to engage in experiences that are threatening build a framework of anxiety and aversion.

Children need to be aware of their goals and to feel that they can work toward them. Behavior that is goal-oriented ("If you want the Popsicle, you'll have to pick up your toys first") helps your children measure their own degree of success. It also encourages them to clarify standards ("You didn't pick them all up, therefore you can't have the Popsicle yet"), and to know where they stand ("Now that you've picked them all up, you can have the Popsicle"). Working toward minor (short-range) goals builds the capability to work toward major (long-range) ones.

Children need to feel that they can make sense out of what's going on in their lives. Children become confused and uncomfortable when they experience excessive change, unpredictability, conflict, emotionality, and inconsistency. Under such conditions their anxiety rises because they are unable to make accurate predictions or reach goals. Every child has his own balance point between his need for stability and his need for change.

Children need to know the standards by which their performance will be evaluated. Children are motivated to please and to gain approval from important adults. When standards are unclear, unstated, or inconsistent, children can't tell whether they will receive praise or criticism for what they do. "Misbehavior" is often a child's effort to force others to clarify standards.

Children need to feel that they can learn, and need to know effective ways for going about it. Knowing that one can learn creates the motivation and openness to learn. Children learn not only how to do things—*they also learn how to learn*, and in this crucial task they must be helped by their parents and teachers. Curiosity is an innate human trait, and learning is the way that curiosity is satisfied. Children who learn how to learn are able to organize and direct their curiosity.

Children need to feel a sense of order. The alternative is a sense of disorder that promotes anxiety. By living within a relatively ordered environment at home and school, your children develop skills in organizing, planning, and problem solving, the foundation of effective learning. A sense of order should not be confused with excessive neatness or cleanliness, but arises more from clear communication, predictability, and ready access to important resources.

Whether or not models are useful ones is measured by the successes or failures that children have when they apply them in their own lives. The values that a child has about school (learned from parents and siblings) will influence whether that child believes school is a positive or negative experience. If a child believes school is "good," he will be committed to what he has to do there and will tend to do better at learning tasks.

The models most likely to affect children's behavior and attitudes are those that have been experienced with strong feelings. If a child experiences something that is associated with intense satisfaction, excitement, or warmth, he is likely to retain it, likewise, the things that he experiences with intense anxiety, unhappiness, or frustration are absorbed and imprinted. Even though these negative experiences are often more difficult to verbalize, they strongly influence a child's behavior. Perhaps you can recall some events that influenced your own life—they were probably associated with strong feelings of one sort or another. For example, children who have early positive experiences with books, and whose parents receive much satisfaction from reading, tend to be motivated to read at school. On the negative side, parents who abuse their children tend to have been abused themselves when they were young. The models that children have influence them when they become adults.

Once children have adopted models, it is very hard to change them. They are like information stored in a computer (the brain), and can only be erased or changed by considerable effort. Both teachers and parents know how much time and energy are needed to change a child's behavior. Even more is required to alter feelings or attitudes. Even if a pattern of behavior results in pain or criticism, a child tends to act out the model he has—until he gets a new one that he is convinced (by his own experience) works better for him.

As your children begin to associate with people outside the home, their experience broadens, new learning occurs ("Where did he learn those dirty words?"), and they begin to absorb models that you no longer control. Folk heroes, movie stars, and fantasy characters are adopted as alternatives to real human models. (Who is he this week?)

Children adopt models of all sorts unconsciously. A child's sense of models is not mimicry, which all children do, but is much more infused with his conscious choices. Mimicking family members, culture heroes, and others is a device children use to reduce anxiety, identify with a stronger or bigger person, and experiment with alternative solutions to problems.

Since modeling is unconscious, your children usually learn more by example than by being told. This is especially important when teaching values, religious attitudes, and interpersonal behavior. Unable to fully understand and accept adults' verbal messages about complex issues, children try to make sense from their observations. ("Do what I say, don't do what I do!" often doesn't work.) When parents espouse values and beliefs and act consistently with them so that a child associates those beliefs with strong positive experiences of safety, security, and affection, they will tend to become part of the child's beliefs. When parents' values are not congruent with their behavior, the needs that children have for consistent, predictable models is threatened, often causing them to turn away from the things their parents say are important.

When children are in situations they know are important to their parents, but in which they experience negative or stressful feelings ("Be nice to Grandpa, no matter how he acts"), these negative associations will be "imprinted" on them. In many instances this leads to a continuing aversion to that situation or similar ones ("Visiting Aunt Sally is just like going to Grandpa's! I have to be nice, no matter what"), and a child may either go along with it without enthusiasm or actively reject it. If such experiences are standard family activities, such as going to church, visiting relatives, going shopping, and so forth, they will become negative models, and may ultimately become philosophical principles later in life ("Being too closely attached to one's family is a way of keeping one from changing").

HOW THE FOUR CONDITIONS INTERACT

Achieving high self-esteem requires that each of the four conditions (connectiveness, uniqueness, power, models) be fulfilled, signifying that the majority of your child's needs are being met. Poor self-esteem is an indication that needs within one or more of the conditions are not being met. Usually poor self-esteem can be traced to a major deficit in *one* condition, which we call the *critical condition*.

The degree to which the multiple needs within each condition are met determines the *quality* of that condition. Imagine a thermometer whose mercury rises as each need is satisfactorily met. As the "temperature" rises, the potential for high self-esteem rises. It is not possible that all needs in any condition are not being met, but it is likely that some needs may be being met only minimally, creating a deficit, and "lowering the temperature."

Likewise, because the conditions are not separate, but exist within a *whole child*, they interact with and influence each other. Understanding how this happens will help parents and teachers make sense of their children's behavior. The most important point to remember is that *children may appear to exhibit similar behavior, but do so for different reasons.* How you can use this knowledge to change your children's behavior or improve their performance will be demonstrated in succeeding sections of this book.

Because your child's self-esteem is based on the degree to which his needs are met, and since one of the chief motives for behavior is to feel good, *children are always attempting, through their own actions, to have their needs met.* In our terms this means that if a child has a poor sense of connectiveness, he will always be attempting to fulfill needs in that area. If his sense of power is low, he, likewise, will always be trying to improve it.

Imagine that a child with poor self-esteem is like a hungry person. The longer a person goes without food, the more the demand for food needs to be satisfied. If hunger continues, it becomes the dominating issue in a person's thoughts, feelings, and actions, and the person will begin to do strange, bizarre, or outrageous things to satisfy the hunger. If no one knows that the person is hungry for food, his behavior will not seem to make any sense—it will appear abnormal. But once it's clear that hunger is the issue, then food can be offered, the need is satisfied, and the person's behavior returns to normal. But, if it's understood that hunger is the issue but the need for food is not *significantly* satisfied (offering the starving person one jelly bean), the abnormal behavior will quickly resume as the person continues to seek food.

The starving man syndrome is a useful metaphor for issues of children's self-esteem because we are willing to grant that food is a fundamental need. So are the self-esteem needs. Actually, *the most important needs that people have at any point in time are the needs that are not then being met.*

Our starving man will not need food for a while after he has eaten. People don't need sleep after waking from a good night's rest. People don't get cold when they're clothed appropriately. Water usually quenches thirst. Children don't excessively seek attention if they get enough of it. People who are loved don't ordinarily behave as if they're not.

A child may not have certain needs fulfilled or he may not have a certain need fulfilled *sufficiently*. For example, children need to make significant decisions that affect their lives. All children make some decisions, but a child with a poor sense of power may not be allowed or encouraged to make *enough* decisions in important areas. We have been delighted that the majority of teachers with whom we have worked are (consciously or intuitively) aware of what most children need. But the greatest problems arise when it comes to meeting these needs sufficiently. When a teacher does the right thing, but doesn't do *enough* of it, children's behavior may not change, and frustration ensues. Creative, imaginative, and courageous behavior by teachers is often necessary to effect change.

IDENTIFYING THE CRITICAL CONDITION

The four conditions of poor self-esteem have characteristic behaviors associated with them. These behaviors are symptoms of unmet needs in a child, or evidence that the child is trying to fulfill those needs but is doing so ineffectively or inappropriately.

Any *one* of these symptomatic behaviors is, in itself, *not abnormal*. All children are shy sometimes; all children have some difficulty expressing their feelings; most children experience problems in relationships at some point; all children need to be alone sometimes. These three factors will help you determine the critical condition:

- *Repetition.* When a child repeats a certain symptomatic behavior despite varying circumstances, or responds to a specific event in the same inappropriate way again and again, it is evidence of a problem. The existence of a problem is even more obvious if the specific behavior produces dissatisfaction and/or discomfort for the child.

- *Intensity.* When children, behaving in ways that are problem indicators, show strong emotion (anger, being upset, intense embarrassment, frustration, etc.), it is likely that the behavior identifies a critical condition.
- *Amount.* If children repeatedly act in *several* ways that characterize problems with a specific condition, they definitely have problems in that area.

In Chapters 3, 6, 9, and 12 you will find detailed descriptions of the ways children behave when each of the four conditions is a problem.

When one condition of self-esteem is a problem, it colors all other conditions. The critical condition lowers self-esteem so that children seem to exhibit problems in all self-esteem areas. The case studies that follow will show how this occurs.

JOEL: A CHILD WITH CONNECTIVENESS NEEDS

Mrs. Lawson was beginning to give up on Joel. She couldn't seem to keep him functioning at the level she was sure this third-grade boy was capable of. Under some circumstances he showed flashes of real competence, and was even highly creative from time to time. But he would continually slide back into a withdrawn, lethargic, and often disruptive attitude. In order to keep him working, she had to devote an inordinate amount of time to him.

When Joel performed in group settings, he seemed to fall apart. He'd lose the place, recite in a hesitant and low-keyed way, and couldn't seem to retain information. When left to work on his own, his productivity was low and he often didn't seem to understand what he was to do. When the aide worked with him individually, there was some slight improvement, but often accompanied by lots of talking, helplessness, and whining. Joel performed best when Mrs. Lawson herself sat with him. Usually it would take a few minutes for him to warm up, but then he would perform. Often his performance was notable, but confusing. As an example, he could read something from his reader to Mrs. Lawson with great fluency and assurance that only minutes before, in the reading group, he had stumbled over.

Mrs. Lawson might get him to do several math problems accurately as she sat huddled with him at his desk, and then leave him to work out the rest by himself. She would come back later only to find that he had done almost nothing on his own, with the excuse that he had forgotten how.

Joel's relations with his classmates were not great, but they weren't bad. Little conflict occurred between him and others, but little of anything else either. He'd play with others during recess, but usually in a halfhearted manner. He was not considered very good in sports, even though Mrs. Lawson had seen him once at school on a weekend, playing by himself and demonstrating great speed, agility, and grace. Children tended to leave Joel alone.

It was in the creative realm that Mrs. Lawson had the most questions about Joel. From time to time he'd show up after school and hang around the doorway of the room. She'd invite him in, and often let him draw or color (she knew his mother worked and wasn't home when he left school). He sometimes created drawings that were so imaginative that Mrs. Lawson was amazed. But he *never* did them in class during the day, no matter what the assignment. In one-to-one discussion he demonstrated a quick and subtle sense of humor that was missing during school.

Joel demonstrated problems in all four conditions of self-esteem. Connectiveness was poor as shown in his fragile peer relations. Uniqueness was a problem in that he rarely showed evidence of creative self-expression, except under highly special circumstances. Power was definitely low as his poor performance, low productivity, and helpless attitude evidenced. His confused, disorganized, and purposeless behavior showed that his sense of models was also amiss. But there were clear features in his behavior that gave the clue to the critical condition.

The most apparent one was his change in attitude and performance when he worked alone with Mrs. Lawson. She noticed that when she sat close to him, even touching him, he focused better and tried harder. It was strange; the closer she sat to him the better he worked. His imaginative and unique drawings only occurred when he was alone with her in the room. Mrs. Lawson was a touchstone to his feelings of safety and security.

Why didn't he perform when working by himself? Mrs. Lawson observed him carefully over several days and found that he spent most of his time watching others in the class-room. He'd look at his paper or book from time to time, but as soon as some noise occurred, he would quickly look up to see what was going on. He especially would stare wistfully for long periods of time at children talking or playing with each other. In addition, he would *always* respond to any overtures made to him by others. When another child showed him something, he'd really pay attention. Even when the other child would move on Joel would keep looking at him or her for a while.

Joel would hang around other kids, even when he was supposed to be working. He might go to the pencil sharpener and take some time to return to his desk, stopping several times to watch what others were doing. These were times when Mrs. Lawson would get on him to get back to work. She saw how her efforts to constantly prod him were making her most frustrated and resentful of him.

Joel's problem with his sense of connectiveness was the critical condition. Trying to connect absorbed so much of his time that there was little left over for productive work. Only when he felt safe and secure, with someone he trusted—Mrs. Lawson—was he able to expose the many good qualities and capabilities he had. Joel's senses of uniqueness, power, and models were being suppressed by his strong connectiveness needs.

* * *

Joel's behavior is representative of many children who are having problems learning. But his own particular need was not going to be satisfied by focusing more on academic issues, but by satisfying his need for human connections. Greater emphasis on academics would only result in more frustration for everyone, including Joel.

It would be silly to put a Band-Aid on a sore throat, burn salve on an upset stomach, or give an aspirin to stop a cut from bleeding. When parents and teachers try to treat one condition of self-esteem when another is the critical one, the results often are disappointing. When a child's dysfunctional or inappropriate behavior does not change it is evidence that the important needs he is seeking to fulfill are still not being attended to. Even though a child may appear to perform at a high level in many areas of his life, he may still have unmet or insufficiently met needs in another. Parents and teachers may be undermining a child's ability to fulfill certain needs, despite their sincere and compassionate intentions. Children may be more competent and responsible than we think they are, like Terry in the following case study.

TERRY: A CHILD WHO
NEEDS TO BE ALLOWED TO GROW UP

Mr. and Mrs. Loman finally went to see a family counselor. Terry, their ten-year-old daughter, was giving them fits. The things that upset them most were Terry's periodic bursts of uncontrolled anger, her picking at her younger brother, and the recent assertion of herself through nasty back talk to both her parents, sometimes accompanied by striking her mother.

What was confusing and disconcerting to the Lomans was that these aspects of Terry's behavior *only* occurred at home, and were periodic and unpredictable. Living with Terry was like walking on egg shells! The Lomans were anxious and confused.

Adding to this confusion was the fact that Terry was a

superior student at school (actually the best in her class), well behaved, popular, and good at sports. Parents of Terry's friends were laudatory in their comments about her. All of this added to the Lomans's frustration, resentment, and guilt. "Who's the problem," they asked, "Terry or us?"

The Lomans felt that Terry's self-esteem was a problem. "She's so hard on herself," they reported, "and sometimes she gets into black moods for no apparent reason." Recently she had been helping her father put an addition on the house. She took responsibility for nailing the plywood on a section of wall. As usual her work was excellent, but her only comment about it when Mr. Loman praised her was that she had left one "shiner" among all the nails she'd placed. This kind of self-criticism bothered her parents.

When the Lomans tried to talk with Terry about their concerns, she clammed up or gave some smart-aleck answer. Only direct punishment, threat of the loss of special privileges, or Mrs. Loman's fury and screaming would seem to move Terry when she was in one of her moods. They were really worried that there was something wrong with her.

In consultation the Lomans became aware of how they dealt with Terry. Mrs. Loman recognized that she had a tendency to consider Terry to be a problem, and had done so since Terry's first expressions of anger as a toddler. Because of this she tended to go easy on her—she felt that she'd been tiptoeing around Terry for years. Even though Terry was not spoiled, there was, nevertheless, a way in which Mrs. Loman tended to overexplain things to her, presuming she needed things to be extra-clear and required extra prodding. She tried to teach Terry, and often found herself lecturing rather than listening. She tended to tell Terry things that she already knew, and was effusive in her praise of Terry's successes. It seemed to the counselor that Terry might be feeling a bit smothered by this.

Terry's self-esteem problems, her self-critical attitude, reflected high standards she had for herself. The Lomans saw that rather than help Terry to meet her high standards, they frequently tried to get her to lower them. Both parents felt they had suffered from having overly high standards set for them when they were young, and were bound and determined not to do it to their daughter. In reality, Terry had higher standards for herself than her parents did for her. She was really modeling how her parents were, rather than listening to what they told her.

Things began to change in the Loman household when her parents began to give Terry *more* responsibility and stopped trying to explain things to her. It started the night they told her, "Terry, we really don't know how to solve the problems we're having with you. We want to know what you think needs to be done to stop this arguing and fighting. What do you think *we* ought to do, and what are *you* willing to do?"

Terry didn't have much to say about it that night, but over the next several days there were no hassles. One night Terry approached Mrs. Loman and said, "I've decided that when I begin to get angry, I'm just going to leave the room. I'll go to my room, but don't you tell me to—that gets me angrier."

As the days passed, the Lomans began to notice subtle changes in Terry. She might tell her mother something and then wait for a reaction. When Mrs. Loman would say, "Oh, that's interesting," and not ask questions or prod, Terry would say more. Once she came into the kitchen when her mother and younger brother were playing a game. This was a characteristic time for fighting and squabbling to occur between the siblings. On this occasion Terry asked, "Will you play that with me when you're done with Joey?" Upon receiving an affirmative answer, Terry left the room quietly.

Terry, who was so superior in many ways, was nevertheless suffering from a lowered sense of power at home. When her parents permitted her to make decisions about the important features of her relations with them, they gave her an opportunity to use her intelligence and self-control in productive ways. Even though Terry was able to manifest her sense of power in other areas, the conditions her parents created kept the lid on her growth. She knew she needed to grow up—her parents needed to let her.

Many children are like Terry in that their behavior is so inconsistent that parents and teachers can't make sense of it. Terry's didn't begin to make sense until it was looked at from the perspective of the needs that Terry herself was trying to fulfill. Then her aggressive, angry behavior could be seen as evidence of a low sense of power. She was trying to assert herself under circumstances that did not permit her to.

THE THREE DOMAINS

Self-esteem waxes and wanes, and is determined not only by children's feelings about themselves, but also by the things that happen to them. No matter how solid a person's self-esteem might be, if the circumstances of his life become difficult enough his self-esteem will be undermined.

You need to be cognizant of three domains that influence children's self-esteem and to understand the distinctions among them in order to meet your child's needs creatively and flexibly.

The *personal domain* is represented by feelings, perceptions, attitudes and expectation within the child. You understand what is going on within the child by seeing and hearing what the child does and says. Learning how to analyze and evaluate the four conditions in the personal domain requires that you understand the way children go about fulfilling their needs. Observing the behavior of children is the tool that is used. You "read" a child's behavior in order to identify the critical condition. The introductory chapter in each of the succeeding sections provides specific lists of things to look for.

The *interpersonal domain* has to do with the way that you relate to a child in order to influence his self-esteem in positive ways. You will see that there are many ways to relate to children, and different ones influence different conditions of self-esteem. When you attempt to alter a child's self-esteem, it is essential to know how to produce specific results. It is also important to understand how various ways of relating to children diminish their self-esteem. Direct one-to-one relationships with children are the most powerful arenas for influencing self-esteem, yet they are not enough.

The *organizational domain* is concerned with the context in which children find themselves. Classrooms, families, institutions, and all the human groups that people live within have rules, procedures, policies, and opportunities that influence the way people act. These features of social systems affect the way people feel, thus, the way they feel about themselves. Children must live with and react to the rules and standards established by adults at home and in school. Their self-esteem is affected by decisions we make for them. All social systems (including families) tend to have the characteristics that allow people to meet some personal needs within them, and not others. Self-esteem either suffers or prospers according to the way we manage the organizational domain.

Much of the balance of this book will be devoted to providing ideas and insights about the organizational domain in families. *How* things are done at home affects self-esteem.

THE WHOLE CHILD: FEELING CONNECTED

3

Do Children Feel
They Belong?

The roots of your child's feelings of connectiveness rest in his earliest relations in the family. By the time your child begins school, his level of connectiveness will influence his relations and performance in school, and that experience in turn can enhance or diminish his feelings associated with this sense of connectiveness.

The sense of connectiveness is the critical condition of infancy. There is abundant evidence to show that infants respond to the interpersonal climate into which they are born. The foundations for future self-esteem are laid at that time, when the infant is totally dependent on others for safety, comfort, and physical needs, and must be able to trust his environment and the people in it for the satisfaction of these basic needs.

A child whose early years were characterized by a nurturing, safe, good-humored atmosphere, in which conflict was low (or quickly resolved), communications were clear and consistent, and emotional and physical needs were appropriately responded to tends to have a high sense of connectiveness as a foundation for self-esteem. On the other hand, if a child's home was characterized by excessive conflict and change, tension, poor communications, disregard for personal, emotional, and physical needs, and mistrust, he is likely to have a low sense of connectiveness and be poorly prepared for the high degree of social interaction that schooling requires.

When the early conditions necessary for developing a good sense of connectiveness have been lacking, you and your child's teachers will have to take an active role in altering your child's feeling of being unconnected. This chapter will describe the characteristics of children who have connectiveness problems—children whose feelings of belonging are not firm and consistent. Sammy is a case in point.

SAMMY: THE CASE OF
THE DISAPPEARING CHILD (PART I)

Sammy, a six-year-old, hardly ever said anything. During the first three months of first grade, his teacher, Miss Clarke, rarely heard his voice. He never recited or shared in class, spoke so softly in reading group that he could usually not be heard, and would only respond "yes," "no," or shrug when dealt with on a one-to-one basis by Miss Clarke or her aide. Early in the fall, Miss Clarke tried everything she knew to bring Sammy out (touching, talking to him, putting him with the sociable kids, choosing him to lead things, and so on), but each experience seemed to create so much embarrassment and stress for Sammy that she gradually stopped her efforts. It was so hard to tell what was going on inside this slight, pale, little boy.

Several contacts with Sammy's mother did not produce any change in his behavior. In fact, Miss Clarke wasn't sure if she really connected with Mrs. Holcomb, who was herself a shy, diffident person. She expressed concern about Sammy, but felt that living out in the country, where there were few children Sammy's age, was the reason he had no friends. When Miss Clarke suggested that she could give Mrs. Holcomb the names of parents of some children who might be good playmates for Sammy, so that she might invite the children over, Mrs.

Holcomb thought it was a good idea, but never followed up on it. Sammy's mother did indicate that she had been like Sammy when she was in school and had outgrown it (Miss Clarke questioned *that* to herself). Furthermore, she said that Mr. Holcomb, who was considerably older than herself, had a hard time relating to Sammy.

Miss Clarke stopped having conferences with the Holcombs because they never seemed to resolve anything. Mrs. Holcomb was so vague and abstract that it was hard to pin her down, and Miss Clarke always felt that she had to work hard to keep the conversation going. She did find out, though, as the result of several conferences, that Sammy was always shy and cling-ing, had cried a lot as an infant, and had a terrible time before the Holcombs removed him from the one preschool they had tried.

At school Sammy seemed to disappear. He would hunch down in his seat and hardly move. During recesses and at lunch he would never play with the other children, but would sit by himself against the wall of the school or hang on to one of the posts that held up the walkways. If other children came near him, he would hold on to the post, if no one was around him, he might swing around it. He would always wear his jacket in class, even on the warmest days, and only remove it if Miss Clarke insisted on it. His work output was very low, and his teacher often noticed him sitting in an abstracted manner at his seat or staring at other children, leading her to question his intelligence level.

He would become absorbed in any little thing. He might have a little car in his desk, and Miss Clarke would notice him turning it over and over in his hands or running it up and down his leg. She frequently had to tell him to get back to work.

The other children tried to engage Sammy in their activities, but finally his shyness and lack of enthusiasm wore them down and they tended to leave him alone. In group games he would only make minimal efforts and would never extend himself.

Miss Clarke really became concerned about Sammy and her relationship with him when she noticed that she was becoming unaware of his presence. When his mother called one day after school to find out which bus he'd taken home, Miss Clarke couldn't even remember whether he'd been in class that day! It seemed crazy, but Sammy was disappearing out of her awareness. (The resolution of Sammy's case is presented in Chapter 4.)

Sammy was a child with a very low sense of connectiveness, who was unable to fulfill many of the needs associated with this condition. It was apparent that the level of connectiveness in his family was low. When he started school, he already was firmly stuck into patterns of behavior that reinforced his problems. His low sense of connectiveness restricted and impaired the other parts of his personality.

HOW CHILDREN WITH CONNECTIVENESS PROBLEMS BEHAVE

When children avoid dealing with their unmet connectiveness needs, you will observe the following:

When children attempt to meet their unmet connectiveness needs inappropriately, you will observe the following:

1. They make little or no effort to join group activities and are rarely involved in them.
2. They spend excessive time by themselves, even when playmates are available.
3. They communicate little about themselves or their feelings.
4. They are shy.

1. They disparage the family, racial or ethnic affiliations of others, and themselves.
2. They excessively seek attention in groups in which they feel safe.
3. They want to be in the center of things.
4. They spend a lot of time watching others and/or hang around the fringes of group activities.

5. They have few friends.

6. They try to avoid people or social situations.

7. They don't volunteer to help with chores or classroom duties.

8. They seem uncomfortable around adults.

9. They avoid out-of-school activities that require interacting with others.

10. They have short attention spans at school, and there is no specific evidence that physiological or perceptual disorders are creating the condition.

11. They seem to be lethargic and hold on to, lean on, and touch physical objects (desks, chairs, walls, etc.) that support their weight.

5. They relate more easily to things (material objects, animals) than to people.

6. They try to get other children to notice them.

7. They place a great deal of importance on personal possessions (clothing, toys) and spend time involved with them.

8. They are submissive, dependent, and clinging in relationships with peers and adults.

9. They touch, push, lean, snuggle, seeking physical closeness with peers and adults when *inappropriate.*

When children have connectiveness problems, they become increasingly uncomfortable as the number of people involved in a group activity increases. They may relate well to one person (one-to-one with teacher), or to two or three people (no sign of a problem at home), but, because their feelings of belonging are so fragile, as the group enlarges (and becomes more impersonal), their discomfort rises. The impersonal nature of larger groups, where close, secure, and protective relationships are less likely to occur, creates a problem for low connectiveness children. In larger groups people will pay less attention to them, and they will have more difficulty getting their needs fulfilled. They will often make little or no effort to join in family or school activities, and if the group is very large, will hang around the fringes without participating.

They may voice negative attitudes about the family, class, or school, and demean the accomplishments of others in those groups: "I don't like this class." She thinks that she's so good! She just wants everybody to like her." They will disparage the special characteristics of their families or the racial, ethnic, or religious groups to which they belong: "Black people are so boring." "My parents are really weird." "I hate this Jewish food." "It's stupid to go to church." They will make excuses to avoid significant interpersonal contact: "Do I have to go? I don't feel good." "Okay, I'll go to the picnic, but can I take a friend?" "I don't like to play baseball."

Such children will spend a good deal of time by themselves, even when enjoyable activities are available, if those activities require interaction with others. Their behavior will seem inconsistent and puzzling. A child who has shown an interest in sports may choose not to go to a ball game with a large group. Another child may indicate a great desire to do something that involves other people, only to change his mind at the last minute, as his anxiety about being with the group increases. Children with a low sense of connectiveness isolate themselves and focus on activities that require only one person, for example, reading, collecting, or watching TV. Yet when they are alone, they tend to get underfoot and complain about having nothing to do.

Children who lack connectiveness are poor and/or reluctant communicators. It's difficult for parents and teachers to find out what's going on inside such children, especially when adults *try* to get them to express their feelings. Sharing one's feelings is an act of great intimacy, and often increases feelings of vulnerability. Children must trust the person to whom they express their feelings, and children with connectiveness problems often don't feel close enough to people to trust them— even their parents and teachers. Such children also tend not to volunteer much factual information about their activities. It has to be pulled out of them.

Children with a poor sense of connectiveness desperately need and want friends, but have considerable difficulty making and keeping them. Their anxiety about being close makes them awkward and unsure of themselves. They may be too unassertive or too assertive, too dependent or too pushy, too demanding or too submissive—they will usually be "too" something, so that other children feel uneasy around them.

If a child is taught new ways to relate to people, he may use them *if his relationship with the person trying to teach him is a truly important and positive one.* It will be that warm, secure relationship that prompts a child to try, not the value of the technique itself. If a child does not have such a relationship with a parent, teacher, or counselor, the lesson will fall on deaf ears.

One of the signs that a child has a low sense of connectiveness lies not with the child, but in the way others feel about that child. Teachers and parents and peers do not feel comfortable with such children, but their feelings aren't strongly negative. They are more likely to be uneasy, disinterested, bored, and mildly frustrated about not being able to generate a give-and-take relationship.

Children with a low sense of connectiveness may not know how to relate well. This is learned by observing, modeling, and experiencing nurturing relationships—and then by practicing what they've learned. Low connectiveness children have not had a history of such relationships. Their playmates, parents, and teachers have to take responsibility for promoting, organizing, and maintaining the relationship. When people feel that they are making all the effort in a relationship they become uncomfortable with a child and pull back. Helping a child overcome connectiveness problems requires patience and commitment from parents and teachers.

Feelings and ideas (fear, anxiety, hopes, wishes, and apprehensions) about relationships interfere with and color almost everything these children do. Children with a low sense of connectiveness often seem to be lazy, a characteristic that doesn't distinguish them from lots of children, but the reasons

for it and the *way* they are lazy do. A low sense of connectiveness restricts a child's motivation to *volunteer* for activities that
may involve other people. ("C'mon and help us move this
wood." "Naw, I've got to do something else.") Or the child
may engage in such activities, but doesn't extend himself very
much. A simple act of helpfulness can become a problem for
such children in that it poses relationship dilemmas to them.
Although they may seem to ignore the needs of other people at
home or in school, they are basically avoiding doing things
with others because helping someone is a way of relating.

Another curious attribute of these children is that they *seem*
to be relating when they're not. This often occurs in their
relationships with adults. They may hang around, get underfoot, and "bug" parents and teachers to death, but when we try
to deal with them directly ("Now tell me, Joey, just what is it
that you want to do?"), they will squirm, become silent, and
appear to be uncomfortable and embarrassed. And they often
act in a similar manner with their peers. We all become
enormously frustrated when we know that a child wants
something from us but are not able to find out what that is. If a
child continues to act this way, people begin to avoid paying
attention to him because it's so uncomfortable. Teachers pay
more attention to other children who relate to them, and they
are drawn to those children. Parents often find they enjoy
relating more to other children in the family than to the one
who has connectiveness problems. It's just one of the ways that
these children create their own dissatisfying social climate.
Their ambivalence (wanting to connect, but anxious about
relating) creates a similar ambivalence about them in *others*.

It is this ambivalence that chiefly characterizes children
with connectiveness problems. They always bring both positive and negative feelings to any activity that involves relationships. Because of this, low connectiveness children seem to
create interpersonal situations that don't provide them with
warmth, caring, and nurturing. If they demand attention, they
may get it, but it will be associated with criticism, impatience,

and resentment from parents and teachers who feel forced to give it to them.

They may do poorly in school because their relationship needs take priority over their intellectual ones, but their problems are not fundamentally academic. Children who have a short attention span invariably have connectiveness problems unless there is clear evidence of physiological or perceptual disorders. Children with a low sense of connectiveness do need to pay attention to something, but it is not the work that is laid out before them. Rather, they are paying attention to their own inner processes (daydreams, reveries, fantasies, and fears), or spending an inordinate amount of time being distracted by the actions of others.

These children "connect" with their eyes. Watching others substitutes for their own hopes and desires about relating. Two children laughing at something at the other end of the room may absorb the attention of a low connectiveness child just long enough so that he doesn't hear the teacher's directions. He is reluctant to answer a question because everyone might be watching him. When another child initiates even a brief contact with him, not only is his attention required, but his *feelings* are often stimulated, so much so that it takes time for him to settle down to work again. When he's required to work alone, he feels separate and alone. Just as a hungry person will spend a lot of time thinking about food, a child who is hungry for contact with others will spend a lot of his time thinking about that need.

When human relationships become problems (as they invariably do for such children), they retreat to relating to *things* rather than to people. All children have strong object attachments, but low connectiveness children have substantially stronger attachments, are more emotional about them, and maintain these attachments despite the availability of potentially satisfying human relationships. Pets, toys, objects of all sorts don't talk back, don't demand, and don't confuse, and are easier to relate to than people. Children with connectiveness problems may become obsessively involved in object relationships even when they're not supposed to, in class, for example, instead of listening to the teacher. Strangely enough, their things provide a connection of sorts, and serve to keep their anxiety and security at a level that is acceptable. They have their favorite things, which they hate to be parted from; they may attempt to relate by letting another child play with a favorite object.

While object attachments are normal for all children, they may become quite bizarre in children with a very low sense of connectiveness. One fourth-grade boy was the only child in school who carried a briefcase, which was filled with "stuff" that he periodically riffled through. Many of these children wear hats, coats, or heavy rain gear in class, and rarely remove them. At home a child may seem to have an obsession with some article of clothing or toy. Furthermore, when such children feel isolated, they relate to *themselves*. You will often observe them touching themselves, pulling at their clothing, twining their fingers through their hair, sucking their fingers, pulling up their socks, or retying their shoelaces.

These children like to have physical contact with desks, chairs, walls—any large object that can bear their weight as they lean, sprawl, and lay on it. They will grasp their desk, lean on the teacher's as she corrects a paper, sprawl on the sofa at home, play in the shadow of a building, move toward the edge of the room when others enter, select a seat in class that is near a wall, and so forth. When children feel emotionally unconnected, it promotes a need for physical contact. It seems as if their mistrust of people requires them to connect with objects they can trust not to go away.

Children lacking in connectiveness mistrust their own bodies. They are reluctant to extend themselves physically. Their continuing state of depression (albeit mild) produces a need for physical stimulation that is more safely satisfied by things than by people. Perhaps if they had been touched and held more in comforting and nurturing ways, this way of satisfying their inner needs would be less dramatic.

HOW CHILDREN'S SENSE OF CONNECTIVENESS IS THREATENED

Children's sense of connectiveness can be threatened by events that are outside their control. If their sense of connectiveness is high they can cope adequately with such threats, except if they are continuing, significant, and unpredictable. When children's sense of connectiveness is low, such threats can drive them further into isolation and loneliness.

We need to remember that even though a child has an adequate sense of connectiveness, it may be lost if the threats are significant. These threats are experiences that destroy or weaken children's ability to gain satisfaction from their relationships to important people, places, or objects. Such threats are common and children's mood swings are often explained by them. Think of the child as a vessel, holding within it the water that is the sense of connectiveness. Threats produce leaks in the vessel, requiring parents and teachers to add water at a greater rate than it is flowing out, maintaining the level while the leak is being plugged (healing the child's sense of loss).

The following list is a catalog of experiences that can diminish a child's sense of connectiveness. With the loss of connectiveness a child will demonstrate many of the characteristics that have been described earlier in this chapter.

- Losing an especially valued relative or friend through death, divorce, separation, moving away, etc.
- Having to become a member of a new class or school, and not knowing anyone
- Needing to be held, talked to, sympathized with, encouraged, made to feel secure—and everyone is too busy to do so
- Changing homes, or having to give up one's room
- Having a valued toy taken away as a punishment
- Being restricted or isolated as punishment for long periods of time at home or school

- Losing a loved pet
- Not having toys or personal possessions readily available
- Receiving excessive criticism, punishment, or disinterest from anyone to whom the child is closely attached, be they relatives, teachers, or friends
- When an especially valued toy breaks and is thrown away
- When parents argue, fight, or stay angry at each other for a long time, or when a teacher gets angry or upset
- Having a special hiding place discovered
- Having one's friends criticized or not liked
- Having anything that the child belongs to (class, school, ethnic group, club, team, etc.) disparaged by others who are important to the child
- Being unexpectedly moved to a new environment
- Not knowing and not being able to find out why someone the child has been close to is no longer there
- Losing something of value
- Needing someone, and he or she isn't there

The loss of anything to which your children have formed emotional attachments poses potential threats from infancy through adolescence. Many such attachments are invisible to parents and teachers, because the bond is in children's feelings, and may not be expressed. Children themselves may not be conscious of the importance of someone or something they're attached to until they lose it and experience the feelings of loss.

The next chapter will describe ways in which parents can encourage a good sense of connectiveness in children, and how to deal with children who have a poor one.

At Home:
Being in the Family

How do you build and maintain a child's sense of connectiveness? This chapter will show you, first, how to relate to children, one-to-one, in ways that will insure that your child develops a firm sense of connectiveness. Then we will explore the many things you can do within your family to build connectiveness, including establishing the proper rules, rituals, and special features such as a family council. And last, if your child has connectiveness problems, the section on how to handle threats to this condition is of special importance.

But before moving on to these issues, we will show you how a sensitive and creative teacher handled Sammy, the little boy who, in the last chapter, was shown to have problems relating to people.

SAMMY: THE CASE OF
THE DISAPPEARING CHILD (PART II)

With the help of a consultant, Miss Clarke decided on a long-range strategy to bring about a change in Sammy's ability to relate. The tactics were (1) to deal appropriately with his excessive shyness, (2) to build his feelings of trust, and (3) to reduce threats to his sense of connectiveness whenever possible. Though his work output was so low, special concerns about his academic performance were postponed. Sammy would probably improve academically if his self-esteem improved.

Strange as it seems, Miss Clarke needed to do something to remind herself that Sammy was *there*. She did this by keeping a note on her desk blotter—"Remember S., 2x/day." The note was a reminder to interact at least twice a day with him. She found that she needed the reminder.

During the first week of the experiment, she related to Sammy in ways that acknowledged his presence but posed no threat to him. This approach to shy children is really very simple. Miss Clarke made declarative statements to him, but refrained from asking him any questions. She also walked away from him immediately after saying something. "Hello Sammy, you look nice today" (walk away); or "I like the color of your shirt" (walk away); or "I'm glad you're in class today" (walk away).

Miss Clarke made no academic demands of him during that week. Whatever work he did and handed in received a smile and "Thank you, Sammy." He wasn't excused directly from working (he received paper, books, etc.), she just didn't say anything to him about it. If she returned papers to him, they were placed on his desk without comment. He wasn't called on in groups.

A curious thing began to happen by the end of the first week of this program. Whereas, at the beginning of the week, Sammy had lowered his head and eyes when Miss Clarke spoke to him, by the end of the week she noticed that he watched her as she walked away. Just this subtle variation signaled a change in him.

Miss Clarke altered her approach slightly during the second week. She thought of questions to ask Sammy that he could answer easily, such as "Did you take the bus to school today?" (he always did); "Did you bring your lunch today?" (he always did); "The sun is really bright today, isn't it?" These questions were added to the positive statements she used during the first week. Any response that Sammy gave was acknowledged by Miss Clarke ("That's nice"; "Good"; "Um-hum.") before she walked away. At the beginning of the week Sammy nodded his response; by the end of the second week he gave a verbal "yes" to each question. Miss Clarke continued to make no special demands of him.

During the third and fourth weeks of the experiment, Miss Clarke gradually added new interactions with Sammy. In order, they were:

1. Constructing future-oriented questions. For example, "Are you taking the bus home today?" (he always did).
2. Touching him lightly as she walked past his desk, without looking at him or pausing (at least once each day).
3. Catching his eye (she found that he looked at her more than in the past), and smiling at him.
4. Sitting next to him in the reading group, and touching his arm lightly (without looking at him) several times.
5. Asking him if he wished to read to her at her desk (fourth week).
6. Asking him an easy question in the reading group (fourth week).

As each of these new elements was added, Sammy's demeanor changed. He became more "there" in subtle ways. He began to have more color in his face and worked harder on class assignments. One morning during the fourth week he came running up to Miss Clarke as she was walking toward the room, and blurted out that he had gone to an amusement park on the weekend. It was the longest statement he had ever made to her, and even though he became embarrassed (his face flushed), they smiled at each other.

During the fifth week, Miss Clarke continued her program with Sammy, and his rate of change became dramatic. He initiated conversations with her and other children. He recited in the reading group. He asked questions about his work. Miss Clarke could hardly believe her eyes and ears.

Several weeks later the consultant who had helped her think through the experiment checked with her on Sammy's progress. Miss Clarke was laughing as she reported that she had another problem now—Sammy had become a chatterbox, and she didn't know how to quiet him down! Sammy was making up for lost time.

BUILDING YOUR CHILD'S SENSE OF CONNECTIVENESS

Children need to feel close to both of their parents, if they are available. The permanent absence of one parent through death, divorce, or separation is a difficult adjustment for a child. But children may have even greater problems if both parents are present, and one (or both) of them is so emotionally distant that the child doesn't experience positive, warm contact with that parent.

The following attitudes characterize specific ways for you to connect with your children as a parent. When two parents are available, *both* need to do these things, respecting differences in each one's style. Building children's sense of connectiveness cannot be left to one parent—children seek satisfaction from both.

TOUCHING AND HOLDING

Being touched and held never stops being the primary expression of affection, love, and safety among human beings. *All human beings like to be touched unless it interferes with something important they're doing or it poses a threat to them because they don't know how to react to it or what it means.*

Though many issues complicate people's attitudes about touching and holding children as they mature, being held is critical early in children's lives to their feeling safe, secure, wanted, and connected. (When it is appropriate to touch and hold children varies among cultures and societies. Within each culture children's capacity for physical intimacy is influenced by the family patterns in which they were raised.)

There are lots of ways to touch your children, from a brief pat on the shoulder to a great, big, bear hug of a kiss. Because children's moods and needs change, you need to be flexible in how you touch and hold. When a child is deeply immersed in some activity he might resent the intrusion of a big bear hug, but need that kind of contact when returning from a trip away from home. Children need to know that you will touch and hold them when they need it. *Parents let children know this by reaching out and touching and holding them even when they're not demanding it.* If your child clings, he needs more physical contact than he's getting and his behavior indicates that he *feels* he must demand it before he gets it.

While you need to respect your child's wish not to be touched, you shouldn't be fooled by what appears to be rejection. Children seem to resist being touched for a number of reasons: they're angry at you and are trying to punish you; you distract them from something they find important; your behavior toward them is inconsistent; they believe that you are demanding them to respond to you in ways that they don't want to; and they feel that to be hugged and kissed by parents is "babyish" or "girlish." If a child seems uncomfortable when touched, continue to initiate it in brief but consistent ways, such as a pat on the back, tousling hair, or playful strokes.

Many parents touch their children in a distracted manner, as if it's a bothersome thing to do. You can make touching a more complete and satisfying experience for children by talking to them, smiling, and looking directly at them. Touching children is a good way to get their attention, and for some children it's almost the only way. Touching children and having eye contact with them is a way to insure that they listen to you.

LET YOUR FACE SHOW WHAT YOU FEEL

Children feel confused and insecure when your facial expressions don't correspond to what you are saying. Some parents actually smile when they're angry and frown when they're happy! Many children need visual clues, particularly facial expressions, to tell them how a parent might be feeling when words don't make it clear. You may have noticed your child peering closely at you when you have teased him or made a subtle pun; he may be trying to decipher your meaning by "reading" your face.

Children with a low sense of connectiveness are often unable to interpret subtle or indirect messages about your feelings, so it is very important that you be aware of how your facial expression, posture, and words fit together. You can help such children understand what you're saying so they don't distort your communications and believe you don't like them or are angry when you're not.

Let your face show anger when you feel it and pleasure when you feel that way, so children can learn to distinguish your mood by your expressions. Play a game by standing in front of a mirror with your child and experiment with different expressions that go with different emotions.

TELL CHILDREN WHEN YOU FEEL GOOD ABOUT THEM

Lots of parents fall into the habit of taking their good feelings about their children for granted and not commenting on them to their children. But their negative feelings about them are often expressed in great detail. Children *don't* take positive feelings for granted. They need to hear them—out loud and often. Such positive verbal reassurance can start in infancy (even if you think your child can't understand, watch her face, you'll see evidence that she is responding to your tone and facial expression), and needs to be reinforced through childhood and adolescence.

When you feel good about your children and say so ("I love

you"; "I think you're fantastic"; "You make me feel good") it has an important effect: your children can build a catalog of positive statements that they in turn can say to others, improving their chances for good relationships—and furthering the sense of connectiveness.

MAKE PRAISE AN IMPORTANT COMMUNICATION

Communicating positive feelings is not necessarily the same thing as giving praise. The former reflects your feelings for your child; the latter how you feel about what the child does. Positive feelings may be broad, while praise should be specific. "I like your picture" is different from "You used color so nicely in this. I especially like the red and blue." Children need to know what pleases you so they can choose to do things that make you feel good—with safety and security. Have you ever tried to please someone when you didn't know what pleased them?

Your children need to know that you notice what they have tried to do well. When your praise is specific it's more believable, and helps children develop self-awareness.

Children who have connectiveness problems need to be praised in front of other people. Praise them so that other members of your family hear it. Even if they don't have problems with this condition it's a good idea. Public praise helps children feel they are important to other members of the family.

Praising them for things they don't do, as well as those things they do can be an important strategy. "It made me feel good when you *didn't* fight with your sister." Such praise shows children that you are taking the time to notice them, which is essential to feeling connected to you. The specific quality of their performance is really a secondary issue to them.

Remember to praise children for their personal characteristics, as well as their performance. "Oh, what a big muscle," lets a child know that he's valued for himself, not only for the degree to which he meets your expectations or follows the rules.

LET CHILDREN KNOW WHEN
YOU SEE THEM RELATING WELL TO OTHERS

Children need to know how to relate well in order to have a good sense of connectiveness. Praising them for doing so gives them feedback that encourages them to learn and refine interpersonal skills that work with other people. It also lets them know that the way they conduct relationships is important to you, especially those within the family. Comments about this should be specific: "I felt good when you didn't argue with your brother at dinner"; "The way you shared your toys with your cousins was really nice."

Children who cooperate well are easily liked. Help your child understand that cooperation is an important feature of human relationships by praising them for being cooperative.

Low connectiveness children need continuing and specific definitions of appropriate ways to relate to others. Reinforce their efforts when they do it right, but avoid moralizing and lecturing. When children have connectiveness problems they need lots of this kind of attention, but will need less of it as their sense of connectiveness grows.

SHARE YOUR FEELINGS

Parents have feelings that don't have anything to do with their children (really!). Your children need to know that your feelings aren't always a reaction to what they do. You have bad days and good ones; nice things happen to you as well as bad; sharing some of your joys and trials makes you more human, less threatening.

Parents are sometimes afraid to share negative feelings with children for fear they will undermine a child's security or faith. But most anxiety in children is a result of not receiving clear communications, or not being able to make sense of what's going on. If children sense that a parent is depressed, but don't know why, telling them *why* gives them important information. Hidden resentments in parents are anxiety-provoking to children. Letting them know that you're angry but are still connected to them helps them deal with angry feelings in others. Sharing your feelings helps children feel secure—the root of a positive sense of connectiveness.

SHARE YOUR ACTIVITIES

When you share your interests, hobbies, work, recreational activities, and family experiences with your children, it helps them feel close to you in very concrete ways. You can share activities by talking about them or by participating together. Involving children in what you do, talking to them about how you feel about what you do, and showing them how and why you do things builds a sense of connectiveness at many levels.

Forcing children to do things with you on the other hand, can hinder a sense of connectiveness; furthermore, some adult activities are not suited to children's participation. When you are willing to share in your child's activities, she will be more willing to share in yours.

Sometimes your child's involvement is distracting and intrusive. Parents want to do their own thing too! But when your child continues to put pressure on you, make a special time to expose him to the activity. He may learn about it and like it or may have his curiosity satisfied and lose interest.

BE ABLE TO LISTEN WITHOUT MAKING JUDGMENTS

In our society parents tend to feel obligated to comment about everything children say, making judgments without being aware of it. Even praise can be overdone, since it is a positive judgment. It is possible to acknowledge what children say without having to judge, advise, or comment all the time. Often, a simple response ("Um-hum"; "Yes, I see"; "That's interesting") provides the acknowledgment children are seeking, without parents needing to add any more. Children will frequently continue to talk after receiving this kind of response.

Children can become dependent on parent's evaluations. They can also (especially in late childhood and adolescence) become gun-shy about communicating, if they don't want everything they say to be evaluated. Parents who feel they have to pry information out of their children often are unwittingly overbearing when they talk to them. *Letting* your children talk is an art that can be developed. Sincere interest is of more value to a child, in most instances, than advice or evaluation. (Chapter 5 deals with parent/child communications in detail.)

Children with a low sense of connectiveness are particularly sensitive to criticism. They often distort what parents say, and feel they're being criticized when the statement only intended to instruct them. Reducing judgments reduces threats to their sense of connectiveness.

Since it is impossible never to make a judgmental statement to a child, you can at least avoid criticizing when he already knows he is in error or at fault and, instead, promote self-evaluation. ("I'd like you to think about what just happened, and tell me what you could have done differently."). Discuss your expectations and standards in positive ways, rather than in response to your child's mistakes.

DO SOMETHING SPECIAL

When you do something special for your child, it shows that your feelings of connection are strong—that you are not taking her for granted. When you make a favorite dish, buy something for her hobby, select a shirt in her favorite color—you communicate your special attention.

Children don't know for sure that parents care, unless they see evidence of it. *Sometimes it is necessary to prove to children that you love them.* All the more if such proof only occurs occasionally.

BE GENTLE WITH THE SHY ONES

All children are shy at one time or another. Children with a low sense of connectiveness may be chronically shy. Whether it's an ongoing problem or only a temporary stage, how parents handle shyness is very important to developing children's self-esteem.

Shy children are *not* afraid of people. They are anxious about how to respond to people. The distinction is important because pushing them into relationships, making them the center of attention, and requiring them to be sociable *reinforces the anxiety that is the basis of their shyness.* We all periodically experience anxiety about what others expect of us, and how it is best to conduct ourselves with strangers or in unfamiliar circumstances. It's natural. Shy children have more anxiety, more often, than do children with a good sense of connectiveness.

Being gentle with shy children involves doing the following:

- Try to avoid asking them questions. Questions, by their very nature, demand a response. Severely shy children can become unnerved by such simple questions as "How are you?" Ask necessary questions that only require simple yes or no responses. Don't ask multiple questions.

- Make statements that are clear and declarative. Subtlety, indirect statements, puns, and complicated directives often confuse these children, making them anxious, because they're not sure what you mean. To find out what you mean requires that they assert themselves by asking questions, which is very difficult for them.

- Don't prolong or permit others to prolong interaction with a shy child when you see the child becoming uncomfortable. Stop talking and let the child move on. The longer shy children are required to interact, the more uncomfortable they get—and the more their sense of connectiveness is undermined.

• Be patient with them while they build connectiveness. Very shy children will take a long time to do so. They must feel safe before they can be sociable. They must be able to trust you not to promote or prolong their anxiety.

Don't try to be a perfect parent! First of all, you probably do many of the things we have just suggested, but there are undoubtedly some things in the previous pages you need to do more of. Secondly, your children's sense of connectiveness may be fine, and you needn't be very self-conscious about the way you relate to them. But if you have identified problems with this condition, you may want to select some special ways to relate and experiment with them like Sammy's teacher, Miss Clarke. You will be encouraged.

Even though you try to relate in ways that build your children's sense of connectiveness, there may be general patterns of interaction in your family that stand in the way of your doing so. The next section will help you evaluate them.

BUILDING YOUR
FAMILY'S SENSE OF CONNECTIVENESS

Have you ever noticed that some families seem to have more togetherness than others? Perhaps you've even wished that your family could be more like that. It can, but you may have to give some thought to how you would like things to be in your family, and then have the courage to make changes. What a family does together, and how the family does it determine whether children feel satisfaction in their relations with other members of their family.

The following ideas can result in better relations in your family, and enhance children's sense of connectiveness, if *both what* you do and *how* you do it are considered. You can improve the sense of connectiveness of all members of your family when you combine the suggestions about how to relate to children that were described in the previous section with the activities described below. This combination will increase everyone's feelings of safety, satisfaction, and well-being.

CREATE OPPORTÚNITIES FOR
FAMILY MEMBERS TO WORK AND PLAY TOGETHER

Having opportunities for family members to be together does not insure that everyone will participate all the time. If Mom doesn't like fishing, Dad and the kids can go. If Sarah has play practice, the rest of the family can still go to the movies. It is important, however, to create, coordinate, and carry out activities that can include all family members. The following are some suggestions:

- Make mealtime special so that everyone expects to eat together rather than picking up their own food.
- Plan a special housecleaning day along with a special event (dinner in a restaurant) and divide the chores among everyone.
- Have everyone make some special contribution to planning a picnic.
- Allow the kids to jump into bed with you one morning each week, and read them stories.
- Let everyone voice an opinion about some special event (painting the house, buying a car, etc.) and consider each one's opinion seriously, even though you may have to make the final choice.
- Make one TV night a week special, with soft drinks and popcorn.

No single activity can insure that a sense of connectiveness grows in a family, but an ongoing pattern of such events does. When the members of a family expect to do things together, togetherness becomes a norm, or standard. Ask the members of your family what they would like to do, and *try* to fulfill each person's wishes, including your own. It's more important that everyone experiences a good deal of satisfaction from a few family activities, than there be a lot of activities that people don't care about.

HAVE RULES THAT IMPROVE A SENSE OF CONNECTIVENESS

The standards, expectations, and agreements that a family has both reflect and determine the quality of relations in that family. Rules can keep people separated or encourage good relations. Rules that apply to adults as well as kids create an atmosphere of common endeavor to promote the family's welfare (clean the bathroom when you finish bathing). Having some rules in the family makes children feel that the family stands for something, and introduces order and ritual into family life.

Rules for the home not only control behavior, they promote good relations among family members, by emphasizing cooperation, good manners, consideration, and respect for others' rights.

Rules express values. They communicate parents' attitudes to children in a powerful way. A consistent set of rules and standards is the basic tool that parents have to teach children what they believe to be right and wrong, good and bad, true and untrue.

In Chapter 7, a specific procedure for setting rules and limits in the family will be described. Read that section before creating or changing rules. Here are some rules that enhance children's sense of connectiveness.

1. Rules that promote cooperation:
   - You can borrow or use others' belongings *only* when you have their permission.
   - When more than one person wants to use something at the same time, work out who will use it, at what time, before either person does.
   - When you need help to do something, ask the other person to let you know *when* he or she can. Don't demand.

- When the family does something special together, such as a picnic or trip, everyone is given a special responsibility.

2. Rules that help resolve conflicts:
    - When you are arguing too much, and bothering other members of the family, you will be asked to leave the room until you resolve the argument.
    - You may ask Mom or Dad to resolve something, *only* if you can't agree—and then you have to accept their decision.
    - If disagreements or arguments are not resolved in a reasonable amount of time, both children will spend time in their rooms, until one or the other comes up with an acceptable solution.
    - If you call someone a name, you must pay that person ten cents.

3. Rules that promote respect for others:
    - Knock on the door before entering someone's room.
    - When you borrow something, it's your responsibility to return it in good condition.
    - Name calling or profanity will not be tolerated.
    - No loud music after 9:00 P.M.

ENCOURAGE FAMILY MEMBERS TO
SHARE PERSONAL MATTERS WITH EACH OTHER

Families vary in the expectations that they have for communicating personal issues. Some families discourage talking about personal problems but talk about things they feel good about. Some families talk about feelings more than others. Some families share problems, but don't talk very much about positive experiences. Many of these patterns of communication come from long-standing values and traditions that arise from one's culture, race, ethnic background, religion and place of origin. Conflicts within families often result from differences in the cultural backgrounds of the parents regarding how much and what kind of personal sharing is appropriate.

What's personal? Just about anything that any member of the family finds interesting. Personal matters are not only deeply felt emotional issues that require baring one's soul. Opinions too are personal matters. Do people in your family have the opportunity to share opinions safely? Talking about what one likes or dislikes is a personal matter. If one of the children has said something important about his life to you, encourage him to tell the others at dinner. If a child develops a new interest or friend, have her let the family know about it, at mealtime or at a family meeting. If one parent works late or odd hours, be sure to have a special meal from time to time, so that parent is included.

Parents take the lead and act as models by sharing things from their lives that children don't know about. What happened at work or on trips can be interesting to children. Stories from your past are always winners. It's not the content that is always important; it's your willingness to share that sets a tone, especially if *feelings* are discussed as well as events. Listening uncritically to children's concerns and feelings will encourage them to share more often.

CONSIDER THE ROLES PEOPLE PLAY IN THE FAMILY

Everyone has roles in the family, and they can help or hinder the sense of connectiveness that exists in a family.

Roles are often subtle and ambiguous. They exist, but many of them are not often recognized. They are composed of three factors: (1) what people do, and how they do it, (2) how members of the family see *themselves* in relation to other members of the family, and (3) how each person is seen by the others.

Roles can be subtle and complicated; they may be labeled or not; people can feel good or bad about them; and they can become quite firm so that everyone has a difficult time changing them.

Here are a number of commonplace statements that imply the roles people play:

"Mom's the peacemaker in our family."

"Dad's always working."

"Gerry's the youngest, and is he spoiled!"

"Sammy's the intellectual."

"Alan always drags his feet when we ask him to do something."

"Sara whines a lot."

"He's the strong, silent type."

"She's always bright and cheerful."

"Stanley is moody lots of the time."

"It's easier to talk to Dad than Mom."

"Jack is so irresponsible."

"Wendy is the one who starts the fights."

"You can always depend on Joey."

"He's too sensitive about most things."

"She lives in a dream world."

The role each person plays in your family forms a web of expectations that affect how he or she behaves. Sometimes a role may be a negative one, in that it represents a problem to the person who fills it, as well as to other members of the family. Labeling someone as the goof-off doesn't solve the problem of how he does his jobs. The child who seems to be the most troublesome may be struggling to break free of the negative expectations other members of the family have about him. Mom may get resentful that she's always expected to do things for others; Dad may be hurt when he's overlooked because it's thought he's not interested in partaking in some decision.

The duties and responsibilities that people have in and to the home help to define their roles. When you clarify who does what by when, you help create positive roles for adults and children. The jobs that need to be done at home are activities that can engage everyone in the important enterprise of family maintenance. Creating appropriate chores for children is a way to promote their feelings of connection to the family. Chapters 10 and 11 will give concrete suggestions for doing so.

When circumstances change, roles need to change to fit them. If Mom takes a job, adjustments should be made in her duties to fit the new pressure. Others (including Dad) need to take over some of her responsibilities. Standards and expectations you have for children need to change as they do. Stresses that affect family life should be discussed so that necessary alterations in people's responsibilities occur.

You might try an experiment:

1. List all the things that need to be done in your home to keep it working well.
2. List all the things that people (parents and children) do outside the home.
3. Note who does what in the home, and compare the time and energy required for them with their outside responsibilities.

Is the distribution of duties fair? Do changes need to be made? Do some people need more time for outside-the-home responsibilities; for example, does a child need more time for schoolwork? Does everyone (parents included) have enough time for play and relaxation? Do children need to share more in household duties?

Considering family members' roles means that you think about them, analyze them, and become conscious of the responsibilities, expectations, labels, and attitudes that family members hold for themselves and each other.

FIND POSITIVE WAYS TO RESOLVE
FIGHTS, ARGUMENTS, AND DISAGREEMENTS

While it's natural for disagreements to arise in a family, a family's sense of connectiveness is devastated when chronic problems go unresolved.

When a number of people live in a limited space (a home), it's likely that sometimes they will be trying to occupy the same space at the same time ("Daddy wants to sit in his chair now, Tommy.") Family resources (time, energy, space and material resources, including money) are limited, and it's likely that someone, sometime is going to feel that he's not getting his fair share.

If you avoid disagreements and arguments by not talking about them, then feelings are buried, only to surface later as resentment and frustration. The best goal for family living is to have procedures that serve to resolve conflict, not to eliminate it.

These guidelines will help you develop effective procedures that will resolve conflicts and build a sense of connectiveness in your family.

- Establish a family council or a rule for taking time to talk about a conflict.
- Emphasize problem solving rather than fault finding; have those who are involved in a problem seek solutions together.
- Set rules and limits about fighting and about resolving arguments quickly, so that the incidence of conflict is reduced.
- Give children a time and place to talk things out (often right on the spot), without always providing a solution for them.
- Be a good model for children by practicing what you preach, and by working at problem solving.

THE FAMILY COUNCIL

Regular or periodic meetings in which all members of the family discuss issues of interest or concern will help your family build a sense of connectiveness. They can become an important tradition, aiding families to deal with problems and crises.

Many families try and then reject family councils. The following guidelines may help you overcome the pitfalls and make family councils a valued ingredient of family life.

1. *Start slowly.* If you want to initiate a family council,

start with meetings that are short; handle topics that are fun and easy to deal with; hold them at a convenient time for everyone (during dessert at dinnertime); and don't make a big production of them.

2. *Keep them positive.* Don't confuse the family council with problem solving. The purpose of the council is to have the family get together in a way that promotes good feelings. Discuss positive issues at first: what to eat at Sunday's picnic; planning menus for the week; where to go on next summer's vacation; what to get Grandma for her birthday; what happened today at work or school.

3. *Avoid a "problem" atmosphere.* If family councils become problem oriented, some members of the family will approach meetings with apprehension, and will try to avoid them. If problems must be discussed, balance them with positive topics.

4. *Avoid using them as a soapbox.* Parents often use family councils as an opportunity to make pronouncements. Children feel that they get enough of that in day-to-day relations. Issues don't have to be resolved all the time, they can be discussed; the council can be a time to air opinions.

5. *Give equal time.* Let everyone have his say. Don't let anyone (including Mom and Dad) dominate. Let everyone bring up topics. Don't discriminate by age. If young children have a hard time communicating, help them.

6. *Break bread.* Make council meetings special by serving dessert, popcorn, or other treats.

7. *Be flexible about when they happen.* It's more important that the whole family be present than that councils be held at a special time. As children get older other interests absorb them, and must be considered.

8. *Have a time limit.* If the council is to be over at 8:30, end it then. If family members find that councils interfere with their plans, they'll be resentful about them.

Remember that not everyone will find a council to be the most important activity at that time.

9. *When problems are discussed, avoid placing blame.* Instead, focus on defining the problem and eliciting solutions. It is important to listen to angry feelings, but guide the discussion toward involving everyone in the problem-solving process.

FAMILY OUTINGS CAN BE MORE FUN

Ever have the feeling that you shouldn't have gone? Picnics, camping, a day at the beach or amusement park can be fun, or they can be so filled with arguing and frustration that no one wants to go again. The following suggestions will help make family outings more satisfying for everyone.

1. *Set time limits.* Have a reasonable time for leaving home and returning. Be sure that everyone can meet the schedule without burden, then stick to it.
2. *Anticipate.* Talk about the things you'll do and see ahead of time, as well as the things that each family member would like to do.
3. *Take what you need.* Try to foresee the things you'll need to make it a pleasant outing. A change of clothing can keep an accident from becoming a disaster. Books or toys can help children avoid boredom. A cool drink can help avoid discomfort and save money.
4. *Divide up chores.* All members of the family should take on some responsibility for the outing, to feel that they're contributing to its success. Give children practice in taking this kind of responsibility.
5. *Clarify rules.* "Stay together"; "Let us know where to meet you"; "No arguing"; "Two at a time in the boat." Whatever rules are appropriate to the outing should be discussed and clarified ahead of time. All may not be honored, but they'll be a reference point for making decisions.
6. *$$$.* Who can spend how much for what, when! If

spending money is part of the outing, clarify how much each person has, who can make decisions about money, what happens when it's gone, etc.

7. *Share the baby.* If very small children need continuous supervision, decide who will do so. Mom and Dad can relieve each other; older children may take turns relieving parents. Decide ahead of time who will baby-sit at what times.

TRADITIONS AND RITUALS

Family rituals and traditions are often overlooked as a way to promote children's sense of connectiveness, but they are fundamental to our self-esteem.

All cultures and societies have valued rituals and traditions—they are a universal means by which human beings express their sense of connectiveness in a particular setting and time of history. American society tends to be less committed to rituals in everyday matters than more traditional societies are. Families in which parents share a satisfying and meaningful common heritage find it easier to carry on the traditions and rituals of the past. Modern American families find it difficult to do so for many reasons, including the high degree of mobility that separates people geographically from the cultural roots that feed ritual and tradition, the increase in the number of marriages that combine different heritages, the dissolution of many ethnic ghettos in cities and rural areas, and the high value placed on personal freedom and autonomy that separates individuals from their families.

Not all family traditions or rituals make everyone feel good all the time. Children may not like to go to church every Sunday, especially if their needs and interests are not considered and planned for. Christmas morning may be filled with conflict and argument, mealtime prayers may produce giggling and frustration, going to Grandma's may be a "drag" because there's nothing to do there. But despite such issues everyone gains some important feelings from ritual and tradition that often cannot be stimulated in other ways.

Many traditions arouse feelings of belonging to something. The way we feel when participating in something that is familiar is as important as the feelings we have when we are engaged in something that is unusual. Important rituals stimulate the nonverbal, unconscious sense that we belong to something meaningful and important that makes us feel safe and secure. Feeling part of something that relatives or friends are also a part of, and feeling that we have a special role in a significant event, are among the feelings that ritual and tradition stimulate.

Children's need for feeling part of something is so strong that they spontaneously ritualize their games and play. Observe how they spawn rules and procedures for their games that they repeat each time they play: a certain tree is always "home"; the same game is played again and again; certain words become a ritualized part of a game, and so on. Their sense of tradition is shown by the degree to which they insist that things be done in a certain way, such as their bedtime ritual, the way a certain book is read to them, or wanting pancakes for breakfast every day. Often this sense of tradition can result in highly emotional reactions if parents deviate from some apparently mundane procedure. Traditions, in this sense, increase predictability, which is an important factor in reducing anxiety and fear in children. One of the reasons that family-oriented TV series are so popular with both children and adults is because of the rituals that are carried through the weekly episodes. The very predictability of some elements of the plots produces a feeling of satisfaction in the viewers.

The family watching TV programs that are popular with all members becomes itself a family ritual. The large amount of time many families spend watching TV may very well be evidence of the absence of other important and satisfying rituals and traditions in those families. If you want your children (and yourself) to watch less TV, what can you propose to substitute as a satisfying family activity?

All human beings tend to ritualize most of their behavior. We call the result *habits*, and they connect us to ourselves. The evidence of their importance shows up when we try to change even mundane ones. Have you ever tried to change the way you brush your teeth, comb your hair, or cut your food? Family habits are predictable patterns of interaction which can foster closeness among all members.

Consciously creating rituals and traditions is akin to trying to create good habits; it will seem unusual and awkward to do so. It is easier if you start early in the life of a family, and reach agreements about them. Rituals can be mundane events (mealtimes, activities, family rules, where clothing goes, favorite recipes). They can involve religious expression (church attendance, grace at meals, Bible reading). They can be private family issues (special birthday rituals, pet names). They can connect the family to a broader social context (going to the fireworks display on July Fourth, picnics on national holidays). They can represent the cultural, ethnic or racial roots of the family through dress, food, language, or stories. They can simply be periodic repetition of some satisfying activity. But apart from satisfaction, rituals and tradition must occur consistently (even though a year apart), they must be predictable so that family members' expectations are met, they must engage *all* family members, and they must be satisfying for everyone.

Do you ever get nostalgic for some feelings you had as a child about some family ritual you no longer practice? Have you ever seen disappointment in your children because you didn't follow up on some especially satisfying family activity? Have you been aware of the need in yourself for more ritual and tradition in your life and in the life of your family? If any of these have occurred, you are in touch with the basic human need for tradition and ritual that must be satisfied so that a sense of connectiveness can build.

Family rituals and traditions often are associated with events that occur outside the home. But having rituals and traditions that don't depend on places, events, or institutions outside the home can provide a consistent and predictable family pattern that will be an important hedge against the effect that excessive change has on children's feelings of connectiveness. Change is impossible to avoid.

HANDLING CHANGE THAT
THREATENS A SENSE OF CONNECTIVENESS

In the previous chapter we discussed the things that threaten your children's sense of connectiveness. This section will list some guidelines for dealing with unpredicted or uncontrollable change. Remember that what we mean by a *threat* is the actual or anticipated loss of a valued person, place, or object. Because you may not be fully aware of the things your children have placed value in, their reactions may be surprising and unexpected. Major issues, such as death, divorce, or moving are often easier to anticipate and handle, because they are more obvious and dramatic events in a family's life.

- Even though the object of a child's attachment may seem unimportant to parents, the feelings the child has about it are real and important. Respect the child's feelings.
- Remember that adults have many more experiences involving change than children do, and have found ways to adjust to it. Children are not as flexible nor do they have solid techniques for handling change.
- Keep as many things constant and consistent as possible while moving through major changes. Family rules, rituals, and activities can be anchors for children's security as major changes are weathered.
- Increase other things that support a sense of connectiveness when losses occur. Holding a child who is distraught about a loss is an example. When circumstances keep you from doing certain things that build connectiveness, do more of others.
- Explain the reasons that a loss has occurred (especially a major one). It may help, but don't count on it. More information doesn't necessarily affect a child's emotions. Adults use their minds to override their feelings; children don't.
- Distraction helps young children control their anxiety about change. Distracting a child means unconnecting

him from one object of attention and connecting him with another. Not feeling connected to anything is the most frightening aspect for him.

- Don't panic yourself if you can help it. When children feel their parents have lost control, their main contact with a stable universe is broken. Panic, if you must, when the children aren't around.
- Set limits to the way in which a child expresses his sorrow about the loss, especially when his behavior has an effect on others. Allowing a child to express his feelings doesn't mean that you must tolerate emotional outbursts that interfere with others. Be gentle, but firm.

Improving the Way Children Communicate

THE COMMUNICATION TAPESTRY

Can you think of a time your child had something very important to tell you and you listened carefully, asking questions to clarify your understanding? Perhaps you saw your child's face shine with delight and enthusiasm. At the end of this most interesting conversation your child went off feeling pleased. From this experience you and your child deepened your sense of connectiveness to each other.

Communication is a tapestry that weaves people together. Words, tones, and gestures determine the richness, strength, and flexibility of the cloth. The fabric you weave between yourself and children will, to a large extent, influence how they communicate with others, and determines the strength of their sense of connectiveness. Perhaps you are aware of how your inflection, accent, and use of language are similar to those of your parents. Because most of our communication habits arise through imitation, you should be conscious of how you communicate. Practice the following so that you can pass on this crucial skill to your children:

- Listen carefully to what other people say.
- Describe your needs clearly, in language that attracts interest.
- Disclose your feelings, intentions, and personal experiences to friends, parents, and teachers.
- Describe anger and upset feelings rather than resorting to blaming, name calling, and emotional displays.

As in all learning, children acquire communication skills by watching your habits in this area as well as by being taught.

BUILDING STRENGTH INTO
THE COMMUNICATION TAPESTRY

Listen and respond to what your child is saying. Children need to feel and know that you are listening to them. You can accomplish this in several ways.

1. Look directly at your child when you speak.
2. Paraphrase or feed back to your child what you hear him say.
3. Let her know you sense the feelings she is expressing but not directly describing.
4. Ask questions that help him elaborate his story (for example, "Tell me more about . . ." or "What other things did you do?").
5. Avoid questions that begin with "why" and are slightly accusative (for example, "Why did you think *that*?").
6. Avoid jumping to conclusions about whether she was right or wrong in some action.

How intently you need to listen will vary according to the situation. Often only a quick reply to indicate that you recognize they are present is sufficient. "Hi, Mom, I'm home," requires only an "Okay son," without having to focus on what a child is saying. On the other hand, when your daughter tells you about her pain in being rejected by her best friend, you should listen carefully, indicating you recognize the importance of the experience. People frequently feel relief when they sense someone cares enough to listen. You will become aware of a broad range of emotions and motives as you begin to listen intently. When children repeatedly complain about homework, for example, they may want to keep you in conversation to avoid doing a difficult task. In such cases, let your child know you understand he is frustrated, then encourage him to continue working and indicate that you have a limit on the time you can spend with him.

When your tone of voice, facial expressions, gestures, and words all indicate joy at what your child did, the impact is strong. If you say you're happy and you do not smile, children can be confused, and the effect of what you are saying is reduced. Similarly, when you are angry, let the feeling show in your face, voice, and words.

Telling children how their actions affect you makes a difference to them. Often when you tell a child he should or shouldn't do something, this command is based on a feeling that you have. When you restate a "should" in terms of your feeling, it helps to build a sense of connectiveness, because of the personal quality of the message. "You shouldn't yell in the house" can be restated as "I get upset when you yell in the house." "Don't talk with your mouth full" is more effective as "I cannot understand you when you talk with food in your mouth and, besides, looking at you when you do that disturbs me." Many of us feel that we're being selfish if our criticism is based on a personal feeling. We try to use abstract principles ("Eating with your mouth open is bad manners"), rather than expressing our feelings directly. Remember, a child will sense how you feel even when you try to conceal it.

ADDING RICHNESS TO
THE COMMUNICATION TAPESTRY

Help your child build a varied vocabulary. Preschool children will often mimic words parents use without knowing their meaning. You can and should deliberately use words that are beyond your child's current vocabulary. You might say, "Isn't that a *delicious* pie?" When your child then tries out *delicious* and gets approval and attention, she will use the word in many different settings to see what impact it has. Similarly, children often use profanities they don't understand because they sense the strong reaction they create in adults.

Read stories to your children that vary in word difficulty. They can comprehend the meaning of a story in a variety of ways—through the context, and by making mental pictures are two examples. One of the authors, while reading *The Hobbit* to his six-year-old son asked, "You don't really understand the words do you?" "No, Daddy," he replied, "but I make pictures."

Humor and puns are both a challenge and delight and stimulate children to search for unusual words. Without humor our communication threads would be dull. Many cartoonists use puns in their comic strips that can be shared with the family or class. Kidding with a child, especially young children, can add to the delight of both child and adult. This can take the form of exaggeration. "That apple is so big it is bigger than this house." Or after a child ties her shoes for the first time: "I bet the magic dwarf helped you put on your shoes." "He did not," laughs the child, "I did, all by myself."

Riddles are another source of fun, and intrigue children, particularly when they can stump you on one. Go to your local library with your child to find some riddle books with material that can be used at home or at school.

BUILDING FLEXIBILITY INTO THE COMMUNICATION TAPESTRY

Your children can be taught to satisfy their needs through words. Children are experts at indirect manipulation of others in order to get power. "You don't love me!" often brings the needed holding and comforting from a guilty parent. Whining, pestering, and acting helpless are other ways children use to get their way. "You are always helping Billy, but never me," is cover for a need that can be asked for directly and successfully. You can help them communicate more forcefully and directly by ignoring their habitual manipulations, and by teaching alternative ways of asking.

Encourage your child to be both direct and specific when she wants help. Often you will have to ask the complainer or whiner "What are you asking for?" or "What do you want to do?" Then instruct her to ask directly for it, providing language that she can mimic. For example, your daughter complains (to no one in particular), "Oh heck, this homework is so hard. I can't do it" (deep sigh and slamming of a book on the table). Rather than rushing in and saying "I can help you," ask "Are you asking for help?" If she says "Yes," then ask her to request help directly by saying, "Mom, would you help me with this problem?" Do not respond with assistance until she can ask directly.

Expressing themselves appropriately according to place, time, and audience is an important task to teach your children. Everyone has limits. Children need to know what these limits are in order to adjust their behavior. Yelling is okay in the backyard during the day but not after 9:00 P.M. and not in the house. Talking to your neighbor in the classroom is fine during work period, but not during a test. "It's hard for me to listen to you while I'm cooking; tell me about it during dinner," is an important way to teach your child that you have limits. One of the favorite times for children to talk to you is when *you* are talking on the telephone. This is the time to be clear and firm, telling the child, "I cannot talk to you now but I can in fifteen minutes" (or, "after I finish talking on the phone"). Be certain to keep your commitment to talk to your child when you said you would. If she does not respond to this limit, you need to set a rule about interruptions.

THE THREE D'S THAT HINDER COMMUNICATION AND DESTROY CONNECTIVENESS

The communication fabric you construct can also be destroyed by three habits you may not be aware of. These habits will weaken your children's sense of connectiveness and reduce your effectiveness in teaching them to communicate.

DISINTEREST

You probably can recall a time when you were totally absorbed in a task and your child wanted to tell you something important. What did you do? If you're like most parents, you reluctantly put aside your work, feeling the gnawing pangs of responsibility to the child struggling against your own interests. You then listened indifferently, wondering if you would have time to finish what you had started. Children can sense this disinterest, but because they have *some* of your attention they continue to relate to you. Deep inside, though, is the feeling that something is missing, and children will leave such an interaction with a vague sense of incompleteness. Typically, many parents, when their interest is divided between a pestering child and an important task, will often placate the child with promises that are not kept or remembered. The child will remember, however, and the adult, now feeling guilty over a broken promise, will often placate the child again. What children really need, initially, is your undivided attention when they have something important to say.

DISCONNECTION

Kids are frustrated with adults when we respond to them in a way that is unrelated to what they are saying. For example, Jimmy to teacher: "I wonder why camels have two humps?" Teacher: "Jimmy, would you please close the window. It's getting cold in here now."

Disconnection also occurs when adults abruptly change topics in midstream, without clarifying the connecting links.

"Judy, I saw this dress the other day and I thought it would look great on you. Your hair is messy. When did you last clean it?" Judy does not know that her mother was thinking that the dress would look great on her when she took Judy to see her grandmother, and that Judy would need to clean and comb her hair before going. Her mother had made the unconscious assumption that Judy could read her mind. Judy has to fill in the missing pieces, often inaccurately, and simply gets confused.

DISCOUNTING

Discounting occurs when we attack children's characteristics rather than describe how a particular action affected us. For example: "You are irresponsible!" rather than "When you leave the door to the kitchen open it lets in all the flies and upsets me." Labeling often occurs with very young children whom we feel would not understand a more detailed explanation. "Naughty, naughty" and "bad boy [or girl]" are labels that criticize a child as a whole. Young children can understand specific dos and don'ts without the burden of derogatory names. Sarcasm also discounts a person, even when we are trying to make light of a situation or teach something. "Oh you can't be *that* stupid," is a statement that implies more than that the child could have done something better; it also conveys to the listener that he or she is stupid as a total person. Sarcasm often has such a strong impact that the instructional aspect is lost.

Tone of voice is particularly important in determining how another person will interpret joking. If you are uncomfortable or irritated with what another person is doing, it is likely that your voice will have a sarcastic bite to it.

Another way we discount children is when we use *never* or *always* as in "You always get angry when I speak to you," or "You never finish what I ask you to do." Such statements ignore the many times the child did not get angry or did complete tasks. The rich diversity of your child's behavior is ignored. Such words are often spoken in anger and arouse defensiveness in children, who then engage in pointless argument about how often they did or did not do something.

"Mind reading" is another way to discount a person. Here assumptions about what a person feels or why they did something are taken as fact without checking. We will ask "Why are you angry?" without first checking our perceptions by asking "Are you angry?" Even though parents and teachers may sometimes be accurate in their assumptions, when they are wrong children must try to contradict them or begin to question their own sense of what they feel or think, which is difficult for many children. It becomes even more ridiculous if two people argue about what one of them feels. "Yes, you did feel angry." "No, I didn't." Mind reading discounts your child's ability and responsibility to be aware of and, if appropriate, to report her own feelings accurately.

Imputing motives is also discounting. For example, "I know, Jean, that you are deliberately refusing to do the work; you can do it if you really want to." The teacher had disregarded the fact that Jean had been absent during the class discussion; Jean was confused and scared rather than malicious.

BUILDING COMMUNICATION SKILLS

Intimacy and connectiveness are built only when people can appropriately share the full range of thoughts, feelings, assumptions and opinions, observations of behavior, intentions, and ongoing actions.

Appropriate communication is a key word here.

Name calling is a timeless tradition of children and one that persists despite noble attempts to eradicate it. Of course being called a hurtful name does not build connectiveness, so it is important that children (and adults) realize that name calling or labeling others in a negative way is a cover for underlying feelings of which the speaker is often only dimly aware. We should also realize that the impact of sharing a feeling, even when it is negative, can support a feeling of connectiveness between two people, whereas labeling breaks it.

Almost as dangerous as hurtful communication is the complete lack of it or inappropriate communication. Many relationships have been severed because a person has either revealed so little of his feelings and intentions that the other misunderstood, or so overburdened his listener with a flood of self-disclosures that the other was turned off. There is potential trouble for many people who get in the habit of disclosing only certain things they are thinking about and unconsciously hold back others. For example, a person may state facts about his activities, such as what he did, when, who was involved, and so forth, but fail to mention his own feelings about the events. Others may talk in detail about hurt feelings and what the others did to stimulate these feelings but not say a word about what they intend to do about the situation.

Your children need to learn how to share thoughts and feelings appropriately, and to recognize that appropriateness varies according to the situation. With strangers or casual acquaintances, sharing many intimate feelings might make people uncomfortable; planning a successful family outing requires people to voice preferences. If people vary too widely in their styles of disclosure, that is, if one party shares many personal feelings and the other states only opinions, then it will be hard to establish closeness. You can discuss with your children the kind and amount of disclosure that is needed in any given situation. You, as your child's role model, can strengthen this skill by consciously responding to others appropriately.

We have been discussing the foundation of any skill-building program—modeling good communication. Parents and teachers can add to this discussion by using the following activities to enhance their children's interest and skill in the use of language. Since there is a close relationship between interest in language and reading skill, you can help your child in school with this preparation.

One of the most enjoyable communication-building activities is storytelling. Bedtime stories not only are an enjoyable ritual that eases a child's transition into sleep, but a wonderful method for building vocabulary. A child's interest in the story stimulates curiosity about words. One way to increase your child's fascination with a story is to be dramatic. When your tone and inflection varies and your facial and body gestures reflect the story's action, you capture the child's imagination, even though all the words are not understood. Allowing your voice to vary in pitch, rate, and timbre at first may seem exaggerated, but it will heighten your child's interest. Even though children often enjoy the same story over and over again, introduce a variety of stories, differing in content, style, and vocabulary. Build on these stories by encouraging children to make up their own about the main character in a book. "And what would have happened if————" or "Make up an ending to this story" are helpful lead questions for children to respond to.

Another verbal activity children, especially babies and toddlers, love is to make and imitate sounds. Who has not played "Boo!" with a baby and heard a faint "Boo!" in response? Weave sounds into the stories you read. "And the rooster made what sound?" Encourage your child to imitate the sound of his favorite animal and to make different sounds depending upon the mood of the animal. "How would Billy the Bear sound when he is hungry?" "How would he sound when he is happy?" Many libraries have records of sounds your child can listen to and mimic.

Listening is a skill that aids learning and positive human relations. Your interest and concern for a person is conveyed by listening attentively to that person. Most communication difficulties are the result of a failure to attend to and to be interested in what the other is saying. Listening, like any skill, can be taught. To this end you can help your child learn to pay attention by playing this game: One person tells another a series of commands, such as "Go to the door and open it, then walk to the bookshelf and take out the first book on the end of the bottom shelf." The listener must then perform them in the order presented. The difficulty and number of instructions should vary according to the child's age and abilities. You can construct a graph showing progressively, over time, the number of commands your child is able to perform without error.

SECTION III
THE WHOLE CHILD: BEING SPECIAL

6

Individuality: Plus or Minus?

Many of us believe that those who have unusual style or characteristics have a high sense of uniqueness, but this is not necessarily so. Our sense of uniqueness has to do with how we feel about ourselves, and not with whether we are different. Children and adults may seem to be basically "ordinary," yet have a high sense of uniqueness. Thus we find many people who act in a highly individualistic way may be suffering from a low sense of uniqueness. It all depends on how a person feels about himself.

The images, ideas, and beliefs that children have about themselves are always associated with feelings. Children may have some attributes about which they feel bad (dumb, fat, unlikable, and so on) while knowing they also have good qualities (fast, smart, pretty, for example). Building your child's sense of uniqueness means bolstering those ideas and beliefs about himself associated with strong, positive feelings.

Children's ideas about themselves and, consequently, their sense of uniqueness, develop as their language capability matures. A toddler may express beliefs about himself simply: "Me bad boy!" but as he grows, his range of ideas about himself also expands. At every stage of growth new experiences and demands on children alter their ideas about self, and consequently their sense of uniqueness is being continually renewed.

Children with a *high* sense of uniqueness may be problems for parents and/or teachers. When a child is motivated to "do his own thing," he may not be very adaptive to group activities, or to going along with others. This often is a problem in school. Parents and teachers may believe that a child is *trying to be different* when he is actually *being himself.* The authors estimate that as much as two percent of the children in any school have such a high sense of uniqueness that they appear to be "weird," that is, they are more inclined to follow their own feelings and ideas, rather than submit to the goals or expectations of others.

Children who have *negative* self-concepts are as persistent in acting accordingly as are children with *positive* ones. It may appear that those with negative self-images are "trying to be themselves," when, in fact, they are not at all happy or comfortable with the way they act. A positive sense of uniqueness is fundamental to your child's need to feel good about himself. As with all four conditions of self-esteem, the way parents and teachers treat children can enhance or diminish their sense of uniqueness.

Wendy, the subject of our next case study, is an example of a child with uniqueness problems. She gets her own feelings and self-images all mixed up with other people's images of her. The result is a sad, confused little girl.

WENDY: WONDER WOMAN
UNDER WRAPS (PART I)

Mrs. Crater looked across the fourth-grade classroom at Wendy, who was characteristically staring out of the window with a dazed expression in her eyes, not actually looking at anything. Daydreaming again, Mrs. Crater thought to herself.

But as she watched, Alan walked past Wendy's desk, distractedly looking at his math paper, and accidently brushed her arm. Wendy immediately came out of her reverie, and snapped at him, "You better watch out!" Alan looked at her bewildered and continued toward his seat.

Wendy then got out of her seat and came to Mrs. Crater's desk. "Alan pushed me," she complained in a low voice, and waited for her teacher to react. When Mrs. Crater explained that she was sure it was an accident, Wendy went back to her seat, a resigned expression on her face, and returned to working on her math assignment.

Mrs. Crater was concerned about Wendy, who often appeared to be depressed or inhibited, but also seemed to want so much attention. That was one of the things that confused Mrs. Crater. Wendy might come up to her a dozen times a day with some grievance or complaint or wanting to talk about a topic that didn't have anything to do with what was going on in class. But when Mrs. Crater called on her in reading group, or even praised some bit of work that Wendy did, she would clam up, blush, and seem embarrassed. But if someone else was reciting, Wendy would often interrupt them, or do something that would distract the other children. She would wave her hand wildly to questions Mrs. Crater asked, but if called on, would often not have the right answer, sometimes not even seeming to know what the question was. And if called on after someone else recited, she might just repeat what the preceding child had said.

Because of this behavior Mrs. Crater found herself criticizing Wendy more than she wanted to. And when she tried to avoid doing so her responses were so awkward and contrived that she felt funny: "Well, Wendy, that *is* an interesting answer, but not exactly about the question I asked." Wendy was a problem, but not the sort Mrs. Crater could put her finger on. She wasn't mean or angry, she didn't go out of her way to start trouble, but she required a lot of attention, and often reacted to other children in the same hostile way she had to Alan when he brushed her accidently. Alternating between almost frenetic activity and lethargic daydreaming, Wendy was an enigma.

Wendy's parents were also concerned about her. In fact, some of their reports indicated her behavior at home was more bizarre than at school. She sought attention inappropriately at home as at school, and what with having three other children to look after as well, Mrs. Littleton would blow up at her a lot. An example of Wendy's unusual behavior was the time her mother heard funny noises coming from Wendy's room, looked in the door, and found Wendy jumping around the room karate chopping the air, bouncing on her bed, and uttering strange noises. When Wendy saw her mother watching she screamed at her to go away and slammed the door. Mrs. Littleton blew up at that. Wendy often had to be punished for overreacting to little things that anyone in the family might say to her. Mrs. Littleton thought that Wendy might be "kookie," and would lecture her about being so "crazy."

Wendy's older sister was a model child, responsible at home and motivated in school. The Littletons couldn't understand how they could have one daughter who was so sharp and another who was so "weird." They tried tutors, helped Wendy with homework, applied various punishments, and had lots of conferences at school in an attempt to get Wendy to act more normally. Mostly, though, they left her alone because she demanded so much attention anyway. "We just don't know what's wrong with that child," they told Mrs. Crater.

Wendy was a follower. She was friendly and ingratiating, but rarely took the lead in games or other activities. This same attitude permeated her approach to schoolwork. She would ask again and again, "How should I do this?"; "Is this right?"; "Where should I put the answer?" Even when she was free to do something her own way, in art or writing, she would ask such questions. She checked what others were doing so often that Mrs. Crater was concerned about her copying, although Wendy was at least an average student in all subjects.

But every once in a while Wendy would say or write something that indicated that there was something unusual going on within her. One time she wrote a poem that was a gem, but when Mrs. Crater read it to the class without asking her, Wendy turned beet red, complained of a stomachache, and went to the nurse's office. Her poem: (Misspellings are Wendy's)

Fly through the air grate lady
Save the lives of all
Streek through the water grate woman
Katch them before they fall.
Wondrful lady, heroin without fear
I now in my hart, you allways near
Keep all the childern from crying a tear
You are verry brave and allways hear.
Fly through the air grate lady
Carry me to your hall
Streek through the water grate woman
Show me how to be brave and tall.

Such rare evidence of Wendy's latent creative potential was in sharp contradiction to her usually mundane performance, and only served to further confuse her teachers and parents. Who was this little girl? She surely was different, but was there anything special about her? The answer to who Wendy was is discussed in chapter 7.

Wendy's behavior is not unusual, although she may be an unusual person. There are many children who act in ways that confuse us. Like other children who have uniqueness problems, Wendy exhibits a variety of behaviors that often don't seem to fit together. There are a number of reasons why it is sometimes difficult to identify uniqueness as being the critical condition in a child's low self-esteem.

Children with uniqueness problems may act one way at one time, and in exactly the opposite way at another time. Examples of such bipolar behavior are:

- Acting very conforming/Trying to be different
- Not wanting to be singled out/Showing off
- Disparaging their own creations/Seeking praise excessively
- Following other's wishes/Insisting on doing things their own way.

There are times during childhood when peer pressures are so strong that children may try to squelch their own unique talents or characteristics in order to be a member of a gang or group. This condition seems to accelerate during upper elementary grades and into junior high. When children conform to peer group standards they may appear to be "deviant" with respect to their parents' and their schools' expectations. At such times children seem to be forced into choosing between their connectiveness and uniqueness needs.

Despite these confusing factors, careful and consistent observation of your children's behavior will show the degree to which their sense of uniqueness is present. Parents and teachers need to understand what their children are *feeling*, and whether their behavior is conforming, different, or ambivalent.

HOW CHILDREN WITH UNIQUENESS PROBLEMS BEHAVE

When children avoid dealing with their unmet uniqueness needs, you will observe the following:	When children attempt to meet their unmet uniqueness needs inappropriately, you will observe the following:
1. They do not exhibit much imagination in how they work or play.	**1.** They show off a lot, especially at inappropriate times.
2. They usually do things in the way they're told, rarely in any unique or distinctive manner.	**2.** They seek attention excessively, often about things that are not the focus of interest of the group at the time.

3. They experience embarrassment, confusion, or anxiety when called on or singled out in group activities.

4. They rarely contribute original ideas, tending to mimic others' responses.

5. They tend to conform to others' wishes and ideas, and are anxious if they can't find out what they are.

6. They are uncomfortable when they become aware that they have inadvertently done something that is different from others.

7. They rarely take pride or delight in what they accomplish or produce, and often disparage it.

8. They deny, disregard, become embarrassed by, or undermine praise, especially when it is directed at them publicly.

3. They attempt to be different in dress or behavior to a degree that others feel alienated from them.

4. They insist on doing things in their own way to such a degree that they don't meet standards or expectations of teachers or parents.

5. They act out *negative* roles with great persistence, especially when others expect them to do so.

Children who have a low sense of uniqueness try to correct that condition in active or passive ways and often alternate between one and the other. In their active phase they try to elicit recognition and respect for what they feel are special characteristics, whether they are positive or negative ones. In the passive phase they avoid expressing unique or outstanding qualities, and restrict their own self-expression. Because of this, two children who behave quite differently may both have problems with their sense of uniqueness.

The active phase of a low sense of uniqueness is most dramatically expressed by children who are usually labeled "behavior problems," at home or school. Behavior-problem children persist in acting in ways they *know* will result in pain or punishment to themselves. Why do they do this? The answer is tied up in two issues. One is that some children have a negative sense of self that they try to live up to. The other is that children seek special recognition and attention and are willing to get negative attention if they can't get positive recognition.

Negative roles, negative characteristics, negative attention—what do we mean by "negative"? In general something that is negative with respect to the sense of uniqueness is a quality that is not valued by children or their parents or teachers, actions that result in punishment, criticism, or disapproval, and roles that are disparaged by others.

Examples of negative roles:

class clown	behavior problem
the weirdo	dumbest kid in class
bad kid	irresponsible child
worst athlete	the flaky kid

Examples of negative characteristics:

too fat/too skinny	too sexy/too sexless
too short/too tall	too independent/too conforming
too loud/too quiet	
a physical handicap	too dark skinned/too light skinned
	too different/too similar

Examples of negative attention:

"Not you again!"	"What can I do with you?"
"Since you interrupted me anyhow, what do you want?"	"Go away and stop bugging us!"
	"If you do that once more, you'll have to sit right next to me."

All children need attention and recognition, and when, for any reason(s), they cannot or have not had their virtues sufficiently acknowledged, they will amplify their faults to the point that someone pays attention to them. If their faults don't get enough attention, they will "raise the ante," and express their negative characteristics in more dramatic ways. If, over time, children receive increasingly less attention for their positive qualities, and increasingly more for their negative ones, the negative ones become fixed, and the consequence is a negative self-image. A child *unconsciously* is recognizing that he receives more attention for doing something bad than when he's not doing it and, *voilà*, parents and teachers have a behavior problem on their hands. Most behavior problems are created by children's parents, teachers, and peers being unaware of how they reinforce negative characteristics. Even though children *actively pursue* attention through negative behavior, they, nonetheless, are indicating a low sense of uniqueness.

Children who have a low sense of uniqueness tend not to be imaginative. In school their stories tend to be dull and ordinary, they rarely contribute new ideas to discussions, and they don't seem to enjoy making up fanciful tales. They may have quite an unusual fantasy life, but keep it to themselves. Parents and teachers may rarely, if ever, see evidence of it, and may be quite surprised (even disturbed) if they do. Low uniqueness children feel safe in repetitive play and are uncomfortable with change, since it may challenge their creative and imaginative capabilities. They generally don't enjoy word games, puns, or subtle jokes, and rarely tell them. They usually tell poor lies, since telling good ones requires the imagination and enthusiasm that they restrain. They generally mimic what others do or say. By seeking to be told how to do things, they rarely use their own creativity to fill in information gaps. These children don't have a distinctive style by which they go about life.

Characteristically, they are more comfortable with commonplace solutions to problems than unusual ones, and will not want to go to new or unusual places or try out new activities and experiences. Furthermore, they seem to have little curiosity about a new topic, and don't ask questions or seek new ideas.

Children with uniqueness problems may show off a lot in order to be noticed, but they will do so at inappropriate times or places. Even in showing off, they will be repetitive and mundane, and others will often be able to predict their behavior. The exception here is in the toddler stage when children's sense of uniqueness is developing and forming.

Toddlers may repeatedly show off, seeking to be the center of attention, and perform the same "act" again and again. What they are doing is refining their skill in getting attention and basking in recognition and approval that *they have elicited.* Keep cheering the toddler on, no matter how many times he's done the same act, because in doing so, you're setting the stage for self-acceptance that will reduce the child's need to seek attention inappropriately later in his development. Persistent show-off behavior is a sign that children are not getting the positive, special attention that they need and seek.

All children try to show off at one time or another, but their reasons for doing so are different, based on the self-esteem condition that is most critical for them at the times. Children with a low sense of uniqueness are trying to have some quality about themselves acknowledged by others, and often this is a negative characteristic for which they rarely gain approval. Much show-off behavior in low uniqueness children is regressive; they act as they did in earlier childhood. They're accused, often, of acting "babyish" or "childish" if they are old enough to have more mature standards applied to them.

These children try to conform to the wishes or ideas that others have. While they may adopt the same dress or style of those around them, the reasons for doing it are different from the connectiveness issues that promote the same behavior. This contrast is subtle but significant. Low connectiveness children are drawn *to* a group in order to be part of it, and adopt its standards. Low uniqueness children are trying to bury their feelings of being different in negative ways by membership in a group. It's the fear of being different rather than the need for affiliation that is their motive. When in groups, low uniqueness children will be easily led and avoid leadership roles unless they can check with others about what to do.

When it is pointed out to them that they have said or done something that is different from others, low uniqueness children become uncomfortable, embarrassed, and even apologetic. It is difficult for them to accept public praise ("Everyone, look at the beautiful picture Jane drew!"), since it identifies something different about them in a positive way—something they are unused to dealing with. They will not be able to take much pride in their own unique accomplishments until their sense of uniqueness rises. The way they disparage their own productivity forces others to try to make them feel better by praising them.

Low uniqueness children tend to have a narrow range of emotional expression. They rarely express spontaneous joy or elation, although they may become energized and excited. Similarly they don't become intensely depressed, but quite frequently their tendency to reverie, daydream, and fantasize may result in a lethargic, low energy state. They do not seem to be aware of their own feelings and desires, and don't reflect on their own behavior or feelings; they will mimic what others say about themselves as if it were true for them. ("Yes, I'm sad too, like Jimmy.")

HOW CHILDREN'S SENSE
OF UNIQUENESS IS THREATENED

Even if your child's sense of uniqueness is high, it can be easily diminished. It is a fragile aspect of self-esteem, easily bruised by negative reactions to the child and what he does, especially under certain conditions. Even children with a low sense of uniqueness can deal with criticism if it is about something they don't consider important. But when a child says or does something that *he believes* to be a fine and important expression of himself, and someone *he looks up to* (parent or teacher, for example) *disparages or criticizes* that expression, then his sense of uniqueness is severely attacked, often with long-range consequences. The discrepancy between how a child feels about himself or something he does and how others evaluate it is what makes a child's sense of uniqueness so fragile.

Children don't often make clear distinctions between what they do and who they are. An adult with high self-esteem may weather severe criticism and still maintain good feelings about himself, because he has confidence in his ability to change and improve. Children, not having accumulated enough experience to keep their self-image immune from attack, can be devastated by excessive criticism, even though it may be directed at their performance and not at their character. When children's sense of uniqueness is low, the injunction to "criticize the act not the child" may not work, since they translate criticism into a comment about their self.

The sense of uniqueness has an existential quality that makes threats to it seem to be attacks on one's being. Children with a high sense of uniqueness have the courage to be themselves in a way that children with low uniqueness don't. A firm sense of uniqueness is the basis for children developing the self-actualizing qualities that lead to significant creative expression. A low sense of uniqueness inhibits the expression of children's potential, and later retards the expression of the latent talents of adults. The world profits from the creative contributions of talented individuals whose sense of uniqueness frees them from the straitjacket imposed by conformist, traditional thought.

The following list identifies a number of experiences that can reduce your child's sense of uniqueness:

- When people disparage or criticize fantasies, imaginative play, dreams, and wishes.
- When some accomplishment that a child is proud of is disregarded, criticized, or not taken seriously.

- When a child becomes convinced, through repeated criticism, that something about himself is bad, stupid, wrong, or inadequate.
- When a child must repeatedly forego his own personal wishes or goals in favor of the needs or goals of a group, in the family or in the classroom.
- When resources and opportunities for imaginative, creative expression are limited or denied.
- When a child is locked into a negative role in the family or school and doesn't know how to get out of it.
- When self-expression is encouraged in one important aspect of a child's life (home), but prohibited in another (school) or when one parent encourages it and the other doesn't tolerate it.
- When group membership, associated with peer pressures, becomes the highest value and dominating goal.
- When the family's values, beliefs, behavior, dress, or standards are so different from those of the people with whom a child must associate, for example, in school or in the neighborhood, that the child cannot be comfortable in those relationships, and *tries* to conform to either one set of values or the other.
- When teachers or parents attribute bad motives ("You're just trying to be a smart alec") to a child's *sincere* efforts to express himself in a unique or unusual way.
- When a child's feelings (positive or negative) are not taken seriously.
- When a child cannot consider deviant, unusual, or divergent ideas and feel safe and supported by parents and/or teachers.
- When a child has his faults or weaknesses consistently pointed out, but gets little recognition for his strengths and virtues.
- When a child is called upon to demonstrate some special talent or ability before a group *before he is ready to do so.*

- When a child has few or no limits placed on self-expression (verbally or actively) so that he interferes with other people's interests, and suffers criticism or punishment for doing so.
- When a child is expected to be original or creative in performing a task or solving a problem for which he doesn't have adequate preparation, information, support, or encouragement.

Threats to your child's sense of uniqueness center around the issue of self-expression and how it is handled by you and your child's teachers. In children with low sense of uniqueness it is submerged or expressed inappropriately. The following chapters will show how to encourage and support the sense of uniqueness, so that children feel they are truly special to others, and ultimately gain the self-respect that frees their imaginative, creative, and intellectual talents.

7

At Home: Do You Know Who I Am?

HOW TO RELATE TO YOUR CHILD TO BUILD A SENSE OF UNIQUENESS

Each of the following ways of relating to children is a building block in developing their sense of uniqueness and self-esteem. None of these methods, by itself, is a cure-all for uniqueness problems, but each is a facet of an interlocking set of approaches to children that insure a firm sense of uniqueness. Use these methods as a check list and ask yourself: "Do I do *enough* of this with each of my children, and is there a way I can do more?" (In the next section we outline strategies for combating a poor sense of uniqueness in the family.)

COMMUNICATE ACCEPTANCE

Accepting your children is often confused with being permissive with them. Acceptance is an active *process* in which parents help their children distinguish between their behavior and their character or personality. The phenomenon of a child spilling his milk is a case in point. When a child does so (even frequently) it *does not* mean that he is an incompetent, awkward, sloppy, inconsiderate, troublemaking, malicious person.

It signifies that the child has performed an *act* that needs correcting. The child is still okay, but he needs to stop spilling the milk.

"Accepting the child but not the deed," is expressed in the way parents communicate to their children. Your children experience acceptance as a result of how you react to their feelings, attitudes, opinions, and actions, and how much you show that you understand them. ("I know that you didn't mean to spill your milk, but if you put your glass behind your dish you might not have the problem.") Even when limits need to be set, acceptance of a child and recognition of his dilemma may be voiced. ("I know it's hard for you when your little brother bothers you, but I can't allow you to hit him.")

Communicating acceptance becomes more difficult when children do or say things that conflict with parents' deeply held standards or values. Lying, stealing, conflicts with siblings, and other extremes of behavior will test parents' ability to be accepting of children. Many ideas that will help you handle this will be described in more detail later in this chapter.

A child becomes very upset when adults don't understand *why* he did something, and can't accept his reasons as valid ("Stop using excuses!"). More often they get angry and resentful at not being understood than from being punished.

When their motives (their personal reasons for doing something) are acknowledged, they are more open to exploring new alternatives in their behavior. You need to understand why your child did something, from her point-of-view. Encourage your children to express ideas that may be different from your own.

Even though you don't agree with them, children need to know that you respect their privilege to have and voice ideas that are not like yours. Parents need to remember that thinking something is not the same as doing it, and acknowledging children's ideas and feelings often reduces their need to act on them. How and what a child thinks is a central aspect of individuality, and children whose unusual or special ideas are respected develop a good sense of uniqueness. If you start to do this early in a child's life, it reduces the rebellious nature of early and middle adolescence, when deviant thought is a natural expression of a young person's growing individuality.

Solving problems is an area in which children often attempt to apply new or unusual thinking, frequently trying "weird" solutions to see if they work. If parents give them room to try out unusual ideas safely (for themselves and others), children can test their creative problem-solving skills in a climate of tolerance.

It's especially important to let children know that it's okay for them to have opinions that are different from others—to have their own set of likes and dislikes. Children don't suffer from being different; they suffer from believing that being different is not acceptable. You can help them believe that it is acceptable.

POINT OUT TO CHILDREN THINGS
ABOUT THEMSELVES THAT ARE DIFFERENT OR SPECIAL

Children (and adults) share many characteristics, but each child needs to feel special to himself. Your child needs positive recognition for doing or expressing something in his own way. Pointing out such things as "You were especially polite when Aunt Jane was here" helps a child identify his special attributes.

As children grow and change they need to have their emerging skills specifically pointed out and to receive positive recognition of them; for example, "You weren't able to climb that high the last time we were here; you're sure getting better at it."

Your child's ability to identify what makes her special is often limited by her concepts and language, and by what others say about her characteristics. By using special words to identify virtues, you can impress a child: "You have outstanding perseverance," for example.

When your child's sense of uniqueness is low, and a problem needs to be commented on, it can be reframed in a way that is surprising to them and nonjudgmental in tone ("You fight like a she-bear"; "You bother people like a mosquito buzzing around their ear").

ALLOW CHILDREN TO DO
THINGS THEIR OWN WAY AS MUCH AS POSSIBLE

Increasing your children's sense of uniqueness requires that free expression be encouraged in any activity, within limits that insure that jobs get done well and others' rights are not abrogated. A child's sense of uniqueness is restricted when parents insist that their way of doing things is *the* right way, and require slavish adherence to predetermined standards. Leaving some ambiguity about how things are to be done, gives children the opportunity to try out their own ideas.

All tasks that your children perform permit some degree of free expression, as well as requiring them to adhere to some standards and rules. Every activity varies in the way these two factors are balanced. For example, when a child must clean his room, he may be free to arrange his toys on the shelf as he wishes, but must adhere to the rule that they be placed on the shelf and not on the floor. Allowing children to do things according to their own style and imagination does not preclude that parents set standards and have expectations about how things are to be done.

When adults demand conformity without good reason, children with a high sense of uniqueness are bothered, and children with a low sense of uniqueness may become resistant. Children will be more tolerant of standard procedures if they know they will have many opportunities to do things their own way.

INCREASE OPPORTUNITIES FOR
CHILDREN TO EXPRESS THEMSELVES CREATIVELY

You should have lots of materials available at home so that your children can easily find different ways to express themselves: crayons, paints, different kinds of paper, wood scraps, pencils, and so on. Play music and encourage children to dance to it (initiate it yourself). Have a child make up a story with you. Common activities can become fanciful games (grocery shopping becomes a treasure hunt). Simple toys that allow a child to create fantasies are important (blocks, dolls, balls). Discarded household or clothing items can become valued playthings. Imagination is a substitute for wealth when it comes to providing children with creative play objects.

Imaginative play opportunities are generated by children themselves, sometimes to parents' dismay. A new toy may be found in pieces after a few days, and a child may be using one of the pieces in a way that the original toy was not intended. This may be viewed as the child seeing creative opportunities where adults don't, rather than an example of malicious mischief or "not understanding the value of a dollar."

Helping your children find appropriate ways to express themselves is important, but you should also be tolerant of children who can't wait. Alternatively, parents may see creative potentials in things that children don't, but should not be disappointed if children don't find that the parents' imagination fits their need. *Allowing* creativity in children raises their sense of uniqueness more than *insisting* on it does.

ALLOW CHILDREN TO EXPRESS
THEIR SPECIAL INTERESTS ACCORDING TO THEIR OWN TIMING

The length of time a child may devote to a special interest may vary from slightly more than an instant to his whole childhood (and beyond). Children may use the time they spend on things that interest them in a variety of ways:

- They may passionately insist that an interest be fulfilled but drop it quickly after engaging in it.
- They may get some resource they want (a toy), play with it for a while, appear to lose interest, but periodically take it up.
- They may obsessively devote time (all day, every day) to an interest (*Star Wars*) for short or long periods.

- They may have a consistent interest (collecting), but spend only part of their time with it.
- They may have a special interest for years; it becomes their "thing."
- They may take up an interest to please their parents or follow the lead of a friend (music lessons), seem enthusiastic for a while, but lose interest.

Because of the variability that children exhibit in their devotion to a special interest, parents are often unsure about the amount of resources to invest ("Should we buy her the clarinet?"); the amount of time to spend with children on it ("I'm willing to take you to that movie, but I'm not sure you're really going to like it."); or the amount of encouragement or pressure to put on ("Last week you wanted piano lessons; this week you don't want to practice. You get right in there and practice, now!").

Let your children set the pace when they initiate a new interest, rather than take leadership yourself. Allow children and yourself to test their interest, regulating your investment by continually assessing their commitment as time goes on. Talk with them about the issues involved, and find ways for them to have a share in any potential investment.

DON'T RIDICULE OR SHAME CHILDREN

Childhood experiences of ridicule and shame often are remembered long into adulthood, along with memories of pain and embarrassment. Ridicule or shaming may be effective methods for suppressing behavior, but they also stop children from expressing themselves, lowering their sense of uniqueness dramatically. Ridicule tells them that they've expressed themselves in poor ways; shaming them makes them guilty about not living up to standards other than their own.

Ridicule and shame are communicated to children publicly and privately. Criticism becomes either ridicule or shame when a child's person is attacked, rather than his actions. Criticizing children may be necessary and is least harmful when it is specific, impersonal, and shows children how they can improve.

Some examples of the difference between criticism and ridicule/shame are:

> Criticism—"I'm afraid the windows aren't clean enough. Start again with a clean rag, and stand on the chair. Have another rag to get the streaks. You'll have to do them until they're clean."
>
> Ridicule/Shame—"Are you blind, lazy, or both? You've left those windows dirty."
>
> Criticism—"It's wrong to hit your little brother, because it doesn't resolve anything. You and I are going to have to talk about how you can handle his pestering in a better way."
>
> Ridicule/Shame—"Bullies hit kids who are smaller than they are. I know you don't want to be a bully, so you'd better not do it."
>
> Criticism—"The rule is that people who are talking are not to be interrupted. When you raise your hand I will try to call on you."
>
> Ridicule/Shame—"Well, class, Joey has something so fantastically important to say, that he just can't use good manners. Okay, everyone, we'll stop everything to listen to him. It better be good, Joey!"

Children often interpret teasing, humor, and sarcasm as ridicule, though it is not intended as such. This is especially true if children are unsure of themselves or if the humor is so subtle that they can't decode it. Parents and teachers who have a habit of teasing or being sarcastic may believe that they're enormously funny, but children may be threatened by them. Being straightforward with children is often the safer course, until *their* sense of humor is understood.

There are ways to reduce the likelihood that a low uniqueness child will feel ridicule or shame when being corrected:

1. Attempt to make statements designed to correct errors

or behavior privately to a child, out of earshot of other children.

2. Include some positive observation about the child along with any criticism.

3. Make criticism specific and objective.

4. Indicate positive alternatives the child might employ, if he can't think of any.

5. Allow the child to tell you, if he can, why the error or misbehavior was committed, and acknowledge or accept what he says without challenge, judgment, or criticism.

6. Check with the child after a brief time to see whether he is using a better alternative, and praise him privately if he is doing so. This important factor can apply to behavioral issues also. For example, if a child has misbehaved (pushed another child), and doesn't do it again for several minutes after you have corrected him, call him aside and acknowledge that you have observed him not doing so.

7. Do not use abstract moral or ethical principles in your conversation with a low uniqueness child, because they usually have the effect of shaming him. You may refer to specific rules that apply to the situation to identify the specific consequences of his act to himself or others.

HELP CHILDREN FIND
ACCEPTABLE WAYS TO EXPRESS THEMSELVES

It is usually not *what* a child is doing that is a problem, but rather *how* or *where* he's doing it. The context is always important. A child playing loudly in her room may be okay, but not in the midst of mother's tea party. Painting may be acceptable at the kitchen table, but not on the living room sofa.

Help your children find ways to carry on activities so that they don't interfere with others. Children can be oblivious to their surroundings (including other people) when they get deeply into fanciful play, and need positive alternatives to what they're doing inappropriately. When they use a better alternative, reinforce it with praise and recognition.

USE PRIVATE PRAISE WITH
CHILDREN WHO HAVE A LOW SENSE OF UNIQUENESS

Praise, in order to affect your children's feelings, must give them information that helps them repeat a praiseworthy act. For most children their unconscious motive is to improve their performance, and praise has a positive effect. In low uniqueness children their motive is not to improve performance, but rather to elicit attention. As long as *that* motive remains strong, effusive praise only reinforces their desire for attention and ignores the quality and acceptability of the act.

There are several reasons why children with a low sense of uniqueness have difficulty handling praise:

- The praise contradicts something they believe about themselves. (Catching a ball in a game was a "lucky mistake" to a child who feels he's a poor ball player.)
- The praise comes for something that they have been criticized for previously, and lacks credibility. (A child who's been told that he's a problem reader suddenly is praised for reading well.)
- The praise is given for something that they have been ridiculed or shamed for, and they don't believe it's meant sincerely. (A child who's been laughed at in school for his looks is told by parents that he is handsome.)
- The praise contradicts a role that they have adopted. (A child who's been the class clown is praised for doing something seriously and competently.)

When children with a low sense of uniqueness are praised in front of others, confusion about their roles and how they're seen by others promotes anxiety. Children show this anxiety in their reactions, which may range from mild embarrassment, through denial, to getting downright nasty toward the person who is praising them. They may even misbehave soon after being praised publicly, seemingly in an effort to assert some negative self-image they have.

To alleviate some of these problems you must proceed slowly and use private praise, which is more special, sincere, and meaningful to children with a low sense of uniqueness, especially if it is not overly enthusiastic. A private conversation, a written note, or a quickly whispered aside can surprise and delight a child with a low sense of uniqueness. Any method of praising them that is somewhat unusual has added value ("I'll let you know that you're doing okay by touching my nose!").

TREAT EACH CHILD AS AN INDIVIDUAL

Your children's sense of uniqueness is weakened when they become so immersed in a collective identity that their unique characteristics are overlooked. You may inadvertently deny your child's individuality in a sincere effort to be evenhanded in dispensing time, attention, or material resources to all the children in your family. Even though the children in any family must frequently be dealt with as a unit, parents need to insure that there are many occasions when individual styles, needs, tastes, interests, opinions, and personal characteristics are acknowledged and honored. ("Tonight we are going to have Johnny's favorite dinner, chili with corn bread, in honor of his A in spelling.") When parents respect children's individuality, the children can begin to accept and respect their own individual differences.

Building a child's sense of uniqueness requires that you use a number of these strategies simultaneously. Wendy, the confused and sad little girl described in Chapter 6, is one such child. Her parents found out that they had to be more flexible and imaginative in helping her out of her uniqueness problems, and, as you will see, they needed some help to do so.

WENDY: WONDER WOMAN
UNDER WRAPS (PART II)

Because of the dilemmas posed by Wendy's behavior, Mrs. Crater and Wendy's parents agreed that professional help might be worthwhile. The Littletons contacted a local family counseling agency and made an appointment. They were told to bring Wendy with them.

When Mrs. Littleton told Wendy they were going to see a counselor about the problems she was having in school and the arguments they were having at home Wendy seemed to accept it with a positive attitude. Over the next several days Wendy asked about the time of the appointment, and even mentioned it to her sister. Mr. Littleton, who supported the counseling idea, even had to tell Wendy to stop bugging him about it, as she brought it up several times.

Wendy and her parents were a bit apprehensive on the evening they went to the counseling agency. Wendy chattered away in the car, until her dad teasingly told her to turn off her "motormouth." In the waiting room Wendy paced the floor, looked at the pictures on the wall, played with some toys, and seemed nervous.

At the appointed hour, a young woman greeted them and introduced herself as Sandy Lambert, their counselor. She shook hands with Mr. and Mrs. Littleton and Wendy, and ushered them into her office. After taking some information and engaging in pleasantries about the weather, Miss Lambert posed the question to each member of the family about what had brought them to the agency. Mr. and Mrs. Littleton in turn described the problems they were having with Wendy at home and school, and essentially agreed on the issues: Wendy's oversensitivity at home, her apparent low motivation and mundane performance at school, daydreaming, and her periodic strange behavior.

When it was Wendy's turn to give her opinion she burst into tears, and haltingly restated much of what her parents said, adding nothing of substance to their statements. Sandy gently probed to find out more about Wendy's feelings, asking her questions about school, and the things she liked to do. Most of the answers she received were noncommittal. ("Yes, I like school." "What do you like about it?" "I don't know, I just like it.") Wendy would look at her parents after she gave an answer, as if she were checking with them whether she was right or not. Sandy asked about her favorite TV programs, and Wendy responded with several. When she had gone through her list of favorites, Mrs. Littleton added, "Oh, you forgot one—*Wonder Woman*," and turning to Miss Lambert, said, "She's crazy for that one. She really blows up if she can't watch it. I don't know how she could leave it out."

Sandy Lambert turned, smiling broadly, and told Wendy that *Wonder Woman* was one of her favorites too. Wendy showed real interest when Miss Lambert proceeded to tell her about her collection of old *Wonder Woman* comic books, and related some of her favorite TV episodes. Wendy beamed when Miss Lambert told her how pleased she was to find someone who liked it, since most of her friends thought it was a weird program.

After this interchange, Wendy's demeanor changed for the rest of the counseling hour. She became more lively, and even had some disagreement with her parents about her oversensitivity, protesting that her sister and younger brothers didn't speak very nicely to her sometimes.

When Miss Lambert asked the Littletons had they any observations about Wendy's interests or accomplishments, Mr. Littleton brought up the facts about Wendy's poem, how enthusiastic Mrs. Crater had been, but how Wendy seemed to disparage it. He, along with his wife, felt that Wendy had a lot of potential that was going unused, indicating that they really wanted to help her in any way they could, but were confused about what to do.

While her parents talked about her poem, Wendy looked down at the floor and seemed uncomfortable, but when Miss Lambert didn't comment about it, she relaxed. As the session ended, Wendy and her parents agreed that she would return for some private meetings with Miss Lambert, who told Wendy that she would have some of her *Wonder Woman* comics to lend to her, and laughingly said that she might trade one for a copy of Wendy's poem, if Wendy felt comfortable about showing it to her.

On the drive home Wendy's mother asked her how she liked Miss Lambert. Wendy indicated that she did, very much, but when asked why, responded, "Oh, she's really nice." At home her older sister started to ask her about what happened, and rather than bristling or getting angry, Wendy said, "Well, she likes Wonder Woman too," and proceeded to tell her about Miss Lambert's comic book collection.

For the next several days there were no conflicts or arguments with Wendy. At school she was slightly calmer, although nothing dramatically changed in her behavior. As the time for her next session with the counselor approached Wendy was pretty excited, and again bugged her parents with questions about it.

In a very real way that first hour Wendy spent alone with Sandy Lambert was a turning point in her life, although neither she nor Miss Lambert knew it. Actually, it was quite an ordinary session from the counselor's standpoint, much like many that she's had with ten-year-old girls.

Wendy brought her poem, and Sandy brought the *Wonder Woman* comics. After reading the poem she looked up at Wendy and, rather than commenting on it, asked, "What do *you* think about this poem, Wendy?" Wendy responded by pointing out the spelling errors, and said that Mrs. Crater had liked it in spite of them. She went on to say that she had written it three times before she was satisfied. Miss Lambert asked whether anyone had guessed whom the poem was about, and Wendy responded negatively. Then Miss Lambert said, "Wouldn't it be fantastic to be able to do the things that Wonder Woman does? And be that beautiful, too?" They both laughed.

During their conversation, Wendy became noticeably more relaxed, until she was sitting with her legs curled under her, an open, bright expression on her face. Then Miss Lambert handed her a comic that was rather dog-eared, and said, "Well, here's my part of the deal. Your poem for my comic. This is one of my favorites, but I want you to have it because you'll really appreciate it." Wendy thumbed through the magazine and saw that it was about Wonder Woman when she was a little girl, and how she was trained by the Amazon women in their fictional society. She put it aside when Miss Lambert suggested that she read it at home, as there were some other things they needed to talk about.

The balance of the session was directed by Miss Lambert into the areas that had been raised by Wendy's parents. Wendy spoke forcefully about her confusion about the criticism directed at her. She said that she was bored a lot in school, but felt that she understood most of what was going on, even though her work might not show it. She owned as how she did act "weird" sometimes, but had the keen and unusual insight that it would be more acceptable if she were play-acting with others, because when she played Wonder Woman by herself, people thought she was "nuts". Miss Lambert listened carefully to all Wendy said, rarely agreeing or disagreeing, but acknowledging the validity of Wendy's opinions in a variety of ways ("I can see why you feel that way"; "That makes sense to me"; "I understand").

When asked about her relations with her older sister (the "responsible" one), Wendy indicated that she knew her parents compared them, but that she really loved and looked up to her. The only thing she didn't like was that her sister thought that Wonder Woman was silly, and Wendy was disappointed that she couldn't share that part of her life with her sister. She didn't like it when her sister sided with their parents' criticism of Wendy. Their arguments were unimportant to Wendy, since they usually made up quickly.

When the hour was almost over, Miss Lambert said that she had a few comments and observations to make. She thanked Wendy for being so honest and forthright with her, pointing out that it showed that Wendy was sincere in her interest in talking things out. (Wendy smiled broadly.) She wanted Wendy to know that, in her opinion, there wasn't anything wrong with her, and that she wasn't "crazy" at all. (Wendy agreed by nodding her head.)

"Actually," she went on to say, "Some of what you do is quite remarkable. I would like to tell you my reaction to your poem, if you'd like to hear it." When Wendy indicated her willingness, Miss Lambert told her that the poem was quite precocious (Wendy didn't understand the word, so Miss Lambert explained), and showed that Wendy had a great deal of sensitivity and understanding, and that if she kept at her writing it would get better and better. Miss Lambert said she knew of several well-known women poets who were writing when they were Wendy's age.

"And last but not least," Miss Lambert continued, as she placed her hand on Wendy's shoulder and looked at her, "I think you're great just the way you are." With that tears formed in Wendy's eyes and slowly rolled down her cheeks, but she didn't say anything.

"How about writing me a new poem for next week?" Miss Lambert suggested, as she handed Wendy a tissue. "C'mon, Wonder Woman, you can't go out into that crazy world with water running down your face." As Wendy wiped her tears away, she laughed, got up, gave Miss Lambert a quick hug, and went to see her mother in the waiting room.

Sandy Lambert saw Wendy weekly for several weeks and had several conversations with her parents. Their initial apprehensions about Miss Lambert's youth were dispelled as they saw changes in Wendy occur after her initial session. Her recommendations to the Littletons were pointed and direct. Each was to spend time alone with Wendy, playing a game or just talking with her, but during that time were not to talk about things that would result in criticism, lecturing, or instructing Wendy, unless she asked their opinion.

She recommended they buy a journal so Wendy could have a nice folio for her writing. (Wendy knew that Miss Lambert was going to suggest this, but was nevertheless enthusiastic when she received it.) She talked at length with the Littletons about the things Wendy did at home that were helpful and appropriate. They were embarrassed when they could identify a number of gracious and helpful things Wendy did, and remorseful in admitting that they couldn't remember having praised her for them. Fortunately the Littletons were honest and concerned, so they were able to see how their frequent criticism of Wendy was one-sided. Gradually a new picture of Wendy emerged from these conversations. It was a picture that simply included more of her, and didn't label her as a problem child. The Littletons began to see how their intense focus on Wendy's weaknesses and faults tended to create a negative climate around her, one which she had adopted as her own self-image to a considerable extent.

Sandy Lambert's treatment of Wendy tended to correct a balance in Wendy's feelings; her positive and respectful messages to Wendy affirmed attitudes that Wendy wanted to feel about herself. The frequent criticism she received had made her doubt that there was very much that was good about her.

Wonder Woman was a special and powerful symbol to Wendy. Since she had come to believe that she could do little that was right, Wendy fantasized a lot about someone who never did anything that was wrong. Even though Wendy's outer life was rather ordinary (and subject to frequent criticism), her inner life was rich with fantasy, and often interfered with tasks she had to do.

As her parents began to acknowledge more and more of her virtues, through praise and recognition, Wendy began to relax. This relaxation resulted in less sensitivity to what she had previously taken as criticism, and episodes of explosive anger diminished. Through her writing and opportunities to talk more openly with her parents and Miss Lambert, Wendy found new ways to express herself.

Wendy didn't magically turn into Wonder Woman, but there was a general improvement in her performance at school, and her daydreaming and oversensitivity to the other children was reduced to the point that Mrs. Crater began to see her in a new light, too. Wendy had kept herself under wraps, and as the images that others had of her began to change, her image of herself began to improve.

As you can see, the Littletons needed to change some of the things they did at home in order to give Wendy room to change. Their relationship with Wendy included, so to speak, a number of "bad habits." Wendy had been given a role in the family that continued to keep her sense of uniqueness low. There are a number of things you can do in your family to help you avoid undermining your children's sense of uniqueness.

BUILDING YOUR
FAMILY'S SENSE OF UNIQUENESS

Building your family's sense of uniqueness requires that you all acknowledge and respect the individuality of each member of the family. Mothers, fathers, sons, and daughters—all are unique and special. There are no others on the face of the earth who are just like your family. No label, category, or stereotype does justice to the rich diversity of characteristics that make up an individual human being.

Encouraging a sense of uniqueness in the family means promoting creative self-expression of each family member but you may have to pay a price. If you insist on rigid adherence to rules, excessive neatness, and subordinating personal needs to those of the family as a whole, you will inevitably interfere with the development of your children's sense of uniqueness. To be an individual, a child may need to be out of step with the rest of your family. Their creative expression may result in things getting a bit messy. It may be hard to get everyone to move in the same direction at the same time. A balance must be struck between individual needs and family (group) needs—and parents must find their own most tolerable balance between the two.

The following strategies will ensure flexible parental control so that your children can exercise their own influence and choices. You must discover how different from yourself you are comfortable in allowing your children to be.

CLARIFY AND REINFORCE FAMILY
NORMS ABOUT INDIVIDUALITY

These norms are the rules and expectations (often unstated) that contribute to the atmosphere of your home. How much diversity is permitted in your family? Does everyone have to do things in the same way? Can family members be different from each other without being ridiculed or criticized? Can family members express ideas that may be unusual in the family without being threatening? Are people still respected and valued even though others disagree with their opinions?

Parents take the lead in establishing norms about these matters by respecting themselves and each other, by using the home as a center for their own creative activities, by establishing rules about mutual respect, and by showing active respect for the opinions and attitudes of children. When you develop rules that allow family members to express themselves and deal with others without censoring what they say, having and enforcing limits and rules does *not* interfere with encouraging personal expression.

As with each of the four conditions of self-esteem, family rules and policies can support a sense of uniqueness. Rules for this condition fall into three categories. The examples listed below can guide you in evolving ones that are appropriate for your family.

Rules that respect privacy:

- Knock before entering.
- Get permission before using someone else's belongings.
- You may keep your bedroom door closed as long as you don't break rules (eating, smoking, etc.). You lose the privilege if you abuse it.

- Respect each other's wish to be left alone.

Rules that acknowledge personal styles and taste:

- You can select your own clothes, within the price range that we decide.
- After you have a small portion of everything at dinner, you can have seconds of your choice.
- You will take turns selecting the TV program to watch.
- You can make decisions about buying anything that is purely personal, but must work out compromises on any things that are shared.

Rules that stimulate creative self-expression:

- Everyone will plan one menu (or cook one meal) each week.
- Each person is responsible for keeping his or her own drawers and shelves in order.
- You may select your own chores, as long as the list of duties is taken care of in some way.
- When you are given a job to do, you can do it your own way, as long as it passes inspection.

PHYSICAL ARRANGEMENTS
INFLUENCE THE SENSE OF UNIQUENESS

Every member of the family needs some private space or special place for his or her valued belongings, even if financial considerations limit this to shelves, cupboards, or closets. Personal furniture, even though children may share rooms, is an important symbol of individuality. Children who share rooms don't have to share everything in the room. Your children should have a significant influence on the decorations and arrangements in their own rooms, within the general limits imposed by financial resources and reasonable standards of neatness and aesthetics; for example, parents may permit some posters but draw the line at allowing walls and ceilings to be completely covered with them.

With a little thought you can devise physical arrangements that permit privacy. Often a low partition between beds is all that is possible, but nevertheless symbolizes the value of privacy. Children's needs for privacy and private possessions change as they mature, and older children may need to be protected from younger ones who don't yet respect the value of privacy.

FAMILY AND INDIVIDUAL NEEDS MUST BE BALANCED

Seeking this balance as each problem or situation emerges is a sign that parents acknowledge and respect both the needs of the individual and the family, and wish to avoid undermining either. A child may be permitted to miss a family meal periodically, but not allowed to make it a habit. A large school project may require use of the dining room table, so that others have to find somewhere else to do their homework. Dad may choose to forego his bowling night in order to attend a parent-child event at school.

Beware of using the family and its needs as a method for making your children feel guilty and controlling their behavior. Each individual in the family does and should have an impact on the way things happen in the family. Sometimes the needs of an individual (parent or child) must take precedence over family activities. For example, if a child has had a special disappointment or upset, dinner or bedtime might be altered to take his feelings into consideration.

Enhancing a sense of uniqueness means encouraging individuals to depart from everyday patterns. A child or parent may become deeply involved in some project or task that justifies exempting him or her from a family outing. When respecting individual needs is an important family value, such allowances are made naturally.

EMPHASIZE INCENTIVES FOR GOOD PERFORMANCE AT HOME

Parents often take children's positive performance (chores, interpersonal relations in the family, and personal characteristics) for granted, while noting and criticizing the times that children fail to meet parental standards. Even though limits and rules may require punishing children from time to time, children need to receive rewards which let them know that their special efforts have been recognized and appreciated. Individualize the rewards as much as possible so that they are consistent with each child's special interests or values. Encourage children to use special skills or talents by giving them praise and rewards for doing so. You should never forget that in most instances immediate acknowledgment of a job well done is the most valued reward your child can receive.

CONSIDER CHILDREN'S SPECIAL SKILLS, TALENTS, OR INTERESTS WHEN ASSIGNING DUTIES OR CHORES

If you train your children to do their tasks they are likely to complete them successfully. Their sense of uniqueness increases if they are permitted to do things that are their own "special thing." Some parents carefully teach a child how to start a car on a winter morning, so that it's warmed up when Dad has to go off to work. A child may have a special recipe she prepares well—let her provide it for the family from time to time. Even Mom and Dad have special things that they like to do. Provide recognition for your whole family.

When children (and adults) know that their special interests are considered in household duties, they are more amenable to doing things they don't like. Never having one's preferences and skills acknowledged breeds resistance and produces conflict. *How* people are allowed to do things can be more highly valued than *what* they do. A child, for example, may have an unusual method for trimming the grass that may even be inefficient, but if he gets the job done to acceptable standards, it may be more important to his self-esteem than if he is required to do it the right way.

BE WILLING TO BREAK RULES WHEN UNPREDICTED CIRCUMSTANCES ARISE

Slavishly following rules that interfere with important personal events may deny the unique needs of family members.

Breaking a rule from time to time does not mean that the rule is irrelevant if you make clear that the circumstances are special. Actually, families need some rules about how to break rules! When an unanticipated circumstance (being invited to dinner at a friend's house) keeps a child from fulfilling the rule about coming home on time—a rule about breaking this rule may require that he call home, explain the circumstances, and receive your permission to come home later.

One can conceive of exceptions to just about any rule—and in most families they will occur. If you are being flexible about rules you need not feel you are becoming wishy-washy or inconsistent as long as the rule is the standard by which departures are measured, and you remind children (and each other) that the rule becomes reasserted after the special event passes. Children will press to have the exceptions be the rule, but this leads to chaos and too many "special circumstances" result in confusion in the family.

There is no absolute guideline for making these decisions, but reasonable and appropriate rules can be followed most of the time, permitting you to be flexible in responding to individual needs.

HANDLING THREATS TO CHILDREN'S SENSE OF UNIQUENESS

Children's sense of uniqueness and, thus, their self-esteem, can be threatened and attacked by events that parents have little or no control over. You need to respond to the depression or anger that results from such experiences in such a way that your children's sense of uniqueness is supported.

When children's sense of uniqueness is threatened, they react in the following way:

- They begin to doubt any positive feelings they have had about themselves.
- They begin to question the positive things that others have said to them about themselves.

- A "halo effect" results, so that aspects of their personality or behavior that are not being attacked are also brought into question.
- They become moody or angry, or vacillate between these two states.
- They begin to "turn off," become lethargic, and seek attention inappropriately and excessively.

Attacks on children's sense of uniqueness are like physical wounds—they will usually heal, but proper care and treatment will help avoid permanent damage, and speed the healing process.

The best way to handle a child who has been ridiculed, criticized, or has had a personal expression or creation disparaged is as follows:

1. Encourage the child to talk about his feelings and accept them without judgment, no matter how extreme.
2. If the child is angry or resentful toward the person(s) who have ridiculed him, provide an unusual way to "get back":
   - Write the person's name on a piece of paper and flush it down the toilet.
   - Draw a picture of that person and rip it up or throw darts at it.
   - Have the child beat a pillow that represents the person.
3. When the child is calm again, discuss ways to deal with the situation the next time.

When a child is torn between his loyalty to one group and his wishes to be part of another one (family/peer group conflicts are one example):

1. Listen to the child's feelings about the group, without judgment, and acknowledge his feelings.
2. Ask the child what he would have to do to be accepted in that group, or to be liked by others.
3. Ask the child what he might have to give up in order to

be a member of that group (other friends, activities, etc.), and how he feels about giving them up.

4. If possible, explore with the child how he might be both a member of the group and not have to give anything up.

5. Accept the child's need for acceptance in a peer group, and continue to do the things identified in the first section of this chapter.

When a child is locked into a negative role, such as class clown, and can't seem to get out of it:

1. Listen to the child's feelings, without judgment, and acknowledge her feelings.
2. Encourage the child to think of times or situations when she does not act in ways demanded by that role.
3. Tell the child that she is not one kind of person, but has many facets that are all worthwhile.
4. Let the child know that you sympathize with her problem and approve of her concern.
5. Keep communication open, offer advice *as it is asked for*, and allow the child to grow by working it through.

When a child's opportunities for creative expression are limited by school, other family members, or situations:

1. Give the child increased opportunities for creative expression at times and places when it is possible.
2. Help the child understand the limits imposed on him, and what is possible to do *within those limits*.
3. Encourage the child to fantasize to you what he would do, say or be if he could.

CONFIRMING CHILDREN'S SENSE OF UNIQUENESS: A SPECIAL WAY OF COMMUNICATING

Thoughts and feelings about oneself are often hidden and not presented to the world outside of ourselves. This is our "secret self," containing those ideas and feelings that are unique to us. Yet we wonder if the way we see ourselves is true. "Do others see me as I see myself and do they value the things in me that I value in myself?" is a question that, one way or another, we often wonder about. Others' opinions are important to us because how we feel about ourselves is strongly determined by the way we believe other people evaluate us.

Confirming children's sense of uniqueness is the process by which their thoughts and feelings are validated by others. Insofar as thoughts and feelings are the most direct and basic expression of self, the process of confirming them provides an active message to children that their essential being is valued and respected. Some people, more than others, seem to make us feel good about ourselves. Often it is some indefinable quality in such a person that appeals to us. It may be someone whom we have met only briefly; someone with whom we may not be close or intimate. What is this quality that such people have? What is it they do that results in people feeling so good around them?

One of the authors experienced a case in point many years ago. Through a variety of circumstances he had the privilege of hosting a world renowned psychologist, who, at the time, was at the pinnacle of his career as a dominating influence in intellectual circles. A quiet family dinner was planned that included the author's children in order to provide a respite from a hectic day. Within minutes of entering the living room, our renowned psychologist had several children hanging on his arm or sitting on his lap, and despite their father's efforts to get them to let their guest rest, they refused to move. So, the author, rather than creating an embarrassing scene, let his guest handle the children, as he listened to their conversation.

On the surface it was a casual and friendly conversation between an adult and children. But the loving regard the children showed toward this stranger was unusual. After several minutes it began to be apparent that despite his fame and intellectual accomplishments, this man was dealing with the children with considerable respect and attention. They each were given full opportunity to express their opinions, which were always actively acknowledged by a comment or nod, and frequently our psychologist would contribute a thought that indicated his understanding of the implication of what a child was saying. He told stories that arose from things the children said, and invariably responded appropriately to them. They were quite relaxed and lay against him, looking closely into his face as the conversation continued. When dinner was ready, they graciously escorted him to the table and were models of decorum, for which their parents were surprised and grateful.

This man had the capability to make people around him feel good; his fame was, in part, a result of the fact that his character was uniquely suited to his profession. Thousands of people around the world had been made to feel good by him, and his methods and theories reflected the basic attitude exemplified by his relations with the author's children—that of actively acknowledging and accepting the thoughts and feelings of people he encountered.

The psychologist knew how to boost one of our most precious possessions—our self-image! We hold to it tenaciously, and whether it is a positive or negative one, considerable effort is required before we are willing to alter it. And despite experience that may contradict it, it remains fairly stable, as we seek evidence that we are right about the way we think and feel about ourselves. We want other people to notice the things about us that we feel are special, whether they are personal attributes, possessions, or the things we do. This is true even when we have negative self-images, often believing evidence that fits the images and discounting positive responses from others that tend to contradict our own negative views. A surprising thing, though, is that when we receive confirmation for a negative self-image, something in us is deeply satisfied.

Children seek such notice, and even though they may have negative self-images, they want to have them validated. The simplest form of this is when a child insists that he can't do something, and refuses to agree with parents' encouragement, arguing rather than accepting a more positive assessment of his abilities. In reality, if children or adults cannot gain validation for the things they think and feel about themselves, they can come to only two conclusions—they are either stupid or crazy! Neither of these is very good. There are three levels of confirming that permit you to validate children regardless of whether they say positive or negative things about themselves.

ACKNOWLEDGING

To acknowledge children's communications means (according to Webster's) "to receive with respect." Acknowledging is an action that communicates clearly to children that they were seen and heard when they attempted to say or do something. This action is a verbal response or gesture that lets children know that we received some message they sent to us regardless of whether we liked it or not. We can paraphrase what a child says ("Ah, you don't feel that you can do this homework"; "You say that you're scared of ghosts in your room"; "It seems to me that you're saying you really hate your brother for taking your ball").

Acknowledging lets your children know that you feel that what he or she said or did was important enough to pay attention to. Simple logic suggests that when children believe they're *important*, they feel they're *special*.

This process, while appearing to be self-evident, is very important because it allows parents to respond positively to children, without judging, criticizing, or ridiculing, thereby enhancing children's sense of uniqueness. Acknowledging gives parents a way to deal with self-denigrating thoughts and feelings that children have without denying them the validation they seek. Children's need for attention is satisfied, more often than not, by the simple act of being acknowledged. Furthermore, a communication can be acknowledged even when it's not fully understood.

UNDERSTANDING

Understanding what your children say or do goes a large step beyond simple acknowledging. If acknowledging means communicating that you saw and heard your child, then undertanding communicates, in an active way, that you grasped the meaning of what was said or done and the reasons why.

Understanding children's self-expression does not require us to approve or support the behavior—it is only an expression that we understand it. ("I know that you're angry because I won't let you watch any more TV tonight.")

Children often misbehave for the best of motives: A child may hit or shove another because she feels that doing so would protect or support a friend; another child may tell lies out of loyalty to peers or break rules because of circumstances he feels are extenuating. Understanding that children's negative behavior is often well intentioned means they are understood *on their own terms.* It does not mean analyzing or "mindreading," which involve telling children what they think or feel, and disregard their own perceptions. Being understanding is not dependent on wisdom or psychological expertise, but is actively recognizing what children think they mean.

Since children's motives are expressions of deeply held values and their feelings are (to them) more important than what they do, being understanding is a powerful act of validation for a child, and deepens his sense of uniqueness.

Parents often understand more about what's going on inside a child than they communicate when he is seeking attention. Trying to stop intrusive behavior often leads to an escalation of it, when communicating understanding might reduce it. (At the supermarket: "I know you would love to have some candy or cookies, and I did get you some the last time we were here, but it will soon be dinnertime and I will not let you eat candy now.")

APPROVING

The third level of the confirming process includes the previous two levels but adds the communication that parents find that what children say or do is praiseworthy. Approving is an active process that lets children know they are not being taken for granted, but that their virtues and virtuous behavior are approved and valued by parents. ("It's great that you were able to speak up for yourself at the party.") The magic of this process is that when children know they will receive approval without having to seek it all the time their excessive demands for attention diminish.

Giving approval, though, is not a simple and obvious matter, since children may want approval for things that parents are not comfortable about. A young child may call to his mother from the top of a tall tree, wanting her praise and astonishment at his prowess. Mother may be beside herself with anxiety for his safety, and can only think about getting him down without loss of life or limb. Give approval? Well, under such circumstances, the best she may be able to do is acknowledge his skill!

It is not necessary to choose between praise and criticism in responding to children's behavior. Acknowledging and understanding what children do or say are positive, active reactions to the ways that children express themselves, and provide the basis for confirming their sense of uniqueness. As their self-esteem rises, their feelings about themselves change, and negative self-images automatically become corrected. Validating their inner processes allows them to correct their own behavior.

Stimulating Children's Talents and Creativity

CREATIVITY: HOW DO YOU RECOGNIZE IT?

When you gaze at a painting by Rembrandt or Picasso, you know that you are looking at a creative masterpiece. But when your child hands you his grubby picture of small mice-men who are building a factory, you wonder, is this picture worthy enough to be called "creative"? The awe you felt at Rembrandt's talent was replaced by a gentle laugh and delight when you saw the expressions of the "mice-men." Can both feelings be legitimate reactions to creative expression?

All definitions of creativity have specified that the product be useful or satisfying to those who will use or admire it. If our young artist of the "mice-men" had never seen such a creation but had suddenly imagined these creatures in his mind after hearing a story about mice, his product would be unique. It does not matter if the product had been produced elsewhere as long as the creator arrives at the idea in an intuitive manner.

Our young creator, therefore, having passed one criterion of creativity, has now to face another. What makes a clear-cut definition difficult is that people have different ideas about what is satisfying or useful. Parents and teachers would expect a more sophisticated and refined product from a tenth-grade child than from a second grader. Also people's expectations differ as a function of their background, their need for the product, and their relationship to the creator. The mother of our young artist will have different expectations about his painting than his peers. Fortunately, in our example, the picture of the "mice-men" was satisfying to our young artist's critics. His teachers and parents laughed and smiled when they saw his picture. The adults' satisfaction and pleasure was enough for the label of creativity to be put upon this "master-piece."

Being able to recognize and foster the creative impulse in every child will help build a sense of uniqueness. Your child may have shown creativity when he or she:

- Arranged his or her room to permit a "hideaway cave"
- Created a new game with its own set of rules
- Modified an existing game's rules
- Fantasized an imaginary playmate that helped solve problems
- Told an elaborate fantasy story that contained unusual elements, such as a giraffe who, because of his long neck, helped his lion friend find his way through the long grass
- Developed a new language that was used as a secret code
- Asked questions that demonstrated a curiosity about a common object; for example: "Are rocks alive?" "Is a rock alive when it is moving and dead when it is still?"
- Wrote a poem that showed unusual insight or a novel way of viewing an event

Another way of defining creativity emphasizes the *process* of creation and not the final product, such as an invention, painting, or idea. The creative process starts when a child faces a problem or question that he cannot answer immediately. A period of mental struggle occurs in which the child's habits and ideas seem insufficient to solve the problem. After this period of effort there is often a withdrawal from active wrestling with the problem. Daydreaming or going on to another activity allows the unconscious parts of the mind to take over the creative work. The child, for a period of time, may lose interest in the painting or project. Insight into a solution will often follow this period of withdrawal if the child still has a need for a solution. This insight comes as a complete picture; all the pieces of the puzzle are present without the creator having to search for and fit them together. You can sometimes see this in children when they suddenly smile and comment "Ah ha" or "I got it," stop whatever they are doing, and turn to the forgotten project.

Usually children will then plunge into the final stage of the creative process—trying out the solution to see if it works and elaborating the insight until the project is completed. The painting, game, or story will be pursued with renewed vigor. In any creative expression the stages of *effort, withdrawal, insight,* and *elaboration* may be gone through a number of times.

You may not observe all these stages when watching your child at creative work. He may seem to complete a creative project rapidly in one sitting without a period of withdrawal. It could be that he previously struggled with parts of his project in his own mind, went through withdrawal without being observed, and now, as he is being observed, is putting the ideas together to make the object.

In recognition of these stages, you need to:

- Allow children to struggle on their own by not giving them solutions at the first sign of frustration. It is, however, helpful to encourage the child to continue seeking solutions and to recognize that the task is difficult.
- Challenge children's curiosity by asking them to think

about something in a different way; for example, "Why is a spoon like a car?" "When was tomorrow?"

- Be tolerant and patient when children leave projects standing or indulge in periods of daydreaming.
- Be flexible in time schedules with children when they become deeply engrossed in a project if it does not seriously inconvenience others.

CREATIVITY AND THE SENSE OF UNIQUENESS

Creative ideas come from people who expect to have imaginative ideas, who think of themselves as creative people. Children acquire this expectation when they have been praised and rewarded for expressing novel ideas and creating unique products. Having a strong image of themselves as creative will help sustain them when their ideas are criticized and put down. Unusual ideas will often challenge the way things are done in the family or school and creative children may effect a certain amount of rebuke from peers and those in authority.

Research studies[1] report that one characteristic of creative potential, a rich and unique fantasy life, is possessed by emotionally healthy children who avoid antisocial acts and drug abuse. They can concentrate better than their less imaginative peers. Such research shows that creativity and a high sense of uniqueness do not, as many think, conflict with a child's sensitivity to the needs of others or with appropriate behavior. The struggle to inhibit behavior that is inappropriate may channel energy into the world of fantasy, which is the birthplace of the creative idea.

CREATIVE CHILDREN— A PROBLEM OR BLESSING?

At some time your young artist or inventor may have been so intensely preoccupied that he ignored your requests. You may

[1]Singer, Jerome L. "Fantasy: The Foundation of Serenity," *Psychology Today,* July 1976.

have wondered whether it was worth making a special effort to foster creativity in your child. Special problems do exist in handling creative children.

These children tend to be unpredictable. Their thought-provoking questions can sometimes arouse embarrassment, anger, or frustration. They feel that completing a project is more important than conforming to schedules and requests, and can be intense and "moody." Highly creative children may regress occasionally, appearing to be childish, naive, and playful. Such characteristics tend not to be highly valued by teachers[2] and these children challenge family and school needs for order and regularity.

Creative children are sometimes "strange." The chief characteristic of "strangeness" is not just that the child is doing something that is quite unusual or deviant from what others are doing, but that this odd behavior does not arise from the child's anxiety, need for attention, or from situational demands but is an expression of the child's own highly unique internal imagery, thoughts, and viewpoints. Such a child may be making funny faces while daydreaming, or may be excessively attached to a certain style of outlandish dress, as compared to others. Creative children follow a beat that is different from that which moves others.

Problems often arise when parents are highly creative and their children do not seem to be. Parents may be impatient waiting for the spark of the unusual to appear and may not understand children's greater need for order; they may not value areas in which the children are creative. Frequently, because of parents' high standards in judging a creative act, they will miss the beginning flickers of the creative flame, and, by ignoring or disparaging the child's efforts, blow out the light.

[2]Torrance, E. Paul. "The Creative Personality and the Ideal Pupil," *Teachers College Record*, December 1963 (vol. 65).

FOSTERING CREATIVITY

One of the issues facing adults who wish to see children's creativity grow is *how* to encourage it. If a child is precocious in art, music, or some other area, to what extent is it helpful to emphasize that gift?

First of all, we should be aware of the distinction between *pressuring* and *responding*. When adults *pressure* they usually have an idea or picture in their minds of how, ideally, they would like the child to be. Unless they mold, provide, regulate, cajole, and sometimes berate, they fear that the child will not become that which he is capable of.

Responding means that the adult is able, through observation as well as through discussions with the child, to determine what needs the child has. Such an approach recognizes that the adult's idealized image of the child reflects more of the adult's needs than the child's, who, because of his unique past and ongoing experiences, may have different ones. Responding requires you to listen, to be open to learning *from* your child about her needs, and to recognize that your child is unique. Such an approach can help maximize his creative abilities.

The best way to stifle a creative idea is to criticize it as soon as it appears. Pointing out how silly and impractical it is and that its creator should be attending to more urgent tasks will dry up the wellspring of novel ideas. A child needs room to try out ideas, experiment with them, and discard them when they don't meet his own growing awareness of what the final form should look like.

Don't label a question as stupid even if you think it is irrelevant or it is one you cannot answer. You can always stimulate further search by an answer such as "I don't have an answer to your question but here is a place you can look for it," or "I'm interested in your question—could you tell me more about what you are thinking?" You can ask questions that will encourage your child to elaborate an idea but will avoid trying to pin down the fine details. A new idea often is expressed vaguely and unfolds at its own rate.

Accept unusual approaches to a task. Allow your child to experiment and, as long as life and limb are not threatened, to make mistakes. Errors, when accepted and acknowledged, can provide essential information that can generate new and better ideas. Encourage your child to try new approaches and show you are interested in the outcome, even if the creation seems to be insignificant from your viewpoint.

Experiments have shown that a moderate degree of anxiety is more conducive to creativity than either very low or very high tension.[3] When panic sets in, people will often revert to childlike defenses, such as ignoring, blaming, or excusing oneself, which stop creativity.

You can help your child regulate her anxiety when facing a challenging task in the following ways:

- Acknowledge that the task is difficult and you can understand why she is frustrated.
- Share the information that you've been frustrated too and, by sticking to the task, you found a solution.
- Suggest a rest or play break and show your child some stretching and muscle-loosening movements.

Since children's anxiety is increased in proportion to their parents' or teachers' anxiety, try to regulate your own tension when you see your child's frustration. Remind yourself that a moderate amount of frustration is the start of the creative process. Encourage your child to brainstorm ideas, coming up with as many solutions as possible without judging even silly or outlandish ones. You can help children see disasters as occasions for generating creative ideas when you ask them to help solve the problem such as rain stopping the family picnic or too much noise in the house.

You can also help to stimulate creative ideas as in the following:

[3] Wallach, Michael A., and Kogan, Nathan. A New Look at the Creativity-Intelligence Distinction. Paper presented at the American Psychological Association Meeting, Los Angeles, California, Sept. 1964.

- Keep material that can be used creatively accessible. Paints, paper, scissors, glue, old magazines, yarn, wood, metal bits, spools, leather scraps, broken clock parts, can be put in bins or cupboards convenient to a work area. Make it a habit to drop odds and ends into these bins that can be used in projects.
- Provide a work area where it is all right to be messy and where you don't have to fuss over spilt paint, glue, or worry about breaking fragile objects.
- Stimulate different ways to look at things. Ask your child, for example:
  —If you were a magician, what would you make smaller so that it is nicer? What would you make round so that it would be more comfortable?
  —Suppose you are given these three things: a crayon, a paper bag, and a safety pin. Then you are told that you must give one back. Which one would it be? And why?
  —How many uses of a brick can you name? (Encourage your child to add to the list during the week.)
  —What do the following items have in common: nail, ball, drum?
  (Help your child think of similarities between other seemingly unrelated objects.)
- Encourage children to think metaphorically. That is, where an object or situation is likened to another; for example "All the world's a stage." This ability has been the basis for many new creations. Children trained to make connections between new material and the familiar learn quicker in school. Have your child try these exercises to stimulate metaphoric thinking:
  —Make a comparison between the words listed below and something else. Try to be original in your comparisons.
      Scared as_____
      Funny as_____

Jumps like_____

Angry as_____

—How is the expansion of the American colonies like an amoeba reproducing?

- Pretend situations are fun and give expression to your child's playful impulses. For example:

  —Pretend you are in a room alone with nothing but three pillows, a chalkboard, chalk, doll or stuffed animal, and rocking chair. No one will bother you for twenty minutes. What would you do? What kind of feelings would you have about being in that kind of room?

  —Pretend that you are red all over. What are you? Can you move? How? Do people like you? Why? Will you always be red? Why?

- Encourage children to make pictures inside their minds. For example, before asking your child to write a story about an animal, ask him to see the animal inside his mind, talk to it and find out what it likes to do and what it is afraid of; have your child let this animal show him places it likes to go and let the animal describe what it likes about each place.

- Help children to observe their everyday environment in new ways. Ask your child to look around at everyday things as if she is seeing them for the first time. Have her share these observations with you. Ask her what was "new" about her left shoe, her mother, the front door of her house, the bark on trees, etc.

Remember that in both accepting and stimulating novel ideas, your own creativity will be challenged. Allowing yourself to be different and to change something in your family can foster creative change in your children, especially when the changes can be accomplished in a playful, experimental manner.

THE WHOLE CHILD: DOING THE JOB

9

Feeling and/or Exercising Power

At each stage of growth children naturally seek to acquire new competencies, and as they do so their feelings of self-worth and power increase. As a child moves into toddlerhood, his ability to walk a few steps promotes the same kind of self-satisfaction that a school-aged child experiences when he stays on his skateboard for some time. While the specific activities that contribute to (or diminish) your children's sense of power change as they grow, their inner experiences remain the same—a feeling of satisfaction that results from accomplishing something they set out to do.

While following our discussion about this condition, you need to keep in mind an important distinction that we made early in this book. A sense of power reflects how children *feel* about what they can or can't do. Making something happen, as you will see, does not guarantee that a child will feel a high sense of power, or will do things he is capable of.

A child with a low sense of power will try to control people or things in order to compensate for feelings of powerlessness, while a child who feels powerful will more easily accept realistic limitations because he feels he can accomplish his goals despite them. A sense of power determines *how* children use their capabilities, and how they feel about what they do.

In the following case study, LeRoi demonstrates his poor sense of power in many ways. His case is an example of a chronic problem which plagues our schools—children who don't work up to their potential. Trying to get him to do so makes everyone frustrated and often angry with him.

LEROI: A CHILD WHO WINS THE BATTLES WHILE LOSING THE WAR

As Mr. Todd walked toward the jungle gym he could feel his anger begin to boil. He had kept his eye on LeRoi. He saw him push Carl, a small, studious third grader in LeRoi's class, off the upper rungs of the climbing apparatus for no apparent reason. Fortunately, Carl had caught himself or a real injury might have occurred.

LeRoi was sitting on top of the jungle gym, laughing and threatening everyone who came close to him that he would push them off. He was "king of the mountain," he asserted. Mr. Todd knew that LeRoi would probably stay atop the gym as long as the other children tried to climb it, and would only come down when the others lost interest—and then he'd probably become a bother at some other activity.

With his anger unabated, Mr. Todd shouted up to LeRoi to come down immediately. LeRoi asked, "Why?" in the whiny voice he reserved for times that he was being upbraided. His response only served to make Mr. Todd angrier, who replied, "You get down this instant." LeRoi started to extricate himself from the bars, but seemed to get his foot caught, took several seconds to unhook himself, and then slowly and cautiously got off the bars and came up to his teacher.

"I saw you push Carl, and you darn near hurt him. Don't you know how dangerous that is? What do you think you're doing? I can't trust you for a minute with my back turned."

The rush of words began to relieve the pressure of anger in Mr. Todd.

"It wasn't my fault, and besides, he pushed me first," LeRoi whined, "He wouldn't let me get on top."

"LeRoi," Mr. Todd continued in magisterial tones, "I saw the whole thing, and Carl did none of that. Don't make it worse by lying. It's bad enough that you tried to hurt him. Now, you get on that seat. You're benched for the rest of the week. And if you bother anyone else during recess, it will go worse for you."

Disregarding LeRoi's attempts to explain his innocence, Mr. Todd held him by his arm (with some self-satisfying force) and marched him to the bench. LeRoi, as usual, stumbled and dragged his feet, and then sat sullenly with his shoulders hunched. The other children returned to playing. LeRoi was punished so frequently that they had little interest in the event.

Mr. Todd mulled it over in his own mind as he distractedly watched the others finish their recess. He spent so much time dealing with LeRoi that he was near the end of his rope. He thought about having another conference with the Jacksons, LeRoi's parents, but felt little confidence that anything would come of it. The principal didn't seem to be much help, although LeRoi had been sent to his office innumerable times. He also seemed powerless to deal with the problem.

Mr. Todd felt trapped by LeRoi and his problems. The boy was as much a problem academically as he was behaviorally, although the tests done last year showed him to be above average intellectually. His real deficits in reading and math were beginning to depress the way the third-grader performed in all areas. But he made so little effort that it was difficult to get a clear assessment of his capabilities.

Constantly badgering Mr. Todd, his aide, or other children LeRoi rarely did much work on his own. It was easier to help him than have him cause a disruption. The other children seemed to take care of him, something that Mr. Todd couldn't understand since LeRoi so often tormented them. It seemed unreasonable to punish others for helping LeRoi, and Mr. Todd couldn't control it. His aide also fell easily into LeRoi's traps and spent a disproportionate amount of time with him. Mr. Todd, when helping him, required him to work out his own answers, but that took time too.

The learning disabilities teacher, who had LeRoi an hour each day, had no fewer problems, possibly more. LeRoi was verbally abusive to her and would often refuse to do anything in that class except bother others who were trying to work.

Compounding the whole problem was the fact that LeRoi was black, a fact that made Mr. Todd, who was Caucasian, just a bit more apprehensive about handling him. Twenty-five percent of the students at Emerson were black, and another twenty-five percent were Mexican-American or Oriental. But most of the teachers had been at Emerson during the years when it was primarily an upper-middle-class white school, and they were still making adjustments to teaching a highly diverse student group.

LeRoi was the youngest of three children in a solid professional family. Mr. Jackson was an accountant with a large firm, and Mrs. Jackson was a former nurse who now worked part-time in order to care for her growing family. LeRoi's two older sisters were exemplary students, and the one in junior high was a class officer.

No one, least of all his parents, could understand LeRoi's problem. During parent conferences, Mrs. Jackson had dismissed the idea that she had problems with him at home. "You know how boys are," she said. "It's a struggle to get him to do anything, but if I stay on his back, he'll do his chores." His chores, it turned out, were to feed his dog in the evening and to help his sisters set the table before dinner. Mrs. Jackson or the older girls seemed to do most of the work around the house. Mr. Jackson worked long hours at his job.

The Jacksons had great hopes for LeRoi. Since money was

not an issue, they saw no reason to restrict their children's opportunities, and they delighted in being able to indulge them. The girls were dressed according to the current fads and LeRoi had a roomful of toys, games, and athletic equipment. The latter were not actually used very much because he was not very good at sports, being somewhat awkward and uncoordinated.

Some people who knew the Jacksons felt that LeRoi was a "spoiled brat." He could get his mother or his sisters to do almost anything for him. He would whine and complain until he got his way. The Jacksons had few hard and fast rules at home and never had trouble with the girls, with whom their mother was fairly firm. Mr. Jackson had little patience with LeRoi's whining and foot-dragging, and had spanked him several times. LeRoi tended to hop-to for his dad, but Mr. Jackson wasn't home enough to be consistent with him. His mother kept things that he did from his father in order to protect LeRoi from being spanked.

Mr. Todd had seen evidence of this when a conference with Mrs. Jackson ended with LeRoi making a scene about having to go home to do something. Mrs. Jackson kept her cool, but caved in to LeRoi's emotional demands. But not before she had made clear to Mr. Todd that she expected the school to provide whatever help LeRoi needed in order to bring him up to grade level. She glossed over Mr. Todd's protestations about LeRoi's attitudes and behavior with a veiled implication that perhaps her son was being picked on.

Even after parent conferences, testing, and meetings among the teachers, LeRoi's behavior hadn't changed. He would have some good days when he seemed able to get along well if Mr. Todd "sat on him," but as soon as the teacher's vigilance relaxed, or if LeRoi became frustrated, his aggressive behavior would reassert itself. Talking did no good, since LeRoi would only blame others for his difficulties. Mr. Todd looked ahead to a long, frustrating year.

This one little boy, who couldn't seem to learn effectively or get along with others, nevertheless, could make his parents, teachers, and peers feel powerless to do anything about him. (How LeRoi's problems were handled will be described in Chapter 10.)

Many children like LeRoi pose similar problems for us. But their behavior forms a pattern that is described below. Although children with low power seem to fight an authority like parents and teachers, we can fight back in ways that help the child.

HOW CHILDREN WITH POWER PROBLEMS BEHAVE

When children avoid dealing with their unmet power needs, you will observe the following:

When children attempt to meet their unmet power needs inappropriately, you will observe the following:

1. They blame others for things that are clearly their own fault.	**1.** They are often bossy and aggressive when others (including peers) don't set firm limits on them.
2. They avoid leadership roles that require special responsibilities.	**2.** They take risks in order to prove to others that they are worthwhile.
3. They act as if they are helpless and dependent in areas where they can or should be competent.	**3.** They try to be leaders, but often offend others in doing so.
4. They avoid accepting personal responsibilities, but may do so as part of a group.	**4.** They insist they can do things that are beyond their capabilities and fail at them, while avoiding doing things that are within their capabilities.
5. They do not complete jobs or assignments, because as they proceed through them their fear of failure grows.	**5.** They use voice (loudness, tone), body, or objects to exercise control over others.

6. They lack emotional self-control, and easily cry, get angry, or hysterical.

7. They lack skills that would be appropriate to their age/grade.

8. They avoid challenges and risks in areas where they have the slightest doubt of success.

9. They have a low tolerance for frustration, and give up or become angry when frustrated.

10. They are awkward, poorly coordinated, and lack fine motor control.

11. They react to initiatives taken by others, rather than being initiators.

12. They misinterpret others' behavior or attitudes as being a threat to themselves.

13. They require others to be *very* firm, consistent, and severe in setting limits or conditions for them.

14. They become chronically depressed if conditions that reinforce a low sense of power are severe or long-standing.

6. They bully or torment smaller children or animals.

7. They vehemently deny responsibility when caught lying, cheating, or stealing.

8. They seem highly competitive, but use excuses for avoiding competitive activities if failure seems imminent.

9. They often break rules, but attempt to excuse themselves or blame others for doing so.

Many adults believe that because children are small, dependent, lack experience, and are relatively incompetent by adult standards, they must accept their conditions and resign themselves to a state of powerlessness. But children don't differ one whit from adults in their need to feel an adequate sense of power; they need to have the resources, opportunities, and capabilities that enable them to influence or control the circumstances of their own lives, even though the aspects of life that adults and children need to control are different.

Children who have a low sense of power often make parents and teachers feel powerless as well. Powerlessness is like a communicable disease that infects those who come in contact with such children because we feel responsible for helping a child to be successful, and suffer with him when he fails. Children with a low sense of power are failure prone. They usually don't do the things they're expected to do (chores, schoolwork, and so forth), and exert their control at the wrong times, in the wrong places, and in ways that frustrate and anger us. Their behavior requires us to do things that make us feel bad—be punitive, stay angry, be apprehensive, and keep at them until they do do what they're supposed to. Sooner or later parents and teachers of low power children throw up their hands and say, "I give up! I don't know what to do about him."

An excessive inclination to blame is the most obvious symptom of low power, engaging parents and teachers in fruitless arguments about the validity of some excuse. Low power children act as if they've been treated terribly unfairly if their excuses are disregarded. The pained expressions on their faces may elicit sympathy and guilt feelings in adults who then do not punish them.

Because they don't take responsibility for what they must do or what they have done, they blame people, things, events, or anything else that has a vague connection to something they have done that's wrong or inadequate, or something they should have done. ("I'm late because my mother didn't wake me up." "He called me a name, so I hit him." "You pick up my toys, I don't feel good.")

They act helplessly or incompetently to avoid responsibility, giving up easily to get adults, siblings, or peers to help them do what they should do on their own. Teachers often observe other students caving in to a low power child's demands for answers. Parents wind up doing most of their homework, and other children in the family complain that the low power child is not carrying his fair share of the chores.

Aches and pains abound in these children. If a task is

complex or challenging, they find some excuse to avoid it: they plead ignorance; they defer things until later; they complain about things being unfair; they forget or they create conditions that don't allow them to finish their task ("I lost my pencil, so I couldn't finish the homework"). Usually, the work they're trying to avoid is something they *are* capable of doing, albeit with some extra effort or attention.

These children become helpless in the face of things they perceive as challenging. Even though we may know beyond a doubt that a child is capable of doing something, it's the child's own assessment that influences his behavior. We feel that such a child is lazy. Actually, the child may fear failure more than the wrath of parents or teachers.

The warning signs are diverse: low power children *don't exercise initiative*. They get bored easily. They wait for others to take charge or start things. Even then they will drag their feet, especially if the suggestions offered to them require some effort. They need to be reminded about chores, and kept at them until they finish. They often won't make the simplest effort required to accomplish something they want, such as calling a friend when they need a playmate.

A low sense of power is usually associated with *poor emotional control*. These children cannot lift themselves out of excessive crying, anger, or depressions, and depend on others to make them feel good. A low power child will often react to an apparently unimportant incident with a great show of emotion, and parents are left wondering what it was all about. This occurs because a low power child tends to be unaware of why he's reacting or what it is he's reacting to. This isn't a game. His excessive crying or anger is a result of his low sense of power (which he can't report), rather than the event that seemed to cause the outburst.

Children with a low sense of power attempt to compensate for it by *trying to gain power over others*. They may like to direct and lead, but they are invariably poor at it, interfering with the rights and needs of others. Blindly insisting that they know the right way to do something, they will get depressed when their way fails or is not accepted by others. They are manipulative—a sign that they can't get what they want in more appropriate ways.

Having a low sense of power produces a vicious circle that is caused by and results in poor skills and incompetence in many areas. Thus, children's lack of skills results in failure when they attempt tasks, which, in turn confirms their sense of powerlessness. Learning problems can be traced to a lack of a sense of power. These children have a hard time with any kind of learning, even when they repeat some process over and over again. Only when their sense of power begins to rise can they begin to learn effectively.

Often a child who has a low sense of power is *physically awkward and incompetent.* He will have difficulty in strenuous athletic activities, and try to avoid taking physical risks that his peers perform comfortably, such as climbing or balancing. Such children tend to stumble, drop things, and bump into objects as if they are out of touch with their bodies. This results from anxiety, which produces tension in a child's body so that he cannot be as graceful or adept as peers with high self-esteem.

All of the above characteristics are influenced by a low tolerance for frustration in these children. They frustrate themselves because they don't believe they can do something, and are frustrated by others who may seem (to them) to place obstacles in their paths, however minor.

Since they don't tolerate even minor frustrations, trying to get something they want in appropriate ways (taking time to negotiate or waiting their turn) gives way to bossiness or bullying others. They will be highly competitive (always wanting to win) in safe areas but not in areas where there is a chance for failure.

These children force adults to become more and more punitive before they acquiesce, so that as time goes on punishment becomes more severe with less effect. They maintain some feelings of power by proving to themselves that they can resist punishment, but don't apply those feelings to more useful or productive efforts.

Children with a low sense of power are spoiled in that even though they seem to get their way, they rarely get what they want through their own efforts, and miss that satisfaction. When forced to handle stressful situations without help and support, they may crumble and fail.

Life is generally threatening for children carrying the terrible burden of powerlessness accompanied by fears and anxieties. These and their inevitable psychosomatic complaints and (often) overwhelming feelings of inadequacy may allow them to slide into chronic depression and even more severe emotional disorders if the conditions that promote and maintain a low sense of power are not relieved.

HOW CHILDREN'S SENSE
OF POWER IS THREATENED

Life is filled with threats to our sense of power. The things we set out to do are not always easily accomplished because no one has sufficient skills or competencies to successfully meet all of life's demands. It is easy to feel powerless.

As their bodies and minds develop, children need to extend their range of control and influence. How we respond to this urge can enhance or diminish children's feelings of power. A firm sense of power allows children to deal with threats in ways that enable them to overcome them.

The following list will help you identify and alleviate many of the chief threats to children's sense of power, which, if excessive or unrelieved, will result in the symptoms described above.

- When children are not allowed to make decisions that they are capable of making successfully
- When children are given few resources (toys, money, space, time) over which they can exercise control

- When rules and limits are not enforced consistently
- When rules and limits are arbitrary and children can't influence them
- When children have few or no duties or tasks for which they are held responsible
- When parents or teachers expect children to do things they are really not capable of doing
- When parents do not have emotional self-control, making it difficult for children to predict their mood or reactions
- When children's possessions are arbitrarily taken from them as punishment without prior warning
- When children are not taught how to do the things they are expected to do
- When physical disabilities keep children from performing activities that are normal for their age group
- When parents' fears and anxieties consistently limit children's opportunities to take physical risks (climbing, jumping, etc.) that are within their capabilities
- When children are permitted to interfere with what others (children or adults) are doing, without limits placed on that behavior
- When consequences for misbehavior are unclear and unpredictable
- When children are criticized excessively for choices or decisions they make, without receiving guidance about better ones
- When parents disagree about limits, reducing children's ability to make choices that clearly lead to rewards
- When children are physically abused

10

At Home: I Can Do It!

There is something about children's sense of power that is basically biological. As their physical and mental capabilities expand, they can and must exercise more control and influence over their lives. This control needs to be directed inward, so that they can exercise self-control and discipline, and have ordered mental processes that help them learn, plan, predict, and solve problems. They need to control their bodies so that they can become useful tools in accomplishing their purposes. Children need to direct control outward so that they can manipulate the material world, influence people, develop competence, and accomplish their own purposes. Helping your children develop their sense of power is one of the main functions of being a parent.

BUILDING YOUR CHILD'S SENSE OF POWER

HELP CHILDREN BECOME
RESPONSIBLE BY SETTING LIMITS AND RULES EFFECTIVELY

Being responsible implies that children have a sense that they have considerable influence over the rewards or punishments they receive. You do this by making limits and rules clear and requiring children to do chores that are appropriate to their age and skills. In doing so, you present them with an array of choices that makes them aware of their influence ("Should I do it or not? What will happen to me if I do or don't? How will my parents react to it? What should I do?"). In order to be responsible, children *must* know that the positive or negative consequences they experience are the result of their actions.

Let your children know when they have or haven't acted in responsible ways. Having punishments and rewards helps make this clear.

OFFER ALTERNATIVES WHEN
YOU WANT THEM TO DO SOMETHING

Because their sense of power grows when children have the opportunity to make choices, you must offer them an array of alternatives.

Alternatives can be offered in many everyday situations, such as "Would you like peanut butter or tuna fish for lunch?"; "What would you like to wear, your red or brown pants?"; "Would you like to go to the amusement park or the beach on Saturday?"; "We can go shopping tonight or tomorrow night, which would you prefer?" Offering choices can reduce power struggles by enhancing children's sense of power.

As your children become familiar with having alternatives, their ability to generate their own grows naturally. By carefully choosing the alternatives you offer, you can raise children's sense of power and avoid giving them too much freedom.

LET YOUR CHILDREN KNOW THEY CAN CONTROL
THEIR OWN FEELINGS, AND ARE RESPONSIBLE FOR DOING SO

Many of you are in conflict about how to let your children express emotions. You can accept what children feel at the same time you place limits on how they can express their feelings.

When you require children to calm down before dealing with the cause of an outburst, you help them control their feelings and learn self-restraint ("I will help you with this problem when you stop crying; I'll wait"; "I know you're angry, but I will not discuss it with you as long as you raise your voice").

Children who exercise self-restraint deal more effectively with situations that might provoke anger, fear, resentment or frustration. Those who can't, feel powerless and must blame others for "making" them feel badly.

TEACH CHILDREN HOW TO
INFLUENCE PEOPLE IN POSITIVE WAYS

Children who are skillful in human relations often can get what they want without upsetting other people. But they're not born with such skills; they learn them, chiefly by observing how others relate and being taught simple good manners (learned and reinforced every day).

The most effective way to teach children good manners is to require them to use them at home. You, of course, must reciprocate. Too many parents try to get children to use good manners outside the home, while allowing them to use bad manners at home.

Children can move on to more sophisticated methods of influencing people once good manners are mastered. You can teach them not to interrupt, insist that they make requests in reasonable ways, and show them that you are more amenable to giving permission if they treat you with respect and consideration. Such lessons carry over into their lives outside the home.

When children can use positive ways to influence people, they are more successful at fulfilling their own purposes, thus enhancing their own sense of power.

TEACH CHILDREN HOW TO DO THINGS

The more skills children have, the more flexible they are in finding new ways to be successful in doing things. When they have control over material objects and know how to make things work, children feel competent and build their own sense of power.

Take time to teach your children how to do things that are useful in their everyday activities, such as "Shut off the light when you leave the bathroom"; "Pick up toys that you left on the floor"; "Put your dish in the sink." These competencies can translate to play: "You can climb on the fence by putting this box by it"; "Hold your shovel this way so that the sand doesn't fall off"; "Put this board under your blocks so they don't fall over."

Conflicts arise when parents try to teach, and children don't seem to want to learn. Since children are natural "blotters" when it comes to learning, their resistance may be a sign that you are trying to give them more help or information than they feel a need for at the time. A child may not have the patience to learn how to saw a large piece of wood, but can learn how to use a saw by ripping through a small stick under a parent's supervision. He might not want to vacuum a whole room, but might have the patience to learn how to pick up a few crumbs. She might not be able to learn how to catch a small ball thrown to her from thirty feet away, but will learn how to catch a large ball thrown from two feet.

REQUIRE CHILDREN TO MAKE DECISIONS

Children make decisions all the time, but are usually not aware of the processes they use (weighing alternatives, foreseeing consequences, making choices based on values). Decision making is a skill that can be refined by practice and by being self-conscious about how to go about it. When children complete a task you can point out that the result came from a decision they made; for example, "When you decided to move your bike out of the way, you helped avoid a bad accident";

"When you decided to take your new toy out in the rain, it was likely to get ruined."

Give them practice by discussing impending decisions with them ("Are you going to decide to share your toys when your cousins visit?"). You can review the quality of their decisions together, so that they can learn to correct them.

Require them to make decisions in relationship to you. "I'll play a game with you, but you decide which one"; "You decide what would make me not get angry" are examples. Praise them when they make good decisions.

You can help children increase their ability to make wise decisions by following these four steps:

- Help your children clarify the problem that is creating the need for a decision. Ask them questions that help them clarify what they *see* and *hear*, what it is they *feel* about the situation, and what they want to *change*.
- Help children search for alternative solutions. Adults and children can brainstorm a number of alternatives without feeling they have to be critical of an idea. Although many of the alternatives may seem silly, this step makes children (and adults) realize that there are alternatives and thus choices. You will frequently have to start by suggesting alternatives and gradually encourage children to contribute.
- Help children select one of the alternatives by evaluating the consequences. The best solution is one that solves the problem *and* makes a child feel good about himself. Sometimes the only way your child will find out the consequences of a decision is to make it and see what happens. You need to help evaluate the risks and be supportive and/or approving, depending on the results.

  Older children often need to test adult forecasts in order to find out whether they are correct. Even though they make decisions that you can foresee as questionable, it may be necessary not to intervene. In this way children can learn from their own experience. You don't enhance children's decision-making abilities by requiring that every decision be a good one, but rather by insuring that they are aware of the fact they have made a decision. Suffering negative consequences can motivate children to be more rigorous in evaluating the consequences of future decisions.

- Help your children evaluate the outcomes of their decisions. Evaluating the results of a decision helps children become more aware of the process. Reinforce the positive outcomes to a child's decision. When a decision does not result in positive outcomes, it helps to review the alternatives again and analyze what went wrong.

The basic question is "What went wrong?" not "What did *you* do wrong?" Evaluation means looking at the whole situation, not only the child's part in it. It is useful to have your child review the tactics he will use the next time the problem arises. You can help him prepare for this by getting a clear picture in his mind of *desirable alternatives*, rather than emphasizing what he did wrong.

TEACH CHILDREN TO SOLVE PROBLEMS

In order for children to learn how to solve problems, they need to have problems to solve. This is not as self-evident as it may seem, since many parents quickly become uncomfortable when their children have a problem and provide solutions for them. Helping children think through problems may take longer, but when they know that they have solved a knotty problem themselves, their sense of power rises dramatically.

Don't immediately give advice when approached with a problem unless it's clearly necessary. Ask questions that might help clarify the problem and find the path to the solution; for example, "I know that's a hard math problem, but look at the one you just finished. Is there a clue in that one?"

Children understand problem-solving procedures (taking

time for analysis, calming down so they're not emotional, thinking of several alternative solutions, foreseeing the consequences of a particular solution, and so forth). Teaching children general strategies for problem solving allows them to approach new problems with greater confidence. As their ability to solve problems grows, their sense of power rises.

HELP CHILDREN HAVE SUCCESSFUL EXPERIENCES

When you have your child do some chore, solve a problem, or complete any complex operation, it is best to break down the activity into steps, so that he can successfully complete one stage at a time. Parents frequently ask children very complex things ("Clean your room!"), but don't provide a step-by-step plan for doing it. When children get lost in the midst of a complicated activity, they tend to give up and their sense of power diminishes. Teaching children how to do things well (by words and by example) increases their chances for success. You also need to provide resources that a child might need to perform an activity well, especially if the child is not aware of what resources are available. (Give him a treated cloth rather than a dry rag to dust his room, for example.)

ALLOW YOUR CHILDREN TO DO
THINGS THEY HAVE SHOWN THEY CAN DO WELL

Children take pride in their skills and feel good when they have the opportunity to use those skills, since their sense of power is raised by doing so. All children have some attributes they identify as special skills, from walking along the edge of a curb as toddlers to cooking a special dish when they're older. They may repeat some act again and again, driving parents to distraction. You should try to be tolerant of this, since it's children's way of building their own sense of power.

When your children show skill in some activity, find opportunities for them to do it. Young children may feel that a part of a skill is significant, and are not interested in expanding it under your tutelage, as when a child may be quite happy about *stirring* the hot chocolate but may not show any inclination to learn how to make it. Offer children opportunities to learn new skills, but more importantly, let them use old ones.

HELP CHILDREN SET LIMITS FOR THEMSELVES AND OTHERS

You can demonstrate this by setting clear and consistent limits yourself. Begin by defining personal limits, such as "I can't read to you now because I have to rest. I'll read to you in an hour"; "I'd rather that you didn't chew with your mouth open while I'm at the table with you"; "I don't like you to jump on me when I come in the door. Let me take my coat off and put my things away first."

You can also help children to say no to things that may not be good for them. Children need help to set limits with their peers. ("If Joey asks you to give him answers in class, I think it's okay if you don't. Try it, see what happens, and we can talk about it again.") They also may need continuing support to say no in personal matters. ("You don't have to let your sister borrow your clothes; I'll support you in that"; "If you don't want to play with Andy, you can tell him so.")

Each of these methods for enhancing children's sense of power reflects an attitude about children that presumes children are capable of taking care of themselves in significant ways—and must learn to do so. This directly applies to LeRoi who was introduced to you in Chapter 9.

LeRoi's parents needed to change their attitude toward him, which they did, as you will see. In doing so, they began to help LeRoi solve the problems that his low sense of power was creating.

LEROI: A CHILD WHO WINS THE BATTLES WHILE LOSING THE WAR (PART II)

During the winter and spring the Emerson School Home/ School Club sponsored a series of lectures for parents on issues dealing with their children and schools. The Jacksons decided to attend.

One of the lectures was about delinquency, and was given by a psychologist who worked with delinquents, their families, and local juvenile probation agencies. Dr. Simpson was a personable and entertaining speaker. Because Emerson was an elementary school, Dr. Simpson focused his talk on the childhood antecedents of delinquency, and punctuated his informal presentation with many examples and case studies.

In order to show how delinquency was not only a result of poverty or neglect he quoted studies that pointed out the increasing incidence of delinquency among the children of middle-class families. At one point he described a family that was uncomfortably similar to the Jacksons, whose son had been very much like LeRoi, and had several run-ins with the law regarding drugs and armed robbery.

Dr. Simpson proposed effective discipline procedures for children in the home, as insurance against delinquency in adolescence. He argued that parents needed to start early in a child's life, and consistently maintain fair but high expectations for children. He also described some techniques for improving discipline for young children.

During the discussion period following the lecture, Mrs. Jackson asked a question about LeRoi's behavior. She was a bit nervous in front of the group of parents, and posed her question humorously about "little boys who don't do their chores." Dr. Simpson asked her to describe LeRoi and how she and Mr. Jackson handled him, and before she was aware of it, Mrs. Jackson had revealed a lot of the problems that they and the school were having with her son.

Dr. Simpson thought for a moment before responding to her question. "I hope you're not offended by my answer, but it seems to me that you're describing a very spoiled child," he said. "I don't say this as a threat or to scare you, but the boy you're describing is, in my experience, a high-risk child. If he does not become accountable for his own behavior soon, it will be harder and harder for you to control him."

He then went on to talk about responsibility, how it is built in a child, and what parents need to do to insure it. While Dr. Simpson went on to answer other questions, the Jacksons looked at each other uncomfortably, and Mrs. Jackson, especially, felt quite agitated.

At the conclusion of the evening, the Jacksons stopped Dr. Simpson as he was leaving and asked him why he felt that LeRoi was the high-risk child that he described. Simpson said, "I'll be straight with you folks. In my practice I see a lot of parents like you, who give their kids too much and don't demand much in return. By the time a lot of kids like that become teenagers, they think the world owes them, but they don't owe anything back. Besides which, if they've been allowed to goof off in school, they're so far behind that they're turned off to education, and don't believe that rules apply to them."

"But how can we change things now?" Mrs. Jackson queried. "He's really a good kid. Won't he grow out of it?"

Dr. Simpson replied he had to leave, but gave his card to the Jacksons and invited them to see him at his office, where they could go into the matter at greater length.

The following week the Jacksons made an appointment with Dr. Simpson. During their visit to his office they filled him in on LeRoi's problems in school, their family relationships, and frustrations in trying to change LeRoi's attitudes. When Mrs. Jackson tried to complain about the way the school was handling LeRoi, Dr. Simpson cut her off abruptly.

"Now, don't start blaming the school. I'm no apologist for the school system," he said, "but, it seems to me that they've tried to work with you. Anyhow, they won't have to live with LeRoi years from now, and you will. If I were you, I'd be getting down to the school and working out a plan with them to get LeRoi in better shape."

At the conclusion of the interview, Dr. Simpson recommended several books on discipline to them. He told the

Jacksons that they needed to focus on clarifying their rules and expectations, setting consequences for LeRoi when he didn't meet them, and holding him accountable for the decisions he made about what he did or didn't do.

"Give me a call, if you need to talk more, but I know Mr. Todd at Emerson, and I think he will be able to work with you."

The Jacksons were not ready to talk with the people at school. While she couldn't admit it, Mrs. Jackson was embarrassed to admit that she had been wrong in the way she had handled LeRoi's problems at school, and didn't want to face his teachers yet. But they read the books Dr. Simpson had suggested, and gradually began to form a plan.

After several long discussions with each other they were ready to confront LeRoi. One evening they sat down with him and told him that they'd been doing a lot of thinking about him and were not happy with how they had dealt with him up till now. He wasn't doing well in school, he and his mother argued a lot about chores at home, and he himself didn't seem happy a lot of the time because he got angry too easily.

LeRoi tried to interrupt to complain about the kids at school and his sisters, but his father said, "We don't feel that those are the issues, LeRoi. You do a lot of complaining about what other people do to you. But that doesn't seem to change anything."

As the discussion went on, Mr. and Mrs. Jackson laid out a new set of rules to LeRoi that included some new chores, like setting the table by himself, cleaning his room, and caring for his dog. But the big issue was that they were going to start to impose consequences at home if they received reports that LeRoi's behavior in school was not good.

LeRoi tried to protest through much of the discussion. In his whining voice he complained, "That's not fair," and "Why are you being so mean to me all of a sudden?" When his parents told him about their new attitude toward his behavior at school, he pulled out all the stops.

"That's wrong!" he almost yelled, "Mr. Todd doesn't like black kids; he's always picking on us. The white kids are always picking on us. Don't you want me to fight back?"

Mrs. Jackson could feel her new-found resolve begin to wane as she remembered the discrimination she had suffered as a child. But Mr. Jackson held firm. "Even if that is true, LeRoi, it still is no excuse for not doing your own work at school, and your homework too. Besides, from what we hear, you get in trouble with black kids as well as white."

LeRoi was almost comical as he began to splutter excuses that he now knew were of no avail. Again, Mrs. Jackson's heart began to hammer as LeRoi hung his head and she saw tears forming in the corners of his eyes. She even started to reach out her hand to him, but a look from Mr. Jackson stopped her.

The Jacksons began to follow through with the list of rules and new chores they had designed for LeRoi. It was not easy for Mrs. Jackson, since LeRoi put her to the test the first day. One rule required LeRoi to make his own bed before leaving for school. If he didn't, he had to miss television during the evening. Mrs. Jackson was aware that LeRoi wasn't making his bed the next morning, but didn't say anything to him.

Mrs. Jackson thought about the confrontation that was going to occur after school and didn't look forward to it. Several times during the day she had small bursts of anxiety as she anticipated LeRoi's reaction. But she also strengthened her resolve as she thought about how angry her husband would be if she didn't follow through.

When LeRoi came bounding into the house after school, Mrs. Jackson called him into the kitchen.

"LeRoi, you already seem to have overlooked one of your new chores."

A perplexed look came over his face, but he said, "No, I didn't," in a surly voice.

"Go look at the list in your room," Mrs. Jackson suggested.

When LeRoi returned he said, "Aw, Mom, I forgot this

morning. Besides, it ain't no big thing. I can make my bed now. It's a dumb rule anyhow; I'm just gonna mess it up again tonight."

Mrs. Jackson told him that the rule was the rule, and he had best get his bed made and not expect to watch TV that night.

LeRoi was furious. He ran out of the house and slammed the door. Mrs. Jackson was shaken by the encounter, but felt that she had done what she was supposed to.

That night Mr. Jackson was home and took some of the burden off his wife in imposing the consequence. LeRoi didn't make his bed until just before his dad came home. He had set the table for dinner, although it was a bit messy. After dinner, he moped around the house, complaining that he had nothing to do, and bothered his sisters several times. When they were watching TV he came to the door of the family room and stared at them. Warnings from their mother kept them from teasing him.

Mr. Jackson came into LeRoi's room as he was preparing for bed and told him that he knew that LeRoi had gotten angry about not watching TV, but that in the future he could watch it if he remembered what he had to do. It was really up to him.

"Furthermore," Mr. Jackson went on, "I think that you'd better recognize your mother and I meant what we said last night. If you do the things you're supposed to do, everything will go just fine. If not, you'll be the one to suffer. It's your choice."

During the next week, LeRoi had to be punished almost every night for some chore that wasn't done. Gradually, his vociferous protests diminished to a sort of sullen resignation, and there were no more angry outbursts. The Jacksons didn't hear anything from the school.

Both Mr. and Mrs. Jackson held to the rules. Mrs. Jackson became less apprehensive, but began to wonder if this new approach was going to work. She called Dr. Simpson one day, but he reassured her that LeRoi's reaction was not unusual and that he was waiting to see if his parents would continue to follow through.

During the second week of the new program, LeRoi had several days in which he was not punished, and his parents commented about this to him. He gave a "so what" reaction to them, but they noticed that he was somewhat happier afterward.

By the end of the second week things in the Jackson home had fallen into a routine. LeRoi began to tell his parents, with less rancor, when he had done a chore, and the quality of his performance was beginning to improve.

Mrs. Jackson finally felt that she could see Mr. Todd, and made an appointment with him after school. As she went into his classroom, he greeted her with a smile and asked, "What's going on with LeRoi? Has something happened at home?" When Mrs. Jackson told him what they'd been doing and the way that LeRoi was responding, Mr. Todd exclaimed, "Well, that explains it!"

He told her that LeRoi was acting differently at school. He still had to upbraid him at times, but the incidence of punishable behavior had decreased noticeably and the amount of work that LeRoi was doing was increasing. "No junior Einstein yet," Mr. Todd laughed, "but I can leave him alone for a while, and he'll keep working. He didn't used to do that."

Mr. Todd told Mrs. Jackson that they needed to work out a system to stay in contact with each other about LeRoi's work and behavior. If the Jacksons would support him, he'd start putting some more pressure on the young man and was confident that LeRoi would respond. He also wanted the Jacksons to be able to reward their son if he did well.

Mrs. Jackson was relieved by Mr. Todd's open enthusiasm for what she and her husband were doing. He really did seem to be concerned about LeRoi! She told Mr. Todd about her contact with Dr. Simpson, and he reported that he had met Dr. Simpson at a teachers' conference. Mrs. Jackson and Mr. Todd were getting on quite well when LeRoi came into the class, and, in his whiny voice, asked his mother when they were going home.

She turned to him and said, "Mr. Todd and I are not finished yet. You may wait outside or in the car, but do not disturb me until we're finished."

As LeRoi turned to leave the room, Mrs. Jackson and Mr. Todd looked at each other and burst out laughing. LeRoi looked at them wonderingly but continued out of the room.

More often than not, you need to alter several of the ways you do things at home before you can change a child's behavior. The Jacksons needed to become more precise about rules, build in consequences, control their tempers, and change their attitudes about LeRoi's teachers. A combination of things did the trick.

Everyone in your family needs to have a good sense of power. You can make it happen!

BUILDING A SENSE OF POWER IN YOUR FAMILY

Power in the family is an issue that is usually associated with conflict. Power struggles between parents or among parents and children show that the family climate does not enhance a sense of power in each of its members. When people feel powerful they have less need to "win" because they are already confident that their opinions and contributions to the family make a difference. There are a number of things that your family can do to increase your children's sense of power without giving them control that they're unable to handle wisely.

When conflicts are resolved by having "winners" and "losers," it usually results in inviting more conflict. The pattern is usually set by parents. If they always have to be the winners, it follows that their children have to be losers. If parents are willing to negotiate some things with their children, discuss differences reasonably, and try to clarify opinions and feelings, then children see that there is opportunity to influence their parents. If, as a result of these procedures, a parent gives in or changes an opinion, then children's ability to give in is also enhanced.

You don't have to win in every confrontation with your children in order to gain their respect. Clarity, reasonableness, fairness, consistency, and concern are more likely to result in your children respecting you than using the club of parental authority (not that it isn't required sometimes, but probably less than parents think). When parents can admit mistakes, apologize, and change, it increases their children's faith in them, enhances feelings of security, and increases their sense of power.

AVOID ALTERING RULES AND
PROCEDURES WITHOUT DISCUSSION OR PRIOR WARNING

Being arbitrary, which means using parental authority in unpredictable ways, robs children of their sense of power. It's usually a sign that parents are resentful and frustrated, more often than not as a result of being unclear with children in the first place. Children need to feel that they can influence the rules under which they live. When you act arbitrarily, you erase any rights that your children may have. Children's sense of power is increased when they can plan some of their own activities but if you act arbitrarily and impose unpredicted demands, their ability to plan for themselves is undermined.

FAMILY MEMBERS SHOULD BE
INVOLVED IN SIGNIFICANT DECISIONS THAT AFFECT THEM

It is useful to ask children what kind of rules they believe are needed and what chores they have a preference for. All family members should have the opportunity to indicate preferences about family matters and have them honestly considered. Family outings, vacations, and picnics are splendid opportunities for children to have a say in what happens.

When children know they can influence some decisions, they are usually more accepting of those that parents make for them. Knowing that they can have an effect means their sense of power is high; under these conditions their need to control diminishes.

Allowing children to influence decisions doesn't mean putting everything to a vote; though, when parents don't have a strong vested interest, it is a useful exercise in family democracy. The kind of family democracy we mean is one in which everyone is heard and respected even though you are in charge.

THERE NEED TO BE WAYS TO DEAL WITH GRIEVANCES

Grievances are those chronic issues that we often come to accept: "You'll just have to live with it, that's the way Dad is." "She never puts the top back on the toothpaste." Sometimes it's important to isolate grievances by having only the parties involved discuss them. Sometimes parents have to step in, such as by controlling younger children from tormenting older ones. Sometimes issues need to be aired in a family meeting where everyone can voice an opinion. There are some grievances that can't be solved, but may be tempered by talking about them openly. When grievances are disregarded or suppressed ("Well, it's just too bad you feel that way!"), family members feel that they cannot control their own lives, and their sense of power diminishes.

ENCOURAGE CHILDREN TO TAKE
ON MORE CHALLENGING TASKS AND RESPONSIBILITIES

Children, like adults, are creatures of habit, often being satisfied to stick with what they can do well. With your encouragement they may find they have greater potential than they thought. ("I'm sure you can go down the slide by yourself. Try it, and you'll see.") As your child becomes aware that he grows and changes, his willingness to try new activities increases his sense of power. Often this means that parents need to lead children into taking greater risks without demanding that they go beyond what they feel comfortable with. Your support and encouragement is often enough to get your child to try something new.

In families this should result in older children not only having greater responsibilities, but also more privileges than younger ones. Children need to know that they can gain more of what they want through increased competence and responsibility, and this should be spelled out as clearly as possible. ("Since you've done all your chores without any hassle for some time now, I think that we can allow you to stay up later. You've shown that you can be responsible.") Children seek new privileges. They should be able to get them if they can demonstrate growth in responsibility. ("If you wish to be able to ride down to the store alone on your bike, you'll have to show me that you can be home on time or call me if you can't.")

YOU NEED TO DISTRIBUTE RESOURCES
TO FAMILY MEMBERS IN A FAIR AND EQUITABLE WAY

Money, for allowances or payment for services, is an important resource. But money is not the only resource that a family has. Space and time are equally important. As an example, older children may need special resources because of their special responsibilities. Space for privacy, a quiet place to do homework, special equipment such as desk lamps, books, and a budget for party clothes are needed more by older children than younger ones. Your time and energy are also resources for the family, and children may fight and argue over them. Controlling time is a never-ending challenge to parents, and demands that some structure and order be placed on family activities.

Allocating your time in a consistent and predictable way has a profound impact on your child's sense of power. Spending fifteen minutes every day or two alone with your child, and allowing her to select any activity that is reasonable (a story, game, or just talking), builds trust and a child's sense of power. This time should be sacred, and neither other obligations nor any punishment the child is under should interfere with it. Spending all or part of a day from time to time with each of your children will be even more beneficial.

Children will use special or limited resources effectively and not squander them if they have to show evidence of responsibility before they are allowed to use them. When children know what resources they can get, through the efforts they make, their sense of power is enhanced.

BE CLEAR ABOUT WHAT YOUR CHILDREN'S RESPONSIBILITIES ARE AND WHAT DECISIONS THEY CAN MAKE ON THEIR OWN

A problem area in most families is the way older children take responsibility for younger ones. The older ones are often given the responsibility, but have little authority to control the younger ones. This creates a paradox, because when responsibility and authority are separated, strife and bad feelings are sure to follow.

When a child has the responsibility for some duty, allow him broad latitude in deciding how to do it, if standards and time limits have been clarified. ("I don't care how you do your room, as long as it's done by 3:00 and is clean.") Giving children lots of chores, but not allowing them to have a say in them does *not* build a sense of power. In order to accomplish all of this in a reasonable manner, you need to be very clear in your own minds about what areas you need to maintain control, and what decisions you are willing to let children make. If there is a right way to be a parent, it's by being clear about what you're doing and why, so that children can understand.

Teaching Children to Be Responsible and Competent

When children take responsibility, it is unnecessary to tell them how to act in every situation. They adopt a pattern of appropriate behavior based on your requirements and by reaching realistic conclusions from their own experience.

Your children are responsible when they:

- Perform regular duties without being told every time
- Have specific reasons for what they do
- Do not blame others excessively
- Are capable of making choices among alternatives
- Can play or work by themselves without undue discomfort
- Can make decisions that differ from those of their friends, peer group, or family
- Have various goals or interests that can absorb their attention
- Honor and respect parents' limits without excessive arguing
- Can focus their attention on complex tasks (relative to age) for some time without excessive frustration

- Follow through on what they say they'll do
- Acknowledge mistakes without excessive rationalization

Responsibility implies the *ability to respond*. It suggests that in order for a child to respond well to situations he must make decisions that are appropriate and effective.

Appropriate means that a child makes choices that are within the boundaries of commonly held social norms and expectations that promote his own safety, success, and security.

For example, if a child were to spit on the foot of a stranger who greeted him, it would be considered an inappropriate response, not because there is some absolute rule that a child does not spit on a stranger's foot, but because the relationship between the child and that person would likely become a negative one. On the other hand, if a child who is greeted by a stranger responds with a smile and says, "Hello. How are you?" it is likely that they will develop a positive relationship.

Even though people of goodwill may not reach the same conclusions about what is appropriate in every instance, the overwhelming number of relationships a child has are influenced by social norms, grace, tact, and manners. Success and satisfaction in social interactions are a measure of a child's proper response, and such successes will reinforce his inclination to continue to act appropriately.

A response is effective if it enables the child to accomplish goals that result in enhancing his own feelings of self-esteem. As an example, when a child wishes to visit a friend, she must secure permission from her parents to do so. If she asks without arguing and in a straightforward manner, she is more likely to receive a positive response. When treated with tact by a child, even parents tend to respond amicably to a child's wishes.

In order for a child to respond effectively he needs to

identify the important features of the given situation. Making choices that support the needs and interests of others is an important part of a child's sense of responsibility. If he only exercises his own self-interest and does not consider others' limits, he can create difficulties for himself and for others. For instance, when you need to meet a schedule that involves the whole family, you need to know that your children will be ready on time and that no one member of the family will interfere with the rights of other members.

We all need to be aware of how others view the world so that we can refine our understanding of the way other people think about things. This is especially important for children in that it will increase their ability to be flexible and make them aware that standards and expectations may vary in different situations.

Your children also need to be aware of their own needs and goals. A child is responsible when his actions creatively take into account his own goals *and* others' needs. To arrive at this creative balance between others' wishes and his own needs, a child needs to be able to delay immediate gratification. Accomplishment of this difficult task is easier if, in the past, adults have acted consistently toward him by following through on promised rewards and punishments. It is also essential that you and your child's teachers offer rewards and praise for responsible behavior. Excessive criticism, ridicule, and shame only foment irresponsible acts. Since deferring pleasure is hard, you need to remind your children of times in the past when their discomfort was temporary and their pleasure came later when the job was finished.

Since balancing self-interest with consideration of others is always a creative act that varies from situation to situation, it is difficult to teach. We can help, though, by providing conditions that allow creative decision making. This type of decision making is often stifled under the weight of guilt, and it is essential that we know that teaching children to be responsible is not the same as teaching children to be guilty. Children who have a sense of responsibility have the tools, attitudes, and resources they need to evaluate situations effectively and make choices that are appropriate to themselves and those around them. Children who are motivated by guilt, *seeming* to be responsible, have "special" criteria for making choices.

The differences between guilty children and responsible ones are seen in the following table:

GUILT VERSUS RESPONSIBILITY

	Children Who Are Motivated By Guilt	Children Who Have A Sense Of Responsibility
Goals of Their Behavior	To avoid pain, punishment, criticism, or disapproval	To satisfy needs of themselves or others
Methods They Use	Placating, dependency on others, rigidity in their approach to new situations	Independence, flexibility, being forthright
Focus of Their Attention	In the past: memories of pain or criticism, old situations that are safe	In the present or future: experiencing pleasure now or seeking new goals; remembering successful experiences of the past
Feelings About Themselves	Self-recriminating, anxious and fearful, low self-esteem	Self-approving and positive, high self-esteem

Parents may try to teach children to be responsible, but wind up having their children feel guilty. The following chart summarizes the approaches that produce either guilt or responsibility in children:

PARENTS' ACTIONS THAT PRODUCE
GUILT OR RESPONSIBILITY

Your Motive is:	You can teach your child to feel guilty by:	You can teach your child to be responsible by:
To set limits on behavior and to have children complete their work	1. Punishing inconsistently and excessively	1. Having punishments be consistent and fair
	2. Punishing long after an infraction occurs	2. Punishing soon after infraction
	3. Keeping rules unclear	3. Being clear when rules are broken or obeyed
	4. Having too many arbitrary rules	4. Having a few rules that are known by the children and held to
	5. Protecting children from the natural consequences of their acts	5. Allowing children to experience, within limits, the natural consequences of their acts
	6. Not taking into account your children's level of responsibility	6. Taking into account children's level of responsibility
To let children know how you feel about their behavior	1. Shaming and ridiculing them	1. Describing your feelings without labeling the children
	2. Constantly reminding them of past mistakes	2. Reminding them about positive past behavior to guide them in present and future action
	3. Making them feel responsible for keeping you happy	3. Not making children feel responsible for your happiness
	4. Ignoring their good behavior	4. Praising good behavior
	5. Not letting them know your standards for judging them	5. Clarifying your standards and expectations

	6. Letting them know ahead of time what the consequences are	
To help your children make choices and decisions appropriately	1. Giving your children few choices	1. Offering different kinds of choices
	2. Giving your children choices that are beyond their ability to handle	2. Offering choices and alternatives that are appropriate to children's abilities
	3. Blaming children for wrong choices without helping them to make wise ones	3. Pointing out consequences of their choices; showing them how to think through alternatives
	4. Presenting alternatives that fit your goals but not the children's	4. Presenting alternatives that reflect both the children's and your wishes and needs

HAZARDS THAT HINDER TEACHING RESPONSIBILITY

It is not easy to help children be responsible. Being aware of the obstacles you will come up against along this important but difficult path will help you find your way.

Parental guilt is the number-one hazard, which results when we believe that what we're doing (and how we're doing it) does not measure up to our expectations of ourselves. In order to reduce guilt, you have to lower your expectations to a reasonable level, improve your performance, or do both simultaneously. All of us receive advice from our parents and other experts on how to be good parents, so we have many expectations we are *not* living up to.

When a child hurts, cries, pouts, or makes accusations we often feel guilty. Because guilt is an uncomfortable feeling, we have ways to avoid it. People mask their guilty feelings by:

- Translating guilt into anger and transferring it to someone else. Parents often transfer it to each other: "If it weren't for what you do, our child would act properly (the way I want him to)!"
- Blaming things on circumstances that are beyond our control: "He's just like Uncle Joe; there's nothing I can do about it."
- Developing ailments that excuse us from taking action: "Every time I argue with her, I get a headache; I learned to avoid her."
- Taking all the responsibility, instead of facing conflicts: "When I ask him to do something, he puts up such a fuss that it's better if I do it myself."
- Making up elaborate or unreasonable rationalizations for avoiding situations that produce guilt feelings: "I feel it's very important that she knows I love her, and it's liable to shake her confidence if I punish her."

Guilt makes us change the ways we deal with children. When we do something that causes pain or discomfort to children, then experience guilt or remorse, we tend to alter what we set out to do, relax limits, or not follow through with threats. When we don't do what we said we would, it automatically results in inconsistency, and children know it.

Besides guilt, we have to contend with confusion about how to react to children's manipulation. Here are some of the strategies children—and adults—use.

Children use a "let's be reasonable" strategy in their attempts to avoid responsibility. Adults may feel that a child is purposely making efforts to avoid tasks, but his sabotage tactics may be so subtle that there is little to challenge him about. For example, a child can seem to be working hard on his schoolwork. He says it has to be done tomorrow, and he does not have time to sweep the kitchen. He adds that he needs to get the work done so he can go to bed early because he's tired.

Children sabotage adults' efforts to make them responsible by developing a reputation of incompetence or irresponsibility. If a child consistently does chores poorly, we may conclude that he's incapable of learning, and back off from requiring him to perform certain duties. Any child who is "fortunate" enough to have such a reputation will find himself not being asked to do things, and may be comfortable being the family "idiot."

Foot-dragging is used to avoid completing tasks. When using this strategy, children do things so slowly, or need so many reminders, that people throw up their hands and say, "It's easier to do it myself."

Some children never quite don't do what we ask. They also never quite do it. They appear to make valiant efforts; they make several false starts. In the early stage of doing any task they voice their confusion, frustration, or pain. Children who employ this strategy can rarely be punished for not doing something because they can say, "Look how hard I tried!" They make a great public display of trying to be accommodating, but when they "finish" the task, we observe that it is not completed. It is difficult at that point to berate the child with the fact that something hasn't been done, because so much of it *has* been done. If this strategy is employed regularly by the child, we will soon come to *expect* that the job will not be completely done, and will give it to someone else to complete.

Nitpickers are children who enjoy arguing about tasks, and will invariably find some minor point to haggle about. Even though parents and teachers are reasonable in what they ask, nitpickers will find something unclear or unfair. These children enjoy talking about tasks, rather than doing them, and will talk them to death if allowed to.

"Jailhouse lawyers" will follow the "letter of the law" to extremes, while cleverly avoiding the spirit of a request. An example is a child who dumps things on the bed, dressers, or other places when he has been told to clean them off the floor. Or the child who rakes the leaves from the lawn to the middle of the driveway and reports, "They're off the lawn."

Children use excuses that are not quite irrational. It is difficult to challenge the credibility of a weak excuse. Expressions of hurt and pain on a child's face when his excuse is challenged wring the heart of the hardest adult. For example, a child who has been asked to vacuum the living room may say that she was not able to do it because the dog was very frightened that afternoon, and she needed to spend time with it. Another example is the child who *usually* creates a disturbance when taken to the market by mother. After being told *not* to create a disturbance, he "accidentally" walks into a shelf and stubs his toe. The resulting hysteria is little different from his usual behavior.

Many children appeal to hidden internal processes. They have an ache, feel sick, are afraid, or forget. A person is not able to tell whether these complaints are true or not. This is exemplified by a child who is supposed to do the dishes after dinner, but says that he's not feeling well and needs to lie down. It's hard for us to deny such a request. But if the child is in his room playing actively an hour later (all pain and sickness having disappeared) it's also hard not to be angry.

REMEMBERING

It is important children learn that they are responsible for remembering things. If they forget, they still must experience the consequence of forgetting. Children may be competent and want to please their parents, but if they are not liable for their own memory, they cannot be responsible. We all know that children remember what is important to them. When rules are made important by consistently applied consequences, children will remember them.

Children's sense of time is different from adults'. Very young children live in the present moment, rather than in the past or future, and a child who is totally absorbed in some activity will tend to disregard a future obligation. We have developed a variety of devices that encourage children to remember, and which can be relaxed as your children grow and become better able to assume responsibility.

1. *Write things out and post them.* Keep copies of chore lists. Have a message center. Pin up children's duties in their rooms or on the bulletin board.
2. *Don't remind children after they have assured you they have heard and understood.* Reminding children of their responsibilities can become a bad habit; children then depend on it.
3. *Establish as much regularity as you can.* Scheduling activities at regular, predictable times enhances children's ability to remember. Duties that are associated with regular events tend to be done better.
4. *Don't be afraid to punish if a child forgets.* A mild punishment related to a chore that hasn't been done can act as a prod to the child's memory.
5. *Remember what you said.* When you forget, you give tacit permission for your children to do so. Remember that one of the greatest sins an adult can commit (in a child's opinion) is to forget a promise. Do whatever you have to do to remember what you told a child—write it out, post a note, tie a string on your finger.

BUILDING RESPONSIBILITY THROUGH LIMITS AND RULES

Children can be very responsible in one area of their lives and at the same time show irresponsibility in another. For example, a child may be conscientious in completing school assignments but cannot be counted on to return home on time after playing with his friends. Another child may be friendly and cooperative with her peers but just cannot take responsibility to complete her classroom assignments. Your supervision and direction in setting rules should vary according to situations and need not be applied to all areas of a child's life.

The following guides to effective rule setting cover several situations:

First, and most obviously, you need to decide what rules need to be established. If parents cannot agree on rules and consequences, then children can manipulate to get out of a punishment that will not be consistently applied. You need to define rules before presenting them to children.

The dictates you outline should deal with specific and concrete behavior of the child. Rules that are designed to change attitudes will not be effective because you have no direct control over what goes on in your child's mind or feelings, but you do have control over what the child does. All rules should address specific actions that are required of the child.

What are the characteristics of rules that work?

Rules must be reasonable. Make sure that the resources needed to carry out the rules effectively are available and that you allow them sufficient time for any tasks you set. This does not mean that endless time is allowed, but if a job must be done by a certain time then that time must be reasonable in light of classroom or family functions and the child's other needs and activities. Ask yourself if your child will be able to carry out the rules effectively. For example, if a very short child is expected to do some chore that involves working around high places, you must know that the child has the ability to climb a ladder, or the rule may not be reasonable. For very small children, very heavy work would usually be unreasonable.

You must be sure that you can tell when the rule has been obeyed or when it has been broken. Rules that try to control things that you cannot easily check do not work. You should be able to know whether or not the rule has been met by looking at the clock, or by checking the results of the activity.

The rule must be described in enough detail so that both

your child and you know whether or not your directive has been fulfilled. A rule that states "the garbage must be taken out," is not a good rule. You must specify the conditions under which you will be satisfied with the operation: It is not permissible to have garbage left around the kitchen or under the sink. The top must be replaced on the garbage can. No garbage must be strewn around the garbage can. Fresh garbage bags must be placed in the container, and the container must be replaced in its usual place. This sort of rule defines and describes what you feel is necessary to carry out the chore.

A time limit should be set for all rules. Rules that do not have time limits give rise to arguments about when the job will be done or rule followed. Adding such specifics as: "Before you go to school," "By four o'clock," "Immediately after supper," will help avoid conflicts. Without these guidelines, you will probably have to remind your child to do a chore, thus taking away the child's responsibility to remember. Limits about specific behavior may be stated this way: "If I find that you're doing———, I will warn you and you will have five minutes to stop or else some consequence will occur."

These time limits provide predictability that reduces confusion, helping to promote order and reduce disagreement, anxiety, and guilt. Logically, the best way to monitor time is by the clock. The next best is to use a time limit that is determined by regular activities, such as after supper, before leaving for school, and so forth. The poorest kind is determined by an activity that itself can vary in time: "After you come in from play," "Before you watch television," for example.

Establish firm consequences if the rule is broken. Use consequences that are important to the child. A discipline that may appear to be a punishment for you is not necessarily one to your child. For children who like to watch TV, not being able to watch it is a punishment. For children who rarely watch TV, taking television away from them is not a punishment. Children who don't like dessert will not feel punished if they are not allowed to eat it. You must look at the child's values and interests to determine which ones can be used as a form of punishment.

Punishments or consequences must also be reasonable from your point of view. Punishments that are too severe, that create guilt or excessive concern in you, are not good punishments. Another basic guideline in deciding on punishments is that they do not take too much of your time or energy. Grounding a child in the house for days so he or she can continually "bug" you, is usually a bad choice of punishment.

Don't delay imposing a consequence, and when possible it should be on the day that the infraction has been committed. Since they must be applied consistently, you should set up consequences that you can carry out easily. Punishments that require you to do special tasks or to spend a lot of time watching your child, are inevitably the ones that are not applied consistently. The general rule is that *consistency is more effective than severity.*

Consistency is important not only in applying consequences but also in giving rewards. When you fail to follow through on your promises your child learns that it is possible to say one thing and do another. This is a basis for irresponsibility.

Many times children will misbehave in order to get adults to set limits, and when those are set they will test them to determine whether the adults are trustworthy. Sometimes it seems that no matter how firmly and clearly limits are set, a child will resist following the rule and a power struggle is on until the adult blows up, and heatedly sets the limit. At that point the child will meekly complete the task and the adult most probably will blame himself for exploding and for reinforcing the child's expectation that only negative reinforcement is possible.

Children with a low sense of power generally provoke a high level of punitiveness and anger in their parents. It is okay to be angry and to tell your child how you feel. You can do this with force and still avoid shaming or ridiculing. You can be a useful model for your child to learn assertive behavior. If, however, you find yourself repeatedly getting angry at the same thing, then carefully examine the situation. You may need to set a rule for this situation, as well as check what it is in *you* that is getting you so upset.

Setting limits needs to be balanced with a decrease in the amount of direction given as children gain in responsibility. When children are little, you have to be very directive in setting rules and closely supervising their operations. As children show increased responsibility you can decrease your directiveness and they can be given more influence over rules. As a sense of responsibility grows, you and your child can negotiate with each other and use discussions more than rules to solve problems. Of course, the final goal is to have your child be self-regulating without so much adult support or direction.

BUILDING RESPONSIBILITY
THROUGH FEEDBACK

The consequences you impose on children when limits are broken act as important feedback about behavior they should avoid doing. Children need feedback to know what they *should* do. Children will be responsible if they find that being so results in some advantage to them. Their responsible acts need to be rewarded. Since adults control the resources for rewards, they must be willing to use them in ways that convince the child there *is* an advantage to being responsible.

These resources include your *time, interest, support,* and *goodwill.* Children feel that there is little advantage to obeying you or being responsible if they cannot earn these rewards. Rewarding children for good behavior is important and you need to be aware of the various rewards you can give. Many people believe that rewards for good behavior are a form of bribery. Rewards of a material kind (money, toys, and so on) *may* become bribes if they are the chief technique parents use to motivate children, and if children learn that by holding out long enough they get something for acting appropriately. Rewards are those things a child values—things he wants or needs. We want to emphasize nonmaterial rewards as alternatives:

- *Give children verbal recognition and praise* for jobs that are well done. "You did a fantastic job cleaning your desk."
- *Periodically provide spontaneous recognition* connected to children's accomplishments. "How would you like to go and get an ice-cream cone? You really worked hard cleaning the bathroom."
- *Give children support* when they need it. "Since you helped me weed the garden yesterday, it seems as if I can help you with your homework tonight."
- *Show interest* in what children do, and encourage them. "Since you have to go to a scout meeting tonight, I'll do the dishes for you."
- *Share chores* with children from time to time as recognition of their efforts. "You've really been doing a good job on your room; how would you like some help today?"

It is easy to build a storehouse of resentments and memories of times when a child frustrated you. These memories feed your anger and are dumped on the child at the next infraction. Do you have a similar storehouse of memories about positive things your child has done? If you do, you can remind children of their positive past actions, which they can use as positive alternatives for times they misbehave. Negative reminders emphasize and build in the image of the behavior you want them to avoid. Since images guide behavior, children will tend to behave in accordance with this negative image. By presenting positive images to your children of how they acted in the past you build positive images that can guide their future choices. They also feel good knowing you remember.

Children also need to know how their actions affect others.

A child will often be aware that he's upset you but not be clear what he did to bring this about. Consequences often are not sufficient to help a child pinpoint what he did or said to create the disturbance. You need to help him see the connection between his actions and the effect of these actions on others. You can make such a connection by pointing out to the child two things: What he did, described in terms of his *behavior*, and how you feel about it. "Billy, when you yell loudly and scream, my head hurts and I start to get angry at you," lets Billy know much more than "Billy, how many times have I told you to stop yelling, don't you ever listen!"

THE WHOLE CHILD: KNOWING WHAT'S HAPPENING

12

Good Models/Poor Models

It is difficult for children to make sense out of the world when people often don't mean what they say, when people seem to believe so many different things, and when teachers, parents, TV, and friends say so many different things about what's right and wrong or what's good and bad. To deal with such experiences, our children need values and beliefs that guide their decisions and provide a purpose for their lives. In order to avoid whirling in confusion, floating aimlessly with deep feelings of emptiness, and being overwhelmed by changing and conflicting styles of life, children need a firm sense of models.

A child with a good sense of models will know where he's headed, what activities, experiences and things are most important for him, and how to distinguish between good and bad behavior. He will also know how to go about learning and will have a sense of order that assists him in organizing his time, environment, and activities. Your children's sense of models depends on the quality of the three types of external models they have contact with in their daily lives.

Human models can be parents, teachers, siblings, peers, friends as well as mythical figures from comic books, stories, and tales about ancestors. Children will unconsciously adopt the manners, tone of voice, mood, and style of those people who are important to them. Many of us have been surprised at how our tone of voice, gait, hand gestures and emotional reactions reflect those of our parents or other important figures in our lives.

Philosophical models are the ideas that guide a child's behavior and attitudes. These ideas come from many sources. Adults' casual comments about such values as the worth of schooling, the necessity of fighting for beliefs, and what to feel, think, and do will be incorporated into the beliefs and values of children. Books, pictures, and movies will also present ideas to children, who will then attempt to integrate them into their ongoing daily experiences.

Operational models. Experience creates in children mental structures that unconsciously guide them in how to do things, how to learn and solve problems, how to organize time and their environment, and how to approach unfamiliar situations. These "mental models" grow from everyday, ordinary experiences, especially those that are repeated again and again.

WHAT MAKES A GOOD MODEL

If children can satisfy their needs by putting their internal models into practice, then their models are good ones. Since you are a primary source for your child's sense of models, you might wonder how well you are fulfilling the role. The answer to this question depends upon what's required of the child away from home.

Your behavior may be appropriate and effective for you, but when your children act the same way in another context, they may not be rewarded. For example, a boy who sees his father be tough and assertive in his role as the boss of a local teamsters' union will be punished at school for showing similar behavior. Thus it is possible for you to provide adequately for your children's affectional and security needs at home and yet be inadequate models because of the situations faced by your children outside the home. A girl who learned how to act appropriately in a small farming community in Nebraska may find her models inadequate to handle the hectic pace and the often impersonal quality of relationships in New York City.

The effects of such inappropriate modeling as described above are diluted when children are exposed to a wide variety of situations, people, and ideas. However, breadth of experience by itself is not sufficient to produce a firm sense of models. If the new ideas and events are too radically different from what the child is used to or are experienced chaotically and without some sense of order, then the model will not be helpful. Children who experience the following are more likely to have a good sense of models:

- A variety of experiences
- An orderly environment
- Clear statements of adult expectations
- Affection and support from important adults

Jeremiah's case illustrates how the lack of appropriate models made life difficult for him and for his teacher.

JEREMIAH: A "LOST" BOY (PART I)

Mary Greenburg frowned as she sat in her car outside the home of Jeremiah Brown. She was worried. In a few minutes she would be meeting with Jeremiah's parents to see if all of them could help the second-grade student.

Mrs. Greenburg had noticed Jerry on the first day of school, not just because he had insisted on being called Jerry in class, but because of the anxious, puzzled expression on his face. His quick smile didn't hide the frown on his face or the constantly shifting eye movements as he observed the classroom. He had stood before her, a short, sandy-haired boy with scuffed shoes untied and shirttail flopping over his belt, barely concealing his half-open pants. "My mom and dad call me Jeremiah but I want to be called Jerry," he said. "Other children laugh at my other name."

Somehow Mrs. Greenburg liked Jerry. ("I must remember to call him Jeremiah at home," she reminded herself.) His warm smile was often present despite her frequent reminders to him to keep to the task. Jerry seldom completed his work. He would get absorbed in a math problem and the next moment be in the reading corner looking at a *National Geographic*. Upon checking his work, Mrs. Greenburg would find it to be incomplete.

She shook her head as she recalled Jerry's desk. It reminded her of the junkyard she saw every day alongside the freeway. A clock spring, several crayons, a wrinkled brown apple core, and a tangled ball of twine protruded from the desk, so that the debris forced it to remain permanently ajar.

When Mrs. Greenburg insisted that Jerry clear his desk, he would produce a pile of wondrously incongruous material. Lost papers would be discovered under a pair of mittens, candy wrappers, several oddly shaped rocks, half a deck of playing cards, and some play money.

Jerry was both delightful and frustrating. He had an unusual sense of colors, spending long periods of time filling in the figures in his coloring book. His blending of the hues was often unusual. Often he would have creative ideas for paintings, but would not leave enough space on the paper to include all of his forms. Of course, unless reminded, he seldom cleaned up the scattered papers, spilled paint, or dripping brushes.

She could still recall Jerry's white, scared face, streaked with tears when she had entered the principal's office. Mr. Mooney had called her at home to explain the situation. Jerry, along with three other second-grade boys, had been caught by the custodian breaking into the teachers' room, presumably to steal the candy intended for an upcoming school fair. The other two boys sat stiffly in chairs lined up against the wall, their sullen faces defiant.

Mrs. Greenburg wondered why Jerry had been attracted to that gang, as she opened the ornate iron gate and started toward the house. The gang leader seemed to hypnotize Jerry, who would slavishly follow whatever Tom said. When she had asked Jerry why he had broken into the room, she received a disjointed account of how Jerry had been urged by the bigger boys to squeeze through the half-opened window. At that time, Jerry seemed confused about whether or not he had done anything wrong, and Mrs. Greenburg wondered what his parents would say when they arrived at the school.

It wouldn't be easy talking to two people who were so different. Mrs. Greenburg vividly recalled the anguished look on Mrs. Brown's face as she stumbled into the office and then rushed toward her son, her stringy brown hair askew. She had folded him to her ample bosom and cried. Mr. Brown followed, a small neatly dressed man whose graying hair was brushed carefully in place. He had paused, brushing some lint from his jacket and looking around the room.

The principal and the other boys had left so Mrs. Greenburg answered his questions. His thin mouth was even more stern after she described what happened. He apologized for being ten minutes late, indicating that his wife, as usual, could not find her purse. Looking toward Mrs. Brown, she noted that her flowered blouse was not fully tucked into her slacks. Like Jerry, her shoes were scuffed and one shoelace was untied. The father barely glanced at his son, all but swallowed up in his mother's embrace. Mrs. Greenburg indicated to the parents that they all needed to find some way to help Jeremiah and that she would like to talk to them as soon as possible about her other concerns. As it turned out, the only time Mr. Brown would be home during the next two weeks was today. His salesman's territory, he said with pride, covered all of the western states. Mrs. Brown thought that this hour was free, but wasn't sure because she had forgotten when she had told her closest friend to visit. Breathlessly she had gone into some detail about how much she depended on this childhood companion. She had felt lost in San Francisco, which was so different from the small midwestern community they grew up in.

Mrs. Greenburg rang the doorbell. As she waited she glanced at the blue flowers beside the porch, all but hidden under the robust weeds. She hoped this meeting could really lead to something. (How Mrs. Greenburg handled Jerry's problem is discussed in Chapter 13.)

Jeremiah's poor sense of models was produced by a chaotic home atmosphere and parents who differed widely in values and style. An "open" classroom environment also contributed to his condition.

We must recognize that all children have problems with their models, because they are continually learning, refining what they know, changing, and having new experiences. The nature of childhood is always to be a bit confused. Therefore, everything we describe below about problems with a sense of models actually applies to all children to some degree. But a child has a severe problem in this area when he demonstrates many of these behaviors in most situations, and is severely handicapped by excessive tension and anxiety.

HOW CHILDREN WITH MODELS PROBLEMS BEHAVE

When children *avoid dealing* with their unmet models needs, you'll observe the following:

When children *attempt to meet* their unmet models needs inappropriately, you will observe the following:

---

1. They get confused easily.

1. They often insist there is only one way to do something.

2. They have difficulty discussing goals.

2. They may have very rigid standards, and, if so, get excessively angry with others who do not conform to their standards.

3. They tend to be sloppy, messy, or disorganized with materials and in the way they dress.

3. They fail to complete a task because of obsessive attention to a small part of the task.

4. They are not clear about what is right or wrong behavior.

4. At times they slavishly follow what a "hero" (gang leader, rock

5. They have a difficult time deciding what to say or do.

6. They have difficulty sticking to one topic in conversation.

7. They waste time with apparently aimless activity.

8. They often don't tell the truth.

9. They avoid new situations.

star, movie star) does or says, regardless of appropriateness to a particular context.

5. While espousing high ethical standards, they will often act contrary to them.

6. They take one rule and follow it even when doing so is dysfunctional (trying to be neat while climbing a tree).

7. They rigidly hold to time schedules and become anxious if the schedule is disrupted.

8. They demand that they (and often others) do things perfectly.

Chronic confusion is a major symptom of children with models problems. They have difficulty carrying out even the simplest instructions and appear to become disinterested in most tasks very quickly, even those in which they had previously indicated interest. Keeping them on target is often akin to trying to hold mercury in your hand. This characteristic is the result of a deeper problem, which is a general absence of a goal orientation.

A child with goals has some idea of where he's headed (in a particular task), and some notion of how to get there. Children with models problems usually don't. They will often waste time in aimless activity, or may become involved in an activity that doesn't lead them toward the goal at hand. Even though they appear to be busy (often they don't even *appear* busy), they will move from one activity to another, and not reach the point toward which they were initially headed. The lack of clear goal orientation will also show up in how such a child reports about what he's doing. He will have great difficulty conceptualizing or discussing goals. When asked to specify the purpose of an activity (even if he has been told what it is), he will give vague or inaccurate answers, as if he doesn't have a clue why he's doing it.

Children with models problems get confused easily even about ordinary matters. Such things as when some regular task is to be done, where the family is going next weekend, what time dinner is served, or when special events happen, all get mixed up. These children are not trying to avoid a task or to be manipulative and they often feel depressed or anxious because they cannot keep things straight. These confused children should not be labeled as having low intelligence, even though their behavior might indicate such a judgment. Unfortunately, we measure intelligence on the basis of one's ability to be organized and work toward goals.

When children have a low sense of models, *they tend to be quite disorganized, sloppy and messy.* When their spaces (rooms, desks at school) become disaster areas, and they are required to straighten them, they often take excessive time to do so, and then still don't have them organized in any logical manner. In matters of dress and personal hygiene, they will be found wanting, but tend to mimic parents' standards in this area. They will leave tops off jars, tools lying around, not pick up after themselves, and in general leave a trail of unfinished business as they wander from activity to activity. Yelling and screaming at them doesn't change this pattern. Unfortunately, they may become labeled the "absent-minded professor," and parents resign themselves to the problem.

These children have a hard time making decisions because they lack an organizing principle or sense of direction. They will get deeply concerned about an unimportant aspect of a situation rather than pay attention to what are the most important factors. ("You've spent a half hour straightening out your hairpins, but the rest of the job isn't going to get done on time.") Since we always make decisions in terms of some goal we have, low models children tend to avoid making decisions. Once they decide, the outcomes are often unsuccessful, and, thus, unrewarding. This difficulty even affects the way they communicate. They often can't decide what they want to say or how to say it; they tend to start sentences but not complete them and start ideas but not finish them. When asked simple questions they will shrug, stare blankly at you, or ask you what you mean.

Sometimes children with a low sense of models *become obsessive in insisting that there is only one way to do something.* Once they have discovered a method that helps them deal with a situation or task, they will tend to hold on to it, and apply it at times when it is not totally appropriate. Usually they will not generalize, diversify, or embellish the solution, or be creative in altering it. Moreover, they will often insist that others follow the same solution or have the same idea, and will become angry and frustrated if others don't. As a result of this characteristic, if their solution doesn't work (as is often the case) they will give up rather than seek an alternative.

These rigidly held standards are so important to them, that when they get an idea in their heads, it's hard for them to change. If something's right, it's *always* right; if wrong, *always* wrong. Change makes them anxious. Rigidly held standards are like a life raft they hold on to, even though a rescuer is nearby. Similarly, children with models problems are intolerant of ambiguity. When things become unclear, they become anxious, and retreat to rigidity or leave the scene.

Because they have difficulty sizing up a situation in terms of goals, they can't make good choices about what's important; they can't let something go and get on with another piece of the puzzle. They often become excessively concerned with time, and can't shift schedules easily. Work piles up on them because they can't select the most important thing to do on the basis of priorities that will move them toward a goal. They often demand unrealistic perfection of themselves and others, and, in doing so, insure their own failure or interpersonal problems with others.

Ethics and morals are a problem for children with a low sense of models. They have difficulty making consistent ethical choices because they lack a basic set of beliefs (philosophical models) that act as a reference point for decisions. Characteristically these children tend to be unsure about what it is they believe, their decisions about truth/falsity, right/wrong, and good/bad tend to be contradictory and inconsistent. They may voice high moral standards, but their behavior doesn't correspond to them. They will often be accused of lying or being hypocritical, but will not understand why. They often really *can't* tell what is true and what isn't, and may get events so confused in their own minds, that they truly believe black is white.

Children with models problems *tend to shy away from new experiences* for several reasons. One is because their own experience is probably limited. Secondly, new experiences are only chosen if they make sense in terms of some goal they have. These children's problems about goals often diminish their enthusiasm for new experiences.

Children who have a low sense of models may become "chameleons" around people. Having little sense of an integrated self, they may mimic whomever becomes important to them among their peers or adults. Often they don't have a clear image of their same-sexed parent, and thus seek in others the behavioral reference points they need in order to develop an adequate self-image. They are more than followers; they try to *become* like others with whom they relate. They generally are totally unaware that they are doing this.

HOW CHILDREN'S SENSE
OF MODELS IS THREATENED

There are a number of events that threaten a child's sense of models and make it difficult to strengthen this condition. These events, some of which all children experience, become even more threatening if a child's sense of models is already low, if they last over a long period of time, and if a number of them rapidly follow each other. When you, as a parent or teacher, are aware of such a situation, you need to make use of the special strategies we list in the next chapter to strengthen a sense of models.

Beware of these threats to children's sense of models:

- Living in a house where clothing, books, tools, etc. are scattered around with disorder
- Working in a chaotic classroom
- Trying to follow eating and sleeping schedules that are unpredictable or changing
- Being with parents who disagree over discipline methods
- Having adults frequently change their decisions without warning
- Relating to adults whose facial expressions and tone of voice do not fit with what they say
- Being with adults who lie about things that are important to children
- Losing a parent through divorce, separation or death
- Mistrusting a previously admired adult because of the way that adult acted
- Trying to do a household chore without being shown how to do it
- Attempting to follow a parent's command to "behave yourself" when the parent is not clear how the child can fulfill that expectation
- Not having a chance to practice a skill that they have
- Having to make an important decision without being shown how to think through the decision

13

At Home:
Having Good Sense

Improving a child's sense of models requires a good deal of patience. Changing a child's models and images requires that new models for behavior produce more satisfaction and success than old ones. It takes time for a child to build up this feeling of satisfaction. Because children with models problems have difficulty organizing themselves, learning, and setting goals, you should be ready to work on this condition, anticipating that you might not see immediate results from your efforts.

JEREMIAH: A "LOST" BOY (PART II)

Mrs. Greenburg realized that she needed an attitude of patience when she stepped across the Browns' threshold.

Mrs. Brown breathlessly invited her in, apologizing for the disorder in the hallway as they moved past the roller skates and pile of clothes into the living room. Mr. Brown, who was sitting on what appeared to be an antique chair, got up and shook Mrs. Greenburg's hand, adding that he was hopeful that something could be done for Jeremiah.

Mrs. Brown moved aside her knitting and plumped herself

beside Mrs. Greenburg. She turned to her and said, "I've been really worried about Jeremiah since his attack of asthma two years ago. He's such a small boy and I just cannot understand him. He has attacks of asthma every now and then. . . ."

"When you forget to give him his medicine," Mr. Brown interjected.

Mrs. Brown looked pained as she explained the difficulty she had in handling Jeremiah's baby brother, the housework, and the never-ending invasion of weeds in her garden. "Richard is so seldom home," she added looking obligingly at her stern-faced husband.

Mrs. Greenburg knew, with a sinking feeling in her stomach, that the relationship between Mr. and Mrs. Brown would make it difficult for them to make changes at home, but she had to try to do something.

"I think we can do something for Jerr— Jeremiah if we all put our heads together." She then described her concerns about Jeremiah's classroom behavior. She added that Jeremiah focused on his work when she spelled out carefully the steps he had to do and by when he had to complete his work. Mrs. Greenburg confessed that it had been hard for her to do this because all the other children could make use of the unstructured learning environment she had established. "Also," she added, "it might be useful if Jeremiah could be called by the same name at home and at school. Other children tease him when he uses Jeremiah. Being called two names might be confusing to him."

Mr. Brown stiffened and said, "We called him Jeremiah after his grandfather, Jeremiah Brown, and hoped that the name would bring qualities of honesty, hard work, and responsibility that his grandfather had." Mrs. Greenburg realized that trying to change the parents' mind about the use of the name was probably not the best way to proceed, and so she shifted her approach.

"Jeremiah could use some help from you in getting his homework done. He says that he forgets to do it and at times is confused about what to do, even when I explain it to him."

"What kind of help do you want?" Mrs. Brown asked hesitantly.

"Well, Jeremiah would need to have a regular time and place to do his homework at home and it would help if you could impress upon him how important it is to finish his work, perhaps setting some consequence if he did not finish. You might also help him, when he asks, to think through a problem."

"That's too much for me," groaned Mrs. Brown, "I just cannot think of taking on any more. I'm not getting through now."

"I think helping Jeremiah is a good idea," said Mr. Brown. "When I'm home, I would like to set it up so he can get his homework done. I could let you know when I'm here and you could then let me know what to do. In fact, I'll be back next Monday and could get started then."

Mrs. Greenburg, with a sigh of relief, agreed to let Mr. Brown know what work Jeremiah had to do and some suggestions of how he could help his son.

When Mrs. Greenburg said good-bye and went to her car, her mind was busy with ideas of what she could do in the classroom. She now realized that a great deal of the help Jerry needed would be up to her.

The next day she and her aide outlined a plan so that Jerry could learn to complete his work. This included helping him think through what to put in his work and where to put the odds and ends he had accumulated in his desk. For the latter, ice-cream containers were arranged against a wall so that all children could have extra space for their prized possessions. Then she or her aide began to carefully explain each classroom assignment to Jerry, what he had to do, by when he had to complete it, and what to do after he finished. He was given somewhat shorter assignments than most of the class so he could often receive the praise needed to learn the new behavior.

Over the next week, Mrs. Greenburg often had to remind

herself to be patient, for Jerry still hadn't had a full day where he completed all of his work. It was only after his father had come home and had, for a week, monitored his homework that Jerry finally completed all his assignments for that day.

Well, she thought, as she looked over Jerry's completed work, at least he's doing his work. He's still messy, looks bewildered, and has trouble keeping his desk clean, but we have a start. I just have to continue to be patient with him.

The case of Jeremiah highlights the difficulty of helping children with model problems. Changes in how the parents act toward such a child are crucial in any program. With patience, there are things that parents can do to enhance a child's sense of models.

HOW TO RELATE TO YOUR CHILD TO BUILD A SENSE OF MODELS

HELP CHILDREN UNDERSTAND WHAT THEY BELIEVE

When you encourage children to talk about their beliefs and values, you reinforce the idea that values are important as well as assist them to clarify what their values are. Help them think through why they believe something and how important it is to them. Avoid asking them to justify a belief. Children's beliefs change frequently so you should not demand consistency from them. You can, of course, point out when beliefs do contradict each other.

SHARE WHAT YOU BELIEVE WITH CHILDREN

In their continuing search for making sense of their world, children need reference points provided by the adults they would most like to love and trust—their parents. Sharing your beliefs with children does not mean that they must always act according to what you believe. It only means that they are given some clear messages about your values and attitudes, so they can test them with their own experience. When children know where parents stand they can make better choices about their own behavior.

HELP CHILDREN SET REASONABLE
AND ACHIEVABLE GOALS FOR THEMSELVES

Human beings are goal-oriented creatures. Children with models problems are *not* goalless, they are confused and unsure about what their goals are. They need considerable help to clarify and work toward simple objectives. ("Take your dirty clothes out of the closet, *then* make your bed.") It is most helpful for them to have short-term goals, related to things they have to do. Often parents need only help them clarify what they have to do anyhow. ("Now, what is it that you're trying to do?") Children with a low sense of models need help to set goals for their behavior ("How are you going to act when we get to Grandma's house?"); learning ("How many math problems are you going to do tonight?"); tasks or chores ("Which part of your room are you going to work on first; then which part?"). It is sometimes difficult for parents to remember the degree of confusion these children experience in setting goals. Trying to have such children define long-range goals often leads to frustration.

HELP CHILDREN TO UNDERSTAND
THE CONSEQUENCES OF THEIR BEHAVIOR

Children with a poor sense of models have trouble identifying cause and effect. They are not sure that A leads to B. ("Didn't you know that was going to happen when you opened the window?") They can easily be labeled as not being very bright. They need frequent explanations about how their acts affect others, and need help to foresee the consequences of any intended actions. This is best done by challenging them to think about what they have to do, helping them understand alternatives that they might use, and giving them feedback about what they have done.

LET CHILDREN KNOW WHAT YOU
EXPECT, AND MAKE PERFORMANCE STANDARDS CLEAR

Low models children often do not meet reasonable standards of performance in school or at home. While laziness or stupidity may appear to be the reason, more often it is the lack of clarity about standards. It is important for you to set appropriate standards clearly for all your children; for children with low models it is an absolute necessity. It helps when standards are consistent and reinforced. ("No, your room is not done; there should be *no* papers left on the floor. Remember, I told you that the last time?") If they do a good job, they should know why. ("You did a good job on the lawn. I was especially happy to see that you put the tools away. That's always an important part of a job.") It's always dangerous to leave important decisions to a low models child's good sense. We need to spell out in great detail how we want them to do things; they cannot read our minds.

BE A GOOD MODEL FOR CHILDREN

Since children with low models tend to easily mimic what others do, they may copy some of their parents' least wholesome behavior and attitudes. But being a good model has a more specific meaning than just trying to be a saint. You need to demonstrate to low models children what you want them to do. Showing is better than telling. Walk as well as talk them through a task. You may have to show them how to make a bed several times before they get the hang of it. Complex chores, such as dishwashing, will require you to work with them a number of times before they're ready to try it on their own.

HELP CHILDREN RELATE APPROPRIATELY

How to relate to others is learned even though the need to relate is born into a child. Children with a low sense of models often make others uneasy, because their manner of relating seems strained or awkward. They're trying to do it right, without being really sure what that is in a specific situation. Feedback and praise when they relate well is an important way to help them make sense out of what they do. Help them review what happened when something goes wrong in their relationships with others.

HELP CHILDREN BROADEN THEIR RANGE OF EXPERIENCES

Children with a low sense of models need their experiences enriched. Increasing the diversity of their experiences with people is important. Out-of-school classes, club activities, sports, for example, can be good, especially if conducted by adults who can be patient and tolerant of their slowness.

These children profit from watching parents do things, and need exposure to a wide range of everyday tasks as well as to the special things you do that may be work-connected. These children may not get it the first few times you explain some activity, but allowing them to observe you will add to their sense of models.

Parents teach children primarily by exposing them to experiences. In this way any parent can be an effective teacher. Low models children may be reluctant to enter into new experiences and will need encouragement. They may need rewards for doing something you want them to do. Children will also find it easier to accept new experiences if you can pace them so that the new situation is entered into gradually; for example, watching airplanes land at the airport and showing them pictures of airplanes before taking a flight.

DO NOT LIE TO CHILDREN ABOUT
THINGS THAT ARE IMPORTANT TO THEM

This does not mean that you should tell children everything. Take into consideration how much they can understand. It is important, however, to be clear and honest about things that your child is concerned about, such as who will baby-sit, when you are returning home, whether completed tasks meet standards, how grandfather died, and so forth. Parents often tell white lies about events that may arouse uncomfortable feelings in the child in an attempt to spare the child's feelings. However, when the child finds out that you were not truthful, their confusion and anxiety grow because they now cannot trust you, someone they have to trust in order to feel safe and to get their needs met.

BUILDING YOUR FAMILY'S SENSE OF MODELS

Creating a family climate that enhances a sense of models, depends on three issues:

- *Communications.* Especially regarding rules and limits, standards for performance, and expectations about how people in the family should relate to each other.
- *Planning.* This includes making promises and keeping them, making goals (both short-term and long-range) clear, and letting all family members know how things are to be done.
- *Keeping order.* Physical surroundings that are orderly are important; promote good habits through chores; and schedule family activities so that the important things get done.

These three factors all help family members make sense out of all that happens in the family. If done well, they provide a structure of experience that is the basis for a sense of models. They enable all members of the family to know what is expected of them, to make predictions about the consequences of their actions, to make decisions they can reasonably expect to carry out, and to know what people mean.

Communicating clearly is a skill that can be learned. It is of the utmost importance that rules and limits be made clear to all members of the family—those that have to live by them (everyone) and those who have to enforce them (parents). Parents need to communicate rules so that everyone understands them. You must check to see that what you said is understood. ("Will you please repeat to me what I just said to you?") The greatest confusion can result from lack of clarity about the meaning of two simple words: *yes* and *no*. If parents don't mean what they say, what can a child depend on? If children can't be sure about what a parent means and whether they will follow through on what they've said, their sense of models is undermined.

Planning is an ongoing process in a family, not something reserved for big events. It means that everyone in the family, as much as possible, should be able to know what's going to happen when, why, and how it's to be done. Toddlers make plans that depend on parents' activities ("I want to go to the beach!"); older children are even more autonomous ("Gee, why didn't you tell me we were going shopping? I told Joey that I'd come over to his house"). When members of the family know what's happening, each one can make better plans about his or her own activities.

Good planning by parents is something that children observe and emulate. Since the ability to plan is an important ingredient of a high sense of models, providing them with good examples has a profound influence on their self-esteem. Even more to the point: How can you feel confident about family matters if you can't predict what's going to happen? Unless parents exercise some control over their own activities, the resulting confusion diminishes their self-esteem as well as their children's.

A plan consists of a clear goal that you want to achieve by a certain time (go to the park Saturday afternoon, with all of our family), and defines the steps to reach that goal, including who is going to do what by when (talk to family at Monday dinner to get agreement, Dad shops for the hamburgers Friday night on the way home, and so on).

Children need to know the goals of everyday activities and how to reach those goals. For example, what to do to get your clothes cleaned, the steps to take in cleaning the kitchen, what you need to do when you want to stay overnight at a friend's home.

Keeping order within the family involves more than keeping children from fighting with each other. Orderliness is a personal characteristic that is adopted naturally when people live within orderly surroundings. Being orderly does not mean that a family is never spontaneous or messy; it only means that disorder is not the usual standard.

There are many practical benefits of orderliness: People can find what they need, parents are less likely to have to clean up after others if standards of neatness are upheld, there is often less tension in the home, because periods of work and play are more clearly distinguished. Furthermore, orderliness has an aesthetic aspect that promotes interest and concern for beauty in one's surroundings.

Children learn orderly habits and develop a high sense of models by completing chores according to clear performance standards that are set by parents. Children's participation in keeping things organized helps to make orderliness a personal characteristic. It is not sufficient for parents to keep things neat, clean, and well organized for children to develop a good sense of models. The children must have the experience themselves. Personal experience is the basis of a good sense of models.

Parents who insist that messiness or disorder is more natural than good organization, may not pay a price for it themselves, but their children will suffer. Adults have a much higher capability for keeping things clear in their own minds than children do. ("Leave my messy desk alone; I know where everything is, except when you straighten it up!") What may be orderly confusion to parents, may only be confusion to a child.

Scheduling family activities is another important way in which order is maintained. Have fixed times for meals and bedtimes so that family members can adjust their activities around them, and so that departures from them are clear. It's easy for parents to believe that schedules are for their convenience, but children depend on them too, even if they complain about them. On the other hand, rigid schedules, which are never altered, make no more sense than no schedules. Predictability needs to be high but not absolute. A balance is needed between consistency and change.

14

Values and Goals: Getting From Here to There Safely

"I don't know what to make of this younger generation," said a concerned mother. "I just cannot understand them. They don't seem to have any values. How can I keep my child from becoming like that?"

Parents have tried many ways to teach children time-honored values. These practices have ranged from being good models themselves to physically abusing children to keep them from sinning. "Good" values usually mean that children demonstrate the same values as their parents or teachers. Yet each generation acquires its own values that differ to some degree from those held by the previous generation. Fortunately for the continuation and gradual change of society, children's values evolve so that later adult values reflect many of the preceding generation's concepts. We know that values arising from a child's experience include imitating important models, observing the quality of human relations around him, and participating in the daily procedures of home and school. Direct teaching has little impact. The new generation, therefore, responds more to adult behavior and less to adult words—the two often differing.

Before discussing how we guide children in acquiring values, it is important to define what we mean by values and the relationship among values, a sense of models, and goals.

WHAT ARE VALUES?

Values are the criteria by which we judge whether something is good or bad, desirable or undesirable. A value can determine how one should act, how to think or feel about something, or the ideal way society should function. Values are basic to attitudes, which are thoughts and feelings about specific issues, events, or objects.

A person may be able to verbalize some of his values, such as "Making money is the highest good" or "One should speak out for what one believes," yet may not be able to state others clearly. Not being able to state values doesn't mean they are lacking. Values can be understood by observing the consistent pattern of a person's behavior and choices. Many people will state the importance of a belief, for example, "Honesty is the best policy," but act contrary to this without being aware of a discrepancy.

The kinds of values people hold to seem to develop in stages. Usually the values of a six-year-old differ from those of a twenty-five-year-old, and the changes appear to be orderly, one stage following the next. Kohlberg defines these stages as:

> STAGE 1: The child acts to avoid physical pain regardless of the value determining what is good or bad.
> STAGE 2: The child acts to satisfy his own needs and occasionally the needs of others when doing so will bring rewards. "I'll scratch your back if you scratch mine," is the guiding rule.
> STAGE 3: The child conforms to what will please others: Behavior is good if the person "means well."
> STAGE 4: The child acts out a sense of duty and respect for authority.
> STAGE 5: The child is aware that values differ among

people and that what is right is a matter of personal opinion.

STAGE 6: The child makes decisions on the basis of his or her own conscience and self-chosen ethical principles. Values are chosen on the basis of reason, self-examination, and how comprehensively and consistently they can be applied.[4]

All writers on this subject, including ourselves, have beliefs about what values are most desirable. Kohlberg implies that it is desirable to move from Stage 1 to Stage 6. Carl Rogers suggests that it is important to arrive at one's values through one's own experience rather than by automatically absorbing them from parents, schools, or other authorities.[5] Raths, Harmin and Simon, in discussing the "valuing process," emphasize the importance of a person acquiring values through freely choosing from alternatives one can act on.[6]

VALUES AND THE SENSE OF MODELS

There are certain values that are easily described. These values usually reflect habitual acts that we perform ("It is important to attend church regularly"), culturally supported beliefs ("Honor your father and mother."), and how we generally hope people will act toward each other ("People should be at peace with each other"). We may even share values supported by a subculture that is not accepted by larger segments of our society ("Those who work at regular jobs are suckers").

There are other values that can only be understood by examining the sometimes puzzling decisions we've made or knowing how others see us act (for example, how we acted at a

[4]Kohlberg, Lawrence. "The Child as a Moral Philosopher," in Kirschenbaum, H. and Simon, S., *Readings in Value Clarification* (Minneapolis: Winston Press, 1973), pp. 49–61.
[5]Rogers, Carl R. "Toward a Modern Approach to Values: The Valuing Process in the Mature Person," in Kirschenbaum and Simon, *op.cit.*, pp. 75–91.
[6]Raths, Louis E.; Harmin, Merill; and Simon, Sidney B. *Values and Teaching* (Columbus, Ohio: Charles E. Merrill Publishing Co., 1966).

party). The relative strength and importance of various values may not be clear to us unless we have to face a difficult choice. For example, a person who believes one should "be honest" and also values "not being a fool" would experience a conflict if he were given too much change at a store. How we handle our conflicts would indicate the relative importance of the two values. We usually tend to ignore discrepancies between our values and our actions unless we are directly confronted with the inconsistencies.

A child's sense of models is strengthened when he expresses values for which he is rewarded, when he tries out a new way of doing something that satisfies him, or when he shows traits similar to his human models that bring him pleasure.

HELPING CHILDREN TO KNOW
WHAT THEY WANT AND HOW TO GET IT

Daydreams and wishes are the basis for goals. Everyone has wishes, desires, and hopes for his or her future: An overworked housewife surrounded by diapers wishes for a relaxing evening, a teenager dreams of owning his own car, a young girl daydreams that she is a doctor healing the sick. The difference between a wish and a goal is that a wish is a desire without commitment, whereas a goal involves a wish, plus a commitment to make that wish a reality, plus a plan to reach that goal. Our goals can be short-range (a relaxing evening) or achievable only in the distant future (being a doctor). When we are successful in achieving short-term goals, we then have the faith to strive for more distant ones. Helping children define and reach common, everyday goals will not only give them hope for the future but will clarify their own emerging values. For example: Your child is invited over to his friend's house to play with his new toy train at the same time he has a Cub Scout meeting. Making a choice between the activities will require him to examine his values. By not making the decision for him and by assisting him to examine what is really important to him, you will increase his awareness of what he does value.

Here are some ways you can help young children be aware of goals and values.

Confront children with the discrepancy between stated goals and their behavior. For example, young Hamilton, age four, wanted to stay up one hour beyond his bedtime. His father said he could if he would not bother people, otherwise he would have to go to bed. Hamilton managed to play quietly ten minutes beyond his usual bedtime but soon began to pester his mother and father, who were both watching TV. At this point, Dad reminded him of his goal to stay up late and that the way he was acting would not allow him to do so. Hamilton paused, said "Okay," and resumed playing.

When a child wants to do something or expresses a preference that may be unusual and not consistent with your values, you may require him to explain it. It is important that you avoid moralizing when doing so. Moreover, your response should help the child think about the choice without feeling he has to *defend* his preference. The following are some questions you can use: "Why?" "Do you feel glad about doing this?" "Was there anything else you would have liked to do?"

Set conditions that children have to fulfill in order to reach a goal. For example, "We will play a game with you after dinner if you do not bother us," or "You can play with the clay when you finish your arithmetic problems." Such situations help the child understand (1) how committed he is to reaching the goal, (2) that there are conditions that have to be met to reach any goal, and (3) that you get what you want through give and take. It is important that when such agreements are made, you keep your end of the bargain. Children learn to keep agreements when adults are trustworthy. Trust and keeping agreements are the foundations of any intimate relationship. If children do not learn these qualities, they will experience difficulty in future relationships.

Avoid criticizing a child's long-range wishes. For example, John, who was five and very worried, asked his parents if he would be accepted in astronaut school when he grew up. His father replied, "Of course they will accept you, because you are smart." One may question such a reply when the future is so uncertain. However, John needed to have hope for his long-range goals. It was more important that John's father instill in John feelings of faith in his own goals than to be realistic. Faith and hope in one's ability to reach long-range goals can sustain a person when obstacles are met. A guiding principle is that the more distant the goal, the less realistic you need to be in guiding a child's thinking. You need to increase the emphasis on practicality when the goal is closer to the present.

Remember that you can assist children to reach their goals. This is particularly important with young children. For example, Joan, age four, was having trouble putting away the doll house furniture she had been playing with. Her mother assisted her. Joan proudly proclaimed as the last piece was placed in the cupboard, "I did it!" Young children usually feel they did a task even though parents or teachers assist them. Such a viewpoint changes as they get older. It becomes important that older children be held accountable for completing tasks themselves. However, when older children do have difficulty with tasks show them alternative ways of accomplishing them.

Children learn values when you require them to do tasks consistently. For example, children learn the importance of order and neatness through following rules that require them to be neat and orderly.

Let's face it, despite your help and patience, children will not reach all of their goals. Their sense of models will increase if they learn how to handle disappointments without getting depressed or hopeless. You can help children when they have not reached their goals by reviewing the reasons they do not reach their goals:

- *The goal is not clear.* Many of our goals are vague wishes, so vague in fact that we are uncertain whether we have reached them. Such "goals" as "I want to be popular" or "I want to have people like me" are too vague. Help your child to be clearer; for example, ask "Which people?" or "How will you know they like you?"
- *A child accepts adults' goals in order to placate them.* If this is the case, the child may not be fully aware that with such an attitude he is bound to fail. Helping the child clarify his values and needs when he wants to do something, will guard against a placating attitude.
- *A child wants to reach the goal but other values and needs are stronger.* Here, the child's original commitment to work for the goal is not as high as striving for other goals that take his energy and time.
- *Plans are not realistic and unforeseen events may interfere with the original idea of how to reach the goal.* Since many unexpected events do happen (and can provide a source of excitement) you can help your child be flexible and try alternative paths to the goal or change the goal to take into account his shifting needs.

If not reaching a goal creates a deep sense of failure in you, then your children are likely to feel the same way. Children will then either be afraid to set goals for themselves or, if they do, will make them too high or low for their capabilities. If not meeting a goal is an occasion for learning about yourself and stimulates you to develop better ways to reach your goals then your children will have a very good model.

THE WHOLE PARENT: YOUR SELF-ESTEEM

──15

Nurturing Your Own
Self-Esteem

TREATING YOURSELF WELL WILL
RAISE YOUR CHILDREN'S SELF-ESTEEM

We recognize the intimate connection between how we feel
about ourselves and how we act toward others. The boss
criticizes his employee who then goes home and kicks the
family dog. The teacher who is rejected by a close friend finds
her classroom out of control the next day. The rejected teacher
and the criticized employee were probably unaware that the
lowering of their self-esteem had increased their inner stress.

Such heightened stress can lead parents or teachers to
actions that in turn lower a child's self-esteem. Such behavior
is actually an attempt by the adult to change their feelings of
loss of their own self-esteem conditions. Under increasingly
high stress people either will make an effort to strengthen the
low condition but do so inappropriately and in an exaggerated
manner (bossing someone as a way to magnify a decreased
sense of power), or in feeling the loss of the condition will
avoid situations that will further activate the sense of loss.

An adult's low self-esteem leads to different behaviors
toward children, depending upon the particular self-esteem

condition that is low. You will either exaggerate your efforts to heal the condition or withdraw from taking risks that might satisfy the condition.

When Your Sense of Connectiveness Is Low

Exaggeration: You may be very concerned about whether your child loves you, and be very hurt when the child says, "You don't love me." You may be excessively concerned about your child's safety and welfare, often reminding him to wear sufficient clothes or to be careful about climbing trees, etc. You may be very concerned about your child's social life and get upset if she does not become a member of a club or is not invited to a party—more so than your child is.

Withdrawal: You may avoid being involved in your child's life, seldom asking what he did or how he feels. It is a burdensome duty for you to talk with teachers about your child. When you interact with the child, you are bored, impatient, and try to cut it short.

When Your Sense of Uniqueness Is Low

Exaggeration: You may often change routines and pay little or no attention to schedules. The imaginative child may be ignored or criticized. You may provoke your child into rebelling against rules and conventions.

Withdrawal: You are uncomfortable with and try to suppress your child's attempts at creativity and become anxious when the child stands out in a group. It is important for you to be able to predict what your child will do; routine and schedules dominate home and classroom. You will try to control your child by referring to others: "You don't see anybody else doing that, do you?" for example.

When Your Sense of Power Is Low

Exaggeration: You will bully your child, dominating him through verbal or physical attacks. The child's attempts to reason or express his own views would be viewed as questioning your authority, and that issue becomes more important than the original disagreement. You will allow your child to make very few if any important decisions.

Withdrawal: You find it difficult to be consistent in setting limits, frequently complaining about how frustrating your child is. Decisions about how to treat the child make you feel doubt and despair, and you appeal to others for answers. You ask children to make decisions beyond their capabilities. Your children may feel responsible for your happiness and sanity, a task they fail at when they see your mood fluctuations.

When Your Sense of Models Is Low

Exaggeration: You will hold rigidly to your ideas of right and wrong against all kinds of contrary evidence. In fact, you usually will categorize behavior as "right" or "wrong." You get exasperated at your child's attempts to seek a deeper understanding of your values. You may not be clear about your own beliefs. You often don't encourage your child to seek alternatives, implying that there's only one way to do something.

Withdrawal: Your relationship with your child is characterized by confusion. You don't remember what you promised the child and will justify lying to him sometimes. Your home tends to be chaotic, and you spend time looking for lost things. You often feel so rushed, trying to do all the things you have to do, that your child is uncertain when he can have time with you. You're always pressured by time because you're confused about what is important. Your child is confused by your tendency to act differently from your espoused high standards.

You can guess by the above descriptions that adults with a particular low self-esteem condition will create feelings of confusion and deprivation in their children, causing them to experience a lowering sense of fulfillment in the same self-esteem condition. Enhancing the conditions in your life will allow you to help meet your child's needs in that area.

ASSESSING YOUR SELF-ESTEEM

While reading this book you probably got some ideas about which of the four conditions is lowest in your life. Self-assessment is not easy. Because so many activities in our lives are routine, often we are not fully aware how we feel about them. Frequently we sense that we have done the "same old thing today." We need to take time to be self-conscious about ourselves in order to make assessments. Two ways of doing this will be discussed: the Day Review and the Four Conditions Questionnaire.

The Day Review requires that you set aside fifteen minutes a day for two weeks. The steps are as follows:

1. Get a notebook and keep it handy at your desk at home.
2. At the end of the day, before you fade out from fatigue, take out this notebook and record the day's events, briefly picturing them in your mind. Remember the small, routine things, the morning hug (or lack of) from your mate, how you felt brushing your teeth, your thoughts and feelings while showering, etc. Record how you *felt* about what you did.
3. As you picture each activity, list it in your notebook.
4. When finished with this list, pause and reread what you have written. Answer the following questions:
   • Which self-esteem condition was most evident today?
   • Was there any condition that was neglected?
   • Examine your predominant feelings:
     —if you felt isolated and lonely, you lacked connectiveness
     —if you felt dull, unimaginative, bored, and frustrated with routine, you lacked uniqueness
     —if you felt helpless or awkward or depressed because you couldn't change something, you lacked power
     —if you felt uncertain which choice would benefit you, or what goal to choose, or if you were confused about the steps to take to get toward a goal, you lacked models
5. At the end of two weeks review your answers for each

day and rank the four conditions in terms of how fulfilled each one was for you. Determine if you want to do anything about the lowest condition(s).

You can complete the Four Conditions Questionnaire while doing the Day Review or afterward.

FOUR CONDITIONS QUESTIONNAIRE

Rate each of the items below from 1 to 4, depending on how consistently you are able to perform each behavior.

1 = hardly able to do this
2 = sometimes able to do this, but I still strongly need to increase my capacity here
3 = I can do this fairly often, but feel I could improve in this area
4 = I can do this often and in a manner I am satisfied with

AREA A: CONNECTIVENESS

_____ 1. I am able to ask for help, or can ask someone for something I need without feeling inadequate or guilty.

_____ 2. When I'm with another person, I feel fully there without finding my thoughts drifting away to other things.

_____ 3. When I talk to others, my words and voice match how I feel.

_____ 4. I take an active part in a group or groups and enjoy being involved.

_____ 5. When I like someone, I can show them directly how I feel.

_____ 6. I can be aware of how my body feels, what parts are tense, when I need a rest, etc., and seriously try to follow what my body tells me it needs.

AREA B: UNIQUENESS

_____ 1. I can express my ideas without waiting to hear what other people think.

_____ 2. I can go with my feelings and let myself experience them as an important part of me without getting stuck with or hanging on to any particular feelings.

_____ 3. I take time to show my own taste and interests in such things as how I decorate my office, how I dress, and how I express myself. The expressions of myself in these areas is more important than what others will think of me.

_____ 4. There are times I choose to be alone, to withdraw from others and be by myself—resting, loafing, or doing something I enjoy. At these times I do not feel I have to be productive.

_____ 5. I take time to do imaginative and creative projects.

_____ 6. I can share my point of view even when others differ with me.

AREA C: POWER

_____ 1. I can handle a great deal of pressure without stomach upset, headaches, etc.

_____ 2. I am able to set firm and clear limits for myself and others without trying to make either myself or the other person guilty.

_____ 3. I can express my feelings appropriately without feeling I'm losing control.

_____ 4. I seek and enjoy being in charge of and responsible for projects and activities.

_____ 5. I can make decisions without excessive delay or stress.

_____ 6. I can take risks in new situations and find them challenging and exciting.

AREA D: MODELS

_____ 1. I have several important goals that guide what I do with my life.

_____ 2. I make attempts to clarify what my superiors expect of me and what constitutes a good job.

_____ 3. I am developing a philosophy of life that is helpful in guiding me through periods of confusion and ambiguity.

_____ 4. I find that what I do increases my feeling that my life has meaning and purpose.

_____ 5. I can share my values with those who are close to me in a manner that is satisfying to me even though they may disagree with these values.

_____ 6. I try to put myself into experiences that I feel would challenge, deepen, and enrich my philosophy of life.

HOW PEOPLE DESTROY THEIR SELF-ESTEEM

There are many subtle ways in which people undermine their self-esteem. These often go unnoticed under the pressure of activities, but they gradually add to one's level of tension, and result in illness, rash decisions, and inappropriate behavior. The following are some examples.

DESTROYING CONNECTIVENESS

- Because of the demands of children and household tasks you do not find time for your mate.
- Most of your conversations with your spouse are about who is going to do what, problems with the children, and what to buy.
- There doesn't seem to be a chance to share feelings about each other or yourselves.
- With everyone involved in their own interests there is no time to sit down as a family.
- You ignore the ache in your shoulder, the sniffle and the frequent heartburn and tell yourself that you cannot afford the time or expense to attend to these minor aches. You even pride yourself at not giving in to them and then wonder why you no longer feel connected to your own body.

DESTROYING UNIQUENESS

- Your plans to start into pottery are again pushed into last place by work demands and children's needs.
- You avoid wearing a certain blouse or shirt because you will attract too much attention from co-workers.

- You wanted to buy that unique stationery but did not when your friend said, "That doesn't fit you."
- In a moment of joy you wrote four lines of poetry but put down your impulse to share it with a friend because you were afraid that he or she would laugh at your attempt.

DESTROYING POWER

- Looking around the house you notice all of the jobs you seem unable to finish.
- It seems as if you complain a lot to friends about your job, spouse, and children. You justify doing this in order to get out your feelings, not realizing that you are avoiding decisions.
- Sometimes you suspect that your pride in being spontaneous covers up your inability to control and channel your feelings.
- You vow that next time you will cut short the telephone conversation from that "friend" that goes on and on about his or her problems—but you don't!
- Somehow you are always late.

DESTROYING MODELS

- You know you should get up early to meditate or go to church on Sunday but don't. The bed feels so warm and comforting.
- You avoid talking to your spouse about how you want to spend your money and what is a priority because you always seem to end up arguing about the bills.
- You never seem to know who is supposed to do what around here, and there never seems to be time for you to sit down and work it out. When you've tried to you end up accusing each other about the past.
- When you went into this job you didn't really know who you were or what you really wanted to do. You still don't, but do know that you don't like what you're

doing. Yet you avoid searching for something new. How do you start anyway? You feel so confused.

HOW POOR MARITAL RELATIONS CAN LOWER YOUR SELF-ESTEEM

Many books have been written about what we need to do to make a marriage work and we will not attempt to condense such wisdom into a few paragraphs. It is helpful nevertheless to look at the few ways that we unknowingly do undermine our spouse's (and eventually our own) self-esteem.

Sometimes a couple marries because the spouse fulfills one of the four conditions that is lacking in the other. For example, a husband who feels very plain, ordinary, and unimaginative may find the wild outrageousness of his artistic wife exciting. The artist may value the adoration of her partner for fulfilling her connectiveness needs; so, they marry.

Complementary pairing can sometimes hinder the growth and development of a person's self-esteem. Because one person is seen as fulfilling most of one's needs, one may ignore other resources and avenues for strengthening that condition in oneself. The husband of the artist might neglect his own creative potential or his wife might overlook the strength and satisfaction that comes from finding many different people and groups to connect with. The satisfaction of having the low condition partially met can hinder the complete flowering of that area in one's life. Furthermore, we become very dependent on one person when they are the primary source of satisfaction in that area. This condition can work only as long as the other person fulfills their part of this implicit contract. Even when that person is meeting that need, the dependent person is uneasy—all his eggs are in one basket.

People change; a fact that seems to be forgotten in the initial dreams of "forever after." We would like to cling to the stability that comes from finding each other. Yet the large number of divorces indicates the inadequacy of that dream. If we are unaware how our personal changes can threaten the self-esteem of our partner, we increase the potential for stress in a relationship. In our example, if the husband awakens to his need for self-expression by taking classes and associating with new groups, his wife might feel threatened by the diffusion of his interest. Only by being able to discuss their feelings and the importance of their needs in the critical condition can a couple avoid a serious rift.

SINGLE PARENTS STRESS IN SELF-ESTEEM

Many of the stresses of being a single parent come from the following common experiences:

Connectiveness is threatened when:
- There is no spouse with whom one can share intimate feelings and daily events.
- It seems hard to maintain the same friends you both had when you were married.
- A divorce frequently means one person leaves the house, neighborhood, and city and has to establish new roots.

Uniqueness:
- No one now knows you well enough to confirm that which is uniquely "you."
- The added child-rearing duties leave even less time for special interests.
- You may feel that the split was caused by the expression of your own unique qualities and therefore try to suppress those qualities in any new relationship.

Power:
- You feel helpless having to fulfill both father and mother roles.
- Many jobs around the house that had been done by your ex-spouse are now yours. You feel awkward mowing the lawn, fixing a leaky faucet, cooking, doing the laundry, cleaning house, or calling someone to clean out the furnace.

- It may be hard to get credit. Your credit cards were in your ex-spouse's name.

Models:
- Routines of eating, sleeping, recreation are disrupted.
- Jointly held goals are now in disarray.
- Sexual values are often conflictive. Should men be allowed to sleep overnight at the house? What does it really mean if I have sexual relations with my ex-spouse?

ENHANCING YOUR SELF-ESTEEM THROUGH EVERYDAY ACTIONS

After determining which are your lowest conditions, start thinking through ideas that will strengthen those areas. The myriad of daily, small acts, decisions, and interactions with people will profoundly affect your self-esteem. You can continue the routines that will perpetuate how you feel about yourself or you can change what you do. The changes don't have to be huge. The many everyday acts that you choose to enhance a particular condition of self-esteem and repeat over time will create changes.

ENHANCING YOUR SENSE OF CONNECTIVENESS

When you are lonely in the presence of your family and have a sense of isolation, turn your attention to the quality of your relationship with the people and objects that surround you: your spouse, family, the house, and the community. Determine how satisfied you are in these relationships and then decide what aspects of these relationships you would want to change.

Your relationship with your spouse is essential to a sense of connectiveness and yet one that is often difficult to maintain. One difficulty is that when you see your spouse daily, you have a sense of *familiarity* that can be mistaken for the sense of connectiveness. Familiarity can be associated with feelings of boredom, with the same rituals and taking each other for granted. Such feelings can undercut a sense of connectiveness. Some of the following ideas, small as they may be, when repeated, will keep alive your sense of connectiveness.

- Ask your spouse to share a cup of coffee with you in the kitchen.
- Learn a new skill or study an unfamiliar topic together and be able to share both the excitement as well as awkwardness and fears of failure that such activities often arouse.
- Have you ever had your feet massaged by your spouse? With light oil and tender hands your feet (and all of you) can feel wonderful!
- Share with your spouse what you read in the newspaper, or a poem you delight in, or an interesting fact. Allow time for discussion of each other's feelings and viewpoints without having to decide who is right or wrong.
- Offer to do one of your spouse's chores for a day. You will probably be surprised at his/her reactions.

Many of the ideas discussed previously for enhancing family self-esteem will affect your own and we wish to mention here only a few novel ideas. Here is a trick to enhance togetherness: Turn down the heat in the house and have a big blanket spread on the living room floor that you and your children can climb under. Then read a ghost story and imagine that the blanket has special powers of protection.

Are you ready to take another risk? Ask your children to plan three places they would like to take you as a surprise, specifying how much time, money, and travel distance this adventure can take. Let them know what you like to do and what places you enjoy. Guide them to using neighbors, friends, and other local resources such as Recreation Department, Parks Department, and so forth.

Houses and dwellings can care for you, providing warmth,

protection and visual delight or they can be cold, sterile containers of people and activities; it's up to you to establish your special relationship to your house or apartment. Again, small things can help.

- Take off your shoes and walk barefoot on the rugs.
- When you come home, change from your work clothes into ones that you associate with being home.
- Get a new welcome mat for the front door.
- Have a birthday party for the house on the date when you moved in. Each person can bring a small gift for the house.

Building a sense of connectiveness to the community need not require intense preoccupation with politics or volunteer programs. Small acts can increase awareness of what is going on in your community.

- Take a local newspaper.
- Go to a local flea market and chat with the vendors.
- Go to church.
- When coming home from work, travel on streets you have never been before and notice the houses.
- Write to your state assemblyperson about your feelings regarding a local problem.

UNIQUELY YOURS!—ENHANCING YOUR SENSE OF UNIQUENESS

Have you taken time for you to appreciate you? Most of us have secretly thought, "Wonderful!" or "Was I great!" or "I really did a good job!" after building, cooking, painting, or creating something that delighted us. Such inner praise may have surprised you because our ever vigilant internal critic is usually on guard against such self-love. It is true that a sense of uniqueness can be enhanced by such self-appreciative thought, yet there is another form of self-appreciation. This way is to *express* your uniqueness even though the expression does not meet someone's (including your internal critic's) standards. It is you! What is important is the degree to which you have expressed your own preferences, viewpoints, and style. At home take time to express these inner urgings.

- Select decorated stationery that relates to a special characteristic of yours, or which creates a good feeling in you.
- A specially designed note seal for your letters would add to your uniqueness. This is not being pretentious in the sense of superiority; it is expressing a part of you to the world of friends.
- Cook an exotic recipe you would like to taste.
- Change your furniture around.
- Create a large bulletin board space somewhere in the house that is just for you. Put up pictures, poems, cartoons, whatever you enjoy.
- Schedule time in which you can do anything you want. You probably will have to say no firmly to some surprised children or spouse; explain how important this time is to you. Preparing your family for this decision will help prevent intrusions. It would be useful to get out of the house, because there are so many cues present at home that remind people of incomplete jobs. You are also harder to find.
- The old and familiar piggy bank can help in expressing your uniqueness. In the evening, empty your change into a savings container labeled Just For Me, and at the end of a month, spend the money on a gift that is just for your pleasure.

All of these ideas may sound very selfish, self-indulgent, or just arouse an uncomfortable feeling in the pit of your stomach. Be aware that such words and feelings come from an internal critic, who served us when we were children but now needs to be reeducated. You need to remind yourself that a sense of uniqueness is essential for self-esteem, without which it is impossible to give to others with sensitivity and love. Without a sense of uniqueness "doing for others" leads to bitterness and resentment at being taken advantage of, of being drained, and often unappreciated.

POWER AS THE MOVER OF SELF-ESTEEM

Power! Some people glory in having it; others desperately seek it, and yet no matter how much external power they have, never feel it; and still others are afraid of experiencing a sense of their own power. What is your attitude about having it?

A high sense of power can help you make decisions and bring about experiences that enhance the other three conditions of self-esteem. Power is the mover behind the development of self-esteem.

Enhance this ability to make things happen for yourself through the CPA Formula—Choose, Plan, Act.

Apply this formula to one purpose per day for a week and you can lift lingering depression and feelings of helplessness. Each one of the steps in the formula is important. The first step is to change wishes into decisions. A wish does not bring commitment to a plan of action, and thus usually remains as an unsatisfied feeling unless translated into a decision. Start to know the CPA formula by picking some small, often overlooked wishes and desires:

- I wish one night a week I didn't have to cook dinner.
- I wish I could start exercising.
- I wish I could get up five minutes earlier to meditate.
- I wish I could stop drinking after one martini.
- I wish I could refuse a second helping of food.
- I wish I could set a limit for my child and carry through with it.

Choose! To make these wishes come true you will need to follow each of the CPA steps. Let's suppose you have a wish to exercise. Now pause and deliberately choose to exercise. Remember you are always choosing. At any moment you cannot *not* choose. You have to choose either to exercise or not. Sense the importance of this step. Once you've chosen to exercise—jogging, swimming, Yoga—you must decide (also a choice) how often and for how long. When you are clear about these details you are ready for the next step.

Plan! This step will involve thinking of what you have to do to bring your goal about. We will use the example of jogging. Many of these planning activities will involve minor CPA cycles such as purchasing jogging shoes and equipment, telling your spouse you will be getting up 30 minutes earlier each morning, and finishing that book on jogging. It is helpful to visualize yourself doing these activities so that each of the necessary steps are clear to you. Decide on a definite date to start the jogging and determine what preliminary steps need to be done before that date. Decide when each activity will begin. Every time you take one of these preliminary steps you can experience a CPA cycle and a growing sense of power.

Now act! Doing it is easier after the first two steps have been taken, and yet for many people this step is difficult. Old "failure tapes" in the mind may play litanies of doom: "You've tried this before and you couldn't keep at it." "You'll look silly in that jogging outfit." "It will be painful when you start."

Turn off these tapes by remembering all the past times you actually did choose, plan, and act. Then remind yourself what you want to achieve and visualize yourself reaching your goal.

Start the CPA formula with simple things that can be done quickly. For example, if you want to go shopping for that new sweater you saw, decide whether you will do it now or later. If you decide to do it now, then decide when and what do you need to do before you go; finally, get in the car and enjoy your shopping. You can experiment by using the CPA formula for other acts that will increase your sense of power. Consider reading a book you've been wanting to read instead of watching TV; decide to write a letter to a friend; use CPA to clean out a messy closet, or to pay the bills on time, or to take time to walk in the park or on the beach. After using the CPA in these simple acts you can move to more ambitious programs, such as setting limits for children, losing weight, quitting smoking, deciding on different areas of decision making between you and your spouse.

After each successful CPA cycle, congratulate yourself. Feel good! You have stepped toward power and away from helplessness and depression. If this realization is not strong enough reward for you, give yourself a dinner at a wonderful restaurant.

KNOW WHERE YOU WANT TO GO AND WHY—
ENHANCING A SENSE OF MODELS

Creating a sense of models sounds like a major task, requiring careful thought over a long period of time. Sometimes it does and yet we can enhance this condition of self-esteem through daily acts.

Putting things in order not only brings a sense of satisfaction, it can also make things easier to find. Start small, with such activities as tackling that drawer that you keep stuffing things into or your closet. Later, move on to bigger jobs, such as cleaning out your garage or backyard. The many decisions you have to make in cleaning up an area will help clarify what is or is not important to you. It is a way of knowing more about yourself.

Two tendencies make cleaning and arranging difficult: our reluctance to spend time arranging and the hesitancy to throw things away. It can help if you think of arranging as an opportunity for self-enhancement. The enjoyment of dumping clutter and junking irrelevant objects is far greater than the occasional regret of wishing you hadn't thrown that thing away. Besides, people have reported that getting rid of the old makes it possible for new and more fulfilling objects and experiences to enter their life. How can this happen? When we see a closet or a drawer that is full, we tend to feel satisfied or not wonder what new things can fill that empty space. We have a tendency to fill empty spaces whether they are physical places or time gaps. To have new experiences we need to let go of the old, whether it is an outmoded idea, irrelevant object, or destructive habit.

Here are other ways you can heighten a sense of models:

- Read an autobiography of a person you admire.
- After an event (for example, a conversation, a finished

project, a decision), pause and write down on 4 × 6 cards what you liked and what you disliked about that event. By reviewing these cards you can clarify your preferences. Such preferences point to important values that you may not be aware are guiding your decisions. Clarify your values and goals by answering the following questions (it helps you to clarify the issues by discussing them with a friend):

—What is it about you that you are proud of?

—What would you like to accomplish in the coming year?

—Where is your favorite place to visit?

—What activities and situations get you excited?

MIND PICTURES THAT
ENHANCE YOUR SELF-ESTEEM

Our imagination has a strong influence on how we feel and act. Imagine a depressing past event and soon you are feeling sad; picture a potentially uncomfortable future encounter with your supervisor or friend and you'll start to feel anxious. Most of the time we are not aware how much these inner pictures affect our moods. It is difficult to change things you're not aware of. Thus these pictures control us. It does not have to be that way—you can consciously change these pictures and get control over your feelings and actions.

The following "inner scenes" when visualized regularly can enhance the four conditions. The best time to visualize them is in a relaxed state when your mind is not involved in thinking of all the things you must do or anticipating an unexpected interruption. In a relaxed state your images are clearer and your mind is more receptive.

Here is a method for relaxing your body, before visualizing the images that are designed to enhance various self-esteem conditions. Although it may be easier to start relaxing lying on your back, you can obtain the same results sitting in a chair, feet flat on the floor and thinking the following instructions to yourself.[7]

Take a deep breath, hold it for a moment, and then slowly let the breath out, at the same time letting your eyes close. Take another deep breath, and as you let it out, feel the breath spreading a feeling of relaxation throughout your body. Now breathe quietly and deeply. Follow your breathing, letting the breath breathe you. Notice which parts of your body are beginning to relax.

Focus your attention on your feet and imagine on each exhalation you are sending your breath into your feet, and along with the breath goes messages of relaxation. Notice the change of sensations in your feet. They may feel heavier or lighter, warmer or cooler, or there may be a change in tingling sensations. Now focus on your calves and repeat the relaxation instructions to those muscles. Be aware of the changes in sensation that occur. Notice how you become more relaxed as you continue to send relaxation messages to your feet.

Repeat the above process with the rest of the body parts: knees, thighs, pelvic area, buttocks, stomach, chest, back, shoulders, arms, hands, neck.

Focus on your face and relax your forehead and scalp, then the area around your eyes, the mouth, including the sides of your mouth; feel your jaw relax and drop open and your face becoming calm and peaceful.

Sense how your body is becoming more and more relaxed and heavy. Now deepen these feelings by counting backward from five to zero. As you say to yourself, "five," you are becoming more deeply relaxed; "four," feel the tension leaving you; "three," feel yourself sinking down as you count down; "two," you are more and more relaxed; "one," you are almost fully relaxed; "zero," feel yourself deeply relaxed.

If you have trouble fully relaxing some part of your body, try tensing that part of the body for five to seven seconds, then fully let go of the muscle tension and tell the body part to relax.

[7] A relaxation tape is available from the authors. Write to: APOD, 1210 Brommer St., Santa Cruz, CA 95062. Send $6.00 plus $1.00 for postage and handling.

Focus on the feelings of relaxation which will automatically flow into those muscles as they let go from the tensing. With practice, people have found that relaxation becomes easier and quicker. You may want to record these instructions and listen to yourself, or someone close to you, give these instructions.

Imaging for Connectiveness. Imagine yourself in a very pleasant meadow brightened by a warm sun and the rich colors of wildflowers. A gentle wind feels soft against your cheeks. Now see, on the other side of the meadow, a person you would like to feel closer to. You walk toward each other and you see more and more details of that person's clothes and face. Now imagine a light beam of affection shining from your heart to him or her; the light will arouse in the other person a reciprocal warmth toward you. See that person smile and show other signs of openness toward you. Let the light envelope the other person, and now come as close to each other as is comfortable.

By repeating this exercise daily, you'll begin to experience not only feelings of increased closeness toward this person, but also a change in his or her behavior toward you.

Imaging for Uniqueness. Think of a time when you sensed something special about yourself. Maybe someone pointed out this special quality to you or you had gone through an experience that made you very much aware of this aspect. See the setting you were in when you experienced this characteristic and who else was there. Feel that quality in your body. Now imagine that specialness is a seed of some kind. Feel the seed in your hand as you look at its size, color, and texture. Take this seed and imagine placing it in your body, feeling the body sensations located around the place you put the seed. Feel the seed grow in you and now imagine how you would act, speak, and be with this quality strong within you.

Imaging for Power. Visualize an interpersonal scene in which you did something you rather you hadn't. You made a poor decision or said something you wish you could take back. It might be a scene in which you failed to stand up for yourself and were manipulated to behave or act in a certain way. Look at the scene as it unfolds in its original manner. When it ends see the words (or say them to yourself) "The End—I no longer need to do this." Now replay the scene, this time seeing yourself act in a manner that is more self-esteeming. Notice your posture, dress, tone of voice, and so on, clearly. Replay this again for emphasis. At the end see these words or say them to yourself: "To Be Continued." By emphasizing the positive you avoid a mistake we commonly make—focusing on something we want to avoid doing. "I'll not do *that* again" and we see the mistake clearly in our mind. The mind will, in most people, be programmed more by the picture than the words; besides, the mind has no other model to follow other than the presented negative picture. Seeing the negative increases the potential for it happening again.

Imaging for Models. Place yourself in the pleasant meadow again and see someone you respect and admire very much standing in front of you. Besides being someone you know, this figure could be a historical, religious, or storybook figure you admire, respect, and feel you could learn from. He or she is smiling at you and is eagerly waiting for your questions. Ask this figure for guidance about what to do in certain situations, or ask for help in clarifying conflicts in values and goals. Inside your mind, address the figure in words and accept any thought, feeling, or idea that comes into your consciousness *immediately* following the question, as if it is an answer from this figure. If these answers are not clear, ask for clarification. You can hold an enlightening conversation if you imagine this figure as separate from you—similar to talking to a wise friend. When finished, thank the figure, say good-bye and leave.

Many people will not see the images clearly. Don't worry, as long as you can get a sense of the image it will benefit you. Regular visualization of these images can do much to strengthen your self-esteem.

Enhancing your own self-esteem will pay dividends in terms of:

- better health
- more satisfying relationships
- children who feel better about themselves
- higher income
- more enjoyment in what you do

If these goals are important to you, then the time spent on yourself is well worth it.